How To Use the Uniform Residential Appraisal Report

MARTHA R. WILLIAMS

WILLIAM L. VENTOLO, JR.

Real Estate
Education Company
a division of Dearborn Financial Publishing, Inc.

While a great deal of care has been taken to provide accurate and current information, the ideas, suggestions, general principles and conclusions presented in this text are subject to local, state and federal laws and regulations, court cases and any revisions of same. The reader is thus urged to consult legal counsel regarding any points of law—this publication should not be used as a substitute for competent legal advice.

Acquisitions Editors: Wendy Lochner and Margaret M. Maloney
Project Editor: Timothy Taylor
Interior Design: Lucy Jenkins
Cover Design: Vito DePinto

Printed in the United States of America.

91 92 93 10 9 8 7 6 5 4 3 2 1

Library of Congress Cataloging-in-Publication Data

Williams, Martha R.
    How to use the uniform residential appraisal report / Martha R. Williams, William L. Ventolo, Jr.
        p.   cm.
    Includes index.
    ISBN 0-7931-0113-1
    1. Real property—Valuation. 2. Dwellings—Valuation. 3. Real property—Valuation—Standards—United States. 4. Dwellings—Valuation—Standards—United States. I. Ventolo, Jr., William L.
II. Title.
HD1387.W53 1991
333.33'82—dc20
                                                                    91-14333
                                                                        CIP

Contents

Preface

How To Use the Uniform Residential Appraisal Report is designed to assist both new and experienced appraisers. The new appraiser must learn how real estate appraisal theory relates to appraisal practice techniques. The experienced appraiser may want a "refresher" in this vital area. *How To Use the Uniform Residential Appraisal Report* serves both these needs and is also an easy-to-use reference for the field or the office.

The newly recognized importance of real estate appraisal education has highlighted the need for learning materials that cover the basics as they relate to the "real world" of practice. *How To Use the Uniform Residential Appraisal Report* meets that need by having the reader do more than just read about what must be done to complete a URAR form. The reader practices filling out each form section as it is discussed. As a final project, the reader has the opportunity to complete an entire sample appraisal.

In short, whether used alone or as part of a course, this book helps bridge the gap between the world of the observer and the world of the participant.

Acknowledgments

Preparation of *How To Use the Uniform Residential Appraisal Report* was greatly aided by the comments and encouragement received from those who reviewed the manuscript. They are:

Dean Bishop, I.F.S.
Omaha School of Real Estate

Ronald D. Oslin, President
Tennessee Real Estate Educational Systems, Inc.
Oslin Mortgage Company

Corina D. Rollins, CRPA/R
Marin Community College

Production of this book would not have been possible without the encouragement of Carol L. Luitjens, Publisher, and the capable assistance of her staff, including Wendy Lochner and Margaret M. Maloney, Acquisitions Editors and Timothy Taylor, Project Editor. Our sincere thanks to all of them.

Last (as is usually the case) but certainly not least, go our thanks for the patience and understanding of our long-suffering spouses who must share the tribulations of writing a book without ever fully realizing the pleasure that comes from the accomplishment.

Martha R. Williams, JD
William L. Ventolo, Jr.

Introduction

Most residential real estate loans now are placed on the secondary mortgage market, and many federal and quasi-federal agencies are involved in these and related transactions. Over the years, the need for standardized appraisal documentation became apparent and resulted in creation of the Uniform Residential Appraisal Report (URAR). The URAR has become the key reporting tool for appraisers of single-family residences. Appraisers must learn how to use this tool to its maximum advantage, always keeping in mind the client's requirements as well as those of the agency receiving the form.

Many books have attempted to respond to the need for a URAR text. Some explain the mechanics of completing the URAR form and then list various agency criteria. The better books list agency criteria immediately following discussion of the applicable form section. Some books—but not all—have a sample completed URAR form somewhere in the book. With all of the books, the reader must flip through pages constantly to find explanations, agency requirements or form samples.

How To Use the Uniform Residential Appraisal Report is designed for maximum clarity as well as maximum ease of use.

The text begins with a brief overview of real estate appraisal and the history of the URAR form. Each section of the URAR form is then explained, and the relevant agency criteria are provided. Next, the reader has the opportunity to examine how the technique explained can be carried out in actual practice. Finally, the reader has the opportunity to apply what has been learned.

Sections of the form are covered in the same order in which they appear on the form. In addition, all discussion of a particular topic, including agency criteria, appears in the same part of the book. In this way, the reader need not search through the book to find explanations, agency requirements or form samples.

For ease of reference, a heading at the top of each page shows what section is discussed on that page. An Answer Key and topic Index are located at the back of the book.

With all of these features, *How To Use the Uniform Residential Appraisal Report* takes the reader through a three-step learning process of

- discussion,
- examination and
- application.

Step One: Discussion

The URAR form is broken down into its component sections (thirteen in all). Each section is presented, and the information required for each entry in that section is explained. The URAR is intended for a national marketplace. To the extent that it can accomplish this formidable task, it can be labeled a "generic" document. To use the form effectively, however, the appraiser must know and recognize the diversity of properties and regional marketplaces in which it will be used. As often as possible, the authors point out local variables that will require special attention.

Specific agency criteria are presented immediately following the relevant discussion. Agency criteria are not lumped together in a series of appendixes, and they are *not* simply quoted without commentary. The authors have attempted to present and explain agency criteria in clear, uncomplicated language. The criteria are always placed in the context of the form itself.

Note: Always double-check individual agency requirements. The stated requirements can be ambiguous and may not cover every type of information that must be supplied in completing the URAR. The appraiser always must investigate local needs and preferences, which no "national" form (or text) could ever adequately cover.

Step Two: Examination

How To Use the Uniform Residential Appraisal Report is a practice manual as well as a reference book. Following the discussion of each form section, the reader is presented a sample completed version of that section, identified as Appraisal 1, and the background data that led to the entries shown. The reader thus has the opportunity to observe an example of how the form can be used in practice. Because the example comes immediately after the text discussion it reinforces the information just learned.

Step Three: Application

After each URAR form section is discussed and a completed version of that section examined, the reader is asked to complete a blank copy of the form section, identified as Appraisal 2, using the information supplied. This step provides the ultimate reinforcement of "hands-on" application of what has been learned.

The book concludes with a problem, Appraisal 3, which calls upon the reader to make use of all the information learned to complete an entire copy of the URAR form.

Of course, there is a comprehensive Answer Key at the back of the book for the reader to check the completed Appraisal 2 form sections and Appraisal 3 form against the suggested responses.

How To Use This Book

The easiest way to use this book is simply to begin at the beginning with Part One, which gives an overview of real estate appraisal. Part Two opens with a brief look at development of the URAR form. Experienced appraisers may choose to skip this introductory material and go directly to Part Three, the discussion of the URAR form.

In Part Three, the reader is led through the URAR form by the process of discussion, examination and application explained in this Introduction. Any material that is not completely understood can be re-read before proceeding. It is recommended that answers to the exercises always be checked against the Answer Key at the back of the book before proceeding to the next text discussion.

By the time the reader gets to Part Four, "Putting It All Together," completing the URAR form should be a familiar and nonthreatening task.

Conclusion

The most important point for an appraiser to remember about the URAR form is that it is a reporting tool, not an end in itself. No two-page form—even with legal descriptions, maps, photographs and a variety of other attachments—can ever contain all the information an appraiser relied on to form a stated estimate of market value.

The best an appraiser can hope to accomplish with a form is to have a convenient tool with which to summarize the data that had the most influence on the valuation decision. The best the appraiser's client or form recipient can hope for is to have the necessary appraisal data presented in terms that are readily understood and consistent with those used in other appraisals.

This book is intended to help ensure that the Uniform Residential Appraisal Report is completed properly and used productively.

PART ONE

What Is a Real Estate Appraisal?

THE REAL ESTATE MARKETPLACE

Real estate, real property, land, terra firma. No matter what it's called, it's an inescapable part of our daily lives. Every human activity takes place on some form of real estate.

Over the centuries, fortunes both vast and modest have been made through real estate ownership. Nevertheless, relatively little has been done to identify how real estate serves as a financial force. Only in recent decades, for example, has research been launched on components of the real estate marketplace and questions raised about underlying assumptions that, among other things, have helped establish our national housing policy.

Residential Property

In 1949, Congress acknowledged in the National Housing Act that decent, safe and sanitary housing is a right of every citizen of the United States. Over the last 40 years, federal, state and local governments have attempted to bring decent, safe and sanitary housing to all citizens by a variety of building construction, financing and related programs. Direct funding, bond programs, tax credits and relaxation of zoning constraints are only some of the methods used to meet this priority. There are many other ways government has imposed itself on the real estate marketplace, of course. Interest rates paid by property owners and investors reflect the prime rate set by the Federal Reserve System and charged by member institutions to their best-rated commercial borrowers. Federally insured and guaranteed home and farm mortgages have helped popularize the benefits of real property ownership and investment. So have similar state programs and the enormous secondary mortgage market.

Despite these measures, the continued rise in real property prices in the past few years has caused a nationwide downturn in home ownership. Prospective first-time homebuyers can't finance the down payment and/or monthly payments for a "starter" home. Current homeowners who were lucky enough to enter the market when housing was more affordable now find it difficult to "sell and move up." Not only is the market for their present homes unfavorable, but in some cases these owners are also limited by incomes that have failed to keep up with housing prices.

All is not lost, however. As the 1990s get underway, traditionally heated market areas—California for example—are cooling down to more manageable rates of price growth. The tidal wave of baby boomers that pushed housing prices to ever higher levels is now subsiding. New economic and political concerns and their recessionary impact have tempered real estate prices in most areas of the country, sometimes with favorable results. Economically depressed areas, such as the oil states that suffered a roller-coaster price ride during the previous decade now are beginning to show more promising price movements.

Commercial Property

In many parts of the country the commercial real estate marketplace has also been highly volatile. The number of commercial building starts was spurred in the early 1980s by eager lenders from newly deregulated financial institutions and by investors seeking the benefits conferred by tax "shelters." In many areas the result was overbuilding, followed by "see-through" buildings and high vacancy rates that drove down market rents.

The Tax Reform Act of 1986 put the brakes on building development as a means to avoid taxes. Unfortunately, many of the free-spending savings and loans and other institutions have reached the edge of a precipice from which their only rescue is government intervention. The Resolution Trust Corporation (RTC), established by the Financial Institutions Reform, Recovery, and Enforcement Act of 1989 (FIRREA) must now deal with the restructuring or liquidation of hundreds of failed institutions and the disposition of billions of dollars of assets. Most of these assets are real estate, and some are so highly leveraged they are worth less then the amount of their outstanding debt.

Faulty appraisals have been mentioned in the collapse of many institutions. Overinflated portfolios may have resulted from apparent willingness on the part of some real estate appraisers to value property to suit a client's expectation. Such an "accommodating" appraisal might allow a lender to make a loan to a friend or relative, based on collateral that should have been appraised at considerably less. The objectivity that should have been the appraiser's hallmark was compromised for the sake of an appraisal fee.

No appraiser has a crystal ball of course, but there are generally accepted appraisal techniques that, if followed with objectivity and skill, can lead to a fair and reasonably accurate valuation.

APPRAISAL REGULATION

In the past appraisers were subject to few legally mandated rules and regulations. Now, the massive federal bailout effort required to salvage or rescue the hundreds of failed financial institutions has led to new regulations for appraisers and appraisals.

As of July 1, 1991, appraisals of property involved in federally related transactions must be performed only by appraisers licensed or certified by the state in which the property is located. Furthermore, the appraisals must be conducted in the fashion prescribed by the state. Each state must require of appraisers a combination of experience and education that at least meets the minimum established by the newly created Appraisal Foundation's Appraiser Qualifications Board. Appraisal standards must meet the minimum level established by the Appraisal Foundation's Appraisal Standards Board.

For purposes of the new regulations, a *federally related transaction* is any real estate–related financial transaction (any sale, lease, purchase, investment, exchange, refinancing or other use of real property as security for a loan or investment) in which the Resolution Trust Corporation or other federal financial institution is involved and which requires an appraisal. Other institutions may include the Comptroller of the Currency, Federal Deposit Insurance Corporation, Federal Reserve System, National Credit Union Administration and the Office of Thrift Supervision. Obviously the new requirements are far-reaching and thus should have an equally far-reaching impact that reflects their intended purpose of raising the level of appraiser competence.

THE LANGUAGE OF APPRAISAL

An *appraiser* is one who makes an estimate of value. An *appraisal* is the process by which an estimate of value is made.

Most often the value sought by a real estate appraiser is *market value.* For many years market value was defined generally as the *highest* price a property could be expected to bring in an arm's-length transaction occurring under normal market conditions. In an *arm's-length transaction* all parties have full knowledge of the property's assets and defects, the parties are unrelated and no party is acting under duress. *Normal market conditions* include a reasonable marketing time and financing terms that are customary for similar properties in the area.

The assumption of market value as the *highest* price a property can command may be acceptable in a time of continuing price appreciation. During a time of declining prices, or even stagnant prices, a property owner may have little hope of attaining an optimum price. Because so many real estate markets throughout the United States have proven to be highly volatile, in 1986 the Federal Home Loan Mortgage Corporation (FHLMC) and the Federal National Mortgage Association (FNMA) changed their definition of *market value* to the *most probable price* real estate should bring in a sale occurring under normal market conditions. This definition takes into account the fact that an appraiser's research and analysis typically result in a range of values and the highest value in that range is not necessarily an accurate indication of market value.

Appraisers are not fortune-tellers, of course. No one can absolutely guarantee the accuracy of an appraisal. What an experienced and capable appraiser *can* do, however, is to know as much as possible about the property being appraised and the pertinent market factors that influence value, and apply that knowledge with skill and sound judgment.

THE APPRAISAL PROCESS: A FLOWCHART

The process by which an appraisal is carried out is shown in the flowchart in Figure 1. The basic process generally is the same, regardless of the purpose of the appraisal or the type of property being appraised. The steps are as follows:

1. State the appraisal problem; that is, identify the property being appraised and the purpose of the appraisal. Most often the appraisal will be conducted to determine market value for purposes of a sale or exchange.
2. Determine the kinds of data required and the sources from which they are to be collected.
3. Gather and verify the necessary data in the most efficient manner.
4. Determine the property's highest and best use. A valuation based on the current use will be meaningless if the property is not being used to its maximum potential.
5–6. Estimate the land value and then estimate the value of the improvements on the property, using any or all of the three approaches to estimating value (discussed below).
7. Estimate a single final value that most accurately reflects the value of the subject property. The final value estimate is not an average but an opinion that the appraiser makes based on the type of property being appraised, the results of the research compiled and the valuation techniques used.
8. Report the final value estimate in one of the formats described under "How an Appraisal Is Communicated," later in this part.

METHODS OF APPRAISAL

The *sales comparison approach* is the most widely used appraisal method and the easiest to understand. The appraiser finds recently sold properties that are comparable to the subject property. Based on sales prices of the comparables ("comps"), the appraiser determines an

Figure 1. Appraisal Flowchart

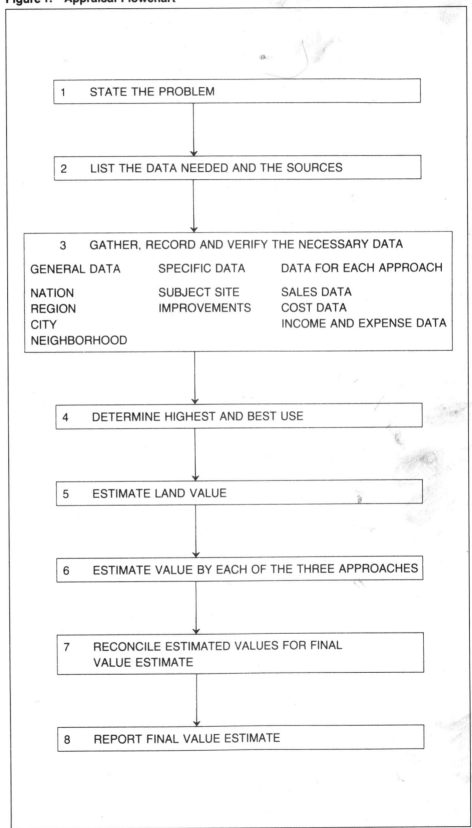

1   STATE THE PROBLEM

2   LIST THE DATA NEEDED AND THE SOURCES

3   GATHER, RECORD AND VERIFY THE NECESSARY DATA

GENERAL DATA	SPECIFIC DATA	DATA FOR EACH APPROACH
NATION	SUBJECT SITE	SALES DATA
REGION	IMPROVEMENTS	COST DATA
CITY		INCOME AND EXPENSE DATA
NEIGHBORHOOD		

4   DETERMINE HIGHEST AND BEST USE

5   ESTIMATE LAND VALUE

6   ESTIMATE VALUE BY EACH OF THE THREE APPROACHES

7   RECONCILE ESTIMATED VALUES FOR FINAL
     VALUE ESTIMATE

8   REPORT FINAL VALUE ESTIMATE

equivalent price for the subject property. The mathematical formula for the sales comparison approach is:

$$\text{Sales Price of Comparable Property} \pm \text{Adjustments} = \text{Indicated Value of Subject Property}$$

The appraiser makes adjustments to the sales price of a comparable by *adding* the value of features that are present in the subject but not the comp, and *subtracting* the value of features that are present in the comp but not the subject.

In the *cost approach*, the present cost to construct the building(s) or other improvements being appraised is first reduced by the amount by which the improvements have depreciated, then added to the property's land value. The formula for the cost approach is:

$$\text{Cost of Improvements New} - \text{Depreciation on Improvements} + \text{Site Value} = \text{Property Value}$$

In the *income capitalization approach*, the net annual income, or investment return, that the property can be expected to produce determines the property's value as an investment. The formula for the income capitalization approach is:

$$\frac{\text{Net Operating Income}}{\text{Rate of Return}} = \text{Property Value}$$

Each valuation technique will be explained in more detail later in this book as you learn how it is used.

HOW AN APPRAISAL IS COMMUNICATED

Several ways exist in which an appraiser can communicate the final estimate of value to the client. The simplest is the *letter of opinion*, in which the appraiser indicates the value estimate for the subject property as of the specified date. The letter of opinion has limited utility, however, because it provides none of the supporting data that the appraiser used to determine the value estimate and includes no discussion of the particular methods used and how any differences in valuation between methods were reconciled.

The most thorough presentation of the appraiser's research and the data that lead to the estimate of value is provided in a *narrative appraisal report*. In a lengthy document (30 to 100 or more pages), the appraiser summarizes important background research and presents all relevant data for each appraisal method that contributed to the final estimate of value. A number of exhibits may be attached, including photographs of the subject property and comparables, as well as maps showing demographic, topographical, soil and other analyses of the subject and comparables.

The narrative appraisal, being the most thorough, also is the most expensive report to prepare. It is an important and frequently necessary tool in the valuation of complex properties, however, particularly for establishing value as part of a legal proceeding. Being the most detailed, the narrative appraisal report makes the most convincing presentation; for the same reason, it is the most difficult type of report to attack.

The third type of appraisal report is the *form report* of two or more pages. It typically is designed in a combination checklist and fill-in-the-blank format and is usually accompanied by one or more exhibits

Figure 2. Appraisal Report Forms

Certification and Statement of Limiting Conditions (1 page)	FHLMC 439/FNMA 1004B Rev. 7/86
Appraisal Report—Individual Condominium or PUD Unit (2 pages)	FHLMC 465/FNMA 1073 9/80
Project Analysis—Condominium or PUD (Addendum) (2 pages)	FHLMC 465A
Analysis of Annual Income and Expenses— Operating Budget (Condominium Project) (2 pages)	FHLMC 465B/FNMA 1073A
Appraisal Report—Residential Income Property (Property Value Under $750,000) (4 pages)	FNMA 1050A/FHLMC 71B Rev. 8/77
Appraisal Report—Residential Income Property (Property Value Over $750,000) (8 pages)	FNMA 1050/FHLMC 71A
Employee Relocation Council Residential Appraisal Report (6 pages)	ERC-2 Rev. 4/86
Land Appraisal Report (1 page)	U.S. Forms Inc. 2 Central Square Grafton, MA 01519
Operating Income Statement (2 pages)	FNMA 216 Rev. 8/88
Residential Appraisal Field Review Report (2 pages)	FNMA 2000 Rev. 11/89
Second Mortgage Property Value Analysis Report (1 page)	FHLMC 704 4/87
Single Family Comparable Rent Schedule (1 page)	FNMA 1007
Uniform Commercial/Industrial Appraisal Report—Existing Property (14 pages plus addenda)	FHLBB—to be revised following test period that ended 12/31/89
Uniform Small Residential Income Appraisal Report (4 pages)	FHLMC 72/FNMA 1025 9/80, Rev. 11/89

depicting the subject property and comparables. There are various types of form report, each designed for a particular kind and size of property.

A form report allows for standardization of information and provides an efficient and uncomplicated way to present a survey of background research and data on the subject property and comparables. In the past it was not unusual for particular institutions to develop their own appraisal forms. Over the years, however, as more properties become involved in government-related transactions, the use of agency-mandated forms has become the rule.

In addition to the Uniform Residential Appraisal Report, the subject of this book, other forms have been developed to expedite real estate appraisals. Figure 2. lists forms developed by the Federal Home Loan Mortgage Corporation (FHLMC), Federal National Mortgage Association (FNMA), Federal Home Loan Bank Board (FHLBB) and other groups. In some cases the forms are required by a particular agency; in other cases they are accepted but not required. Appraisers should be aware of various agency requirements. An appraiser intending to use a preprinted form should always verify that the form is acceptable.

PART TWO

The Uniform Residential Appraisal Report

AN OVERVIEW

At a time when subdivisions of similarly styled and built homes are the norm for new construction, it may be hard to believe that until the 1930s the custom home predominated. A prospective home-owner who failed to find a suitable existing house in the desired area typically would purchase a building lot and then hire an architect and builder.

Methods of financing construction or purchase loans fell far short of the convenient long-term vehicles now available. Mortgages were typically for no more than 50% of property value, with part payable in installments over a relatively short term—perhaps five years—and the entire balance due at the end of that term. The large number of residential loan foreclosures during the Great Depression was surely due, at least in part, to the onerous terms that borrowers were forced to accept.

The collapse and subsequent restructuring of the nation's banking system by the federal government in the early 1930s helped place homebuyers on a more equal footing with lenders. Federal programs that guaranteed repayment of home mortgage loans provided lenders with the incentive they needed to expand their services in this growing market.

The Postwar Housing Boom

In the years to come, the demand for housing soon exceeded available supply. Encouraged by the extraordinary pent-up demand for residential construction that followed World War II, builders and developers learned to make use of economies of scale and standardization in residential construction. Such economies, which included quantity purchases of building materials and application of assembly-line construction techniques, were possible only with homes that offered little individualization.

Levittown, on Long Island in New York, was the first large single-family home tract development. Although Levittown's initial appearance may have struck some as unimaginative, its design and execution enabled thousands of families to become homebuyers. Although the homes were small, they were built on ample lots (at least by today's standards) and provided room for homeowners to remodel and expand over the years as needs demanded and finances allowed.

In both home construction and financing, the move toward standardization broadened the desirability and availability of home ownership. The sheer volume of home loans processed by lenders provided the incentive for finding a way in which to perform the necessary property appraisals as efficiently as possible while providing the information required to make a loan decision.

The Secondary Mortgage Market

The final push toward developing a standard appraisal form came with the emergence of the secondary mortgage market. Prior to 1938 lenders typically retained their mortgage loans in their own portfolios. The risk involved in purchasing mortgage loans meant that few buyers were willing to invest in mortgages on properties outside their immediate area. That risk was reduced markedly, however, by the development of government-insured loans and the creation in 1938 of the Federal National Mortgage Association (FNMA), or "Fannie Mae," to serve as a secondary market for such loans.

In 1968 Fannie Mae was converted partly to private ownership. The secondary market was boosted further with creation of the Government National Mortgage Association (GNMA), or "Ginnie Mae."

The Federal Home Loan Mortgage Corporation (FHLMC), or "Freddie Mac," was created in 1970 as part of the Federal Home Loan Bank System to serve as a secondary mortgage market for savings and loan associations and mortgage bankers.

As a result of these readily available public and quasi-public secondary market sources, many lenders now prefer to transfer the risk of holding mortgages by selling them, even though the lender might retain the tasks (and fees) related to "servicing" the loans (overseeing payment collections, impound accounts, and so on).

Because the majority of today's residential mortgage loans will become part of the secondary mortgage market, the needs of the agencies involved have dictated the manner in which property appraisals are conducted and reported at the time of loan origination. This is not just an instance of "the tail wagging the dog," however. The recent federal mandates on appraiser qualifications and licensing have highlighted the importance of accurate appraisals. The extent to which faulty appraisals may have contributed to the collapse of so many financial institutions will probably never be known. What is known, however, is that a properly researched and documented appraisal estimate is crucial to both the making and guaranteeing of loans based on the value of the appraised property.

Development of the URAR

A Residential Appraisal Report appropriate for single-family residential property appraisals was created by Fannie Mae and Freddie

Mac in the 1970s and revised in 1975 and 1979. The Uniform Residential Appraisal Report (URAR) in use today was issued by FNMA and FHLMC in October 1986 following input from other government agencies and field testing. In May 1987 the URAR became the required form for single-family residential appraisals performed by the Department of Housing and Urban Development (HUD) and the Veterans Administration (VA). It became the required form of the Farmers Home Administration (FmHA) in June 1987.

Certain types of single-family properties, such as condominiums and units in planned unit developments (PUDs), may require special appraisal forms for certain purposes, as listed in Figure 2 on page 13.

SAMPLE FORM AND ATTACHMENTS

Appraisal 1., a sample completed Uniform Residential Appraisal Report and the attachments that accompany it, appears on pages 21–26.

Form Design and Organization

The URAR is designed to record the data collected by the appraiser and to present a summary of the appraiser's findings and final conclusion of value. The current URAR, similar in format to the earlier Residential Appraisal Report, makes use of a combination of checklists and fill-ins in a two-page design that is supplemented by applicable exhibits.

Page 1 of the URAR form, "Property Description & Analysis," includes the following sections:

- **Subject** property and property rights being appraised. A separate section is provided for lender's use so that information on sale price can be recorded.
- **Neighborhood** in which subject property is located. Space is provided for comments on trends and factors not revealed by checklists provided.
- **Site** of property under appraisal.
- **Improvements** of property under appraisal.
- **Room List** (number, use and types of rooms) for the subject property.
- **Interior** specifications (including surface finishes and equipment).
- **Automobile** storage areas.
- **Comments** of appraiser regarding condition of property improvements as well as market conditions, particularly as they relate to financing terms.

Page 2, "Valuation Section," includes the following:

- **Purpose** of appraisal.
- **Cost approach** analysis, including a building diagram and breakdown of reproduction cost figures.

- **Sales comparison** approach analysis, including itemization of factors contributing to price differences between the subject property and comparable properties.
- **Income approach** analysis, using the gross rent multiplier method.
- **Reconciliation** statement, explaining how appraiser correlated values derived by the appraisal approaches used to arrive at a single final estimate of market value. Appraiser signs appraisal, as does the review appraiser (if applicable).

The appraiser includes with the two-page URAR the necessary maps, floor plans and photos of the subject property and comparables. The appraiser also attaches a copy of the Definition of Market Value and Certification and Statement of Limiting Conditions (Form 1004B, shown in Figure 9 on page 122) that specifies the terms under which the appraisal is made.

Figure 3. Appraisal 1.

Property Description & Analysis **UNIFORM RESIDENTIAL APPRAISAL REPORT** File No.

SUBJECT

Property Address	456 CHERRY HILL ROAD	Census Tract 14
City SARASOTA	County SARASOTA	State FL Zip Code 34200
Legal Description	LOT 308 BENT TREE VILLAGE S/D, BK 12, PAGES 12-12 F	
Owner/Occupant	SILAS REMBRANDT	Map Reference G58

Sale Price $ 165,000	Date of Sale OCTOBER 15, 1990	PROPERTY RIGHTS APPRAISED
Loan charges/concessions to be paid by seller $ NONE		[X] Fee Simple
R.E. Taxes $ 1,123.73	Tax Year 1990-91 HOA $/Mo.	[ ] Leasehold
Lender/Client MURPHY MORTGAGE CO., P.O. BOX 134		[ ] Condominium (HUD/VA)
SERRA, FL 34224-1347		[ ] De Minimis PUD

LENDER DISCRETIONARY USE
Sale Price $
Date
Mortgage Amount $
Mortgage Type
Discount Points and Other Concessions
Paid by Seller $
Source

NEIGHBORHOOD

					NEIGHBORHOOD ANALYSIS	Good	Avg.	Fair	Poor
LOCATION	[ ] Urban	[X] Suburban	[ ] Rural		Employment Stability	X			
BUILT UP	[ ] Over 75%	[X] 25-75%	[ ] Under 25%		Convenience to Employment		X		
GROWTH RATE	[ ] Rapid	[X] Stable	[ ] Slow		Convenience to Shopping		X		
PROPERTY VALUES	[x] Increasing	[ ] Stable	[ ] Declining		Convenience to Schools		X		
DEMAND/SUPPLY	[ ] Shortage	[X] In Balance	[ ] Over Supply		Adequacy of Public Transportation	X			
MARKETING TIME	[ ] Under 3 Mos.	[X] 3-6 Mos.	[ ] Over 6 Mos.		Recreation Facilities	X			

PRESENT LAND USE %	LAND USE CHANGE	PREDOMINANT	SINGLE FAMILY HOUSING		
Single Family 75	Not Likely [X]	OCCUPANCY	PRICE $ (000)	AGE (yrs)	Adequacy of Utilities X
2-4 Family	Likely [ ]	Owner [X]			Property Compatibility X
Multi-family 15	In process [ ]	Tenant [ ]	100 Low NEW		Protection from Detrimental Cond. X
Commercial	To:	Vacant (0-5%) [X]	800 High 15		Police & Fire Protection X
Industrial		Vacant (over 5%) [ ]	Predominant		General Appearance of Properties X
Vacant 10			200 — 8		Appeal to Market X

Note: Race or the racial composition of the neighborhood are not considered reliable appraisal factors.
COMMENTS: BENT TREE VILLAGE, A NEIGHBORHOOD OF UPSCALE RESIDENCES SURROUNDING COUNTRY CLUB FACILITIES. THE AREA HAS BEEN DEVELOPED AROUND A CHAMPIONSHIP GOLF COURSE WITH MOSTLY EXPENSIVE SINGLE-FAMILY RESIDENCES. CONVENIENCE TO INTERSTATE 75 IS GOOD, ALLOWING EASY ACCESS TO CENTERS OF EMPLOYMENT.

SITE

Dimensions 125 x 180 x 58 x 139		Topography	LEVEL
Site Area 13,907.50 SF	Corner Lot NO	Size	13,907.50/TYPICAL
Zoning Classification RSF-1/PUD (RES.)	Zoning Compliance YES	Shape	IRREGULAR
HIGHEST & BEST USE: Present Use YES	Other Use	Drainage	ADEQUATE

UTILITIES	Public	Other	SITE IMPROVEMENTS	Type	Public	Private	View	INTERIOR-PATIO-ATRIUM
Electricity	[X]	FPL	Street	ASPHALT	[X]		Landscaping	GOOD/TYPICAL
Gas			Curb/Gutter	CONCRETE	[X]		Driveway	POLYPEBBLE
Water	[X]	S'EAST	Sidewalk	NONE			Apparent Easements	NORMAL UTILITIES
Sanitary Sewer	[X]	S'EAST	Street Lights	NONE			FEMA Flood Hazard Yes*	No "C"
Storm Sewer	[X]	COUNTY	Alley	NONE			FEMA* Map/Zone 1251440170	5-84

COMMENTS (Apparent adverse easements, encroachments, special assessments, slide areas, etc.): NO ADVERSE INFLUENCES, EASEMENTS, OR ENCROACHMENTS VISIBLE ON THE PROPERTY. SITE IMPROVEMENTS ARE ADEQUATE AND THE SITE GRADE PERMITS ADEQUATE DRAINAGE AWAY FROM THE HOME'S FOUNDATION.

IMPROVEMENTS

GENERAL DESCRIPTION		EXTERIOR DESCRIPTION		FOUNDATION		BASEMENT	N/A	INSULATION	
Units	1	Foundation	CONCRETE	Slab	YES	Area Sq. Ft.		Roof	
Stories	1	Exterior Walls	CEDAR/STUCCO	Crawl Space	N/A	% Finished		Ceiling	R-38 [X]
Type (Det./Att.)	DET.	Roof Surface	ASPH SHGLS	Basement	N/A	Ceiling		Walls	R-22 [X]
Design (Style)	RANCH	Gutters & Dwnspts.	ALUMINUM	Sump Pump	N/A	Walls		Floor	
Existing	YES	Window Type	ALUMINUM	Dampness	N/A	Floor		None	
Proposed	N/A	Storm Sash	N/A	Settlement	NO	Outside Entry		Adequacy G [X]	
Under Construction	N/A	Screens	YES	Infestation	NO			Energy Efficient Items:	
Age (Yrs.)	11	Manufactured House	N/A				FANS,	FIREPLACE,	
Effective Age (Yrs.)	5-7							H/C SYSTEM	

ROOM LIST

ROOMS	Foyer	Living	Dining	Kitchen	Den	Family Rm.	Rec. Rm.	Bedrooms	# Baths	Laundry	Other	Area Sq. Ft.
Basement											ENCL.	
Level 1	1	1	1	1				3	2	1	PORCH	2,119
Level 2												

Finished area above grade contains: 7 Rooms; 3 Bedroom(s); 2 Bath(s); 2,119 Square Feet of Gross Living Area

INTERIOR

SURFACES	Materials/Condition	HEATING		KITCHEN EQUIP.		ATTIC		IMPROVEMENT ANALYSIS	Good	Avg.	Fair	Poor
Floors	WD/CPT/G	Type	FA/CENT	Refrigerator	[P]	None		Quality of Construction	X			
Walls	DRYWALL/WP/A	Fuel	ELECT	Range/Oven	[X]	Stairs		Condition of Improvements		X		
Trim/Finish	WD/A	Condition	GOOD	Disposal	[X]	Drop Stair	[X]	Room Sizes/Layout		X		
Bath Floor	CT/A	Adequacy	ADEQ	Dishwasher	[X]	Scuttle		Closets and Storage		X		
Bath Wainscot	CT/A	COOLING		Fan/Hood	[X]	Floor		Energy Efficiency		X		
Doors	INT/HC/G	Central	YES	Compactor	[X]	Heated		Plumbing-Adequacy & Condition		X		
EXT/WD/SC/GLASS/G		Other		Washer/Dryer	[X]	Finished		Electrical-Adequacy & Condition		X		
		Condition	GOOD	Microwave	[P]			Kitchen Cabinets-Adequacy & Cond.		X		
Fireplace(s) STONE/FR/G # 1		Adequacy	ADEQ	Intercom				Compatibility to Neighborhood		X		

AUTOS

CAR STORAGE:			IMPROVEMENT ANALYSIS (cont.)	Good	Avg.	Fair	Poor
	Garage [X]	Attached [X] Adequate [X] House Entry [X]	Appeal & Marketability		X		
No. Cars 2	Carport [ ]	Detached [ ] Inadequate [ ] Outside Entry [X]	Estimated Remaining Economic Life 53-55 Yrs.				
Condition GOOD	None [ ]	Built-In [X] Electric Door [x] Basement Entry [ ]	Estimated Remaining Physical Life 55-60 Yrs.				

COMMENTS

Additional features: FRONT ENTRY PORCH, DRIVE AND WALK PAVED WITH POLYPEBBLE, REAR POOL WITH BRONZE CAGE AND POLYPEBBLE DECK, GLASSED-IN PORCH AREA WITH CARPET AND CEILING FANS, ROOF VENTS, WOOD FENCING, ISLAND KITCHEN WITH EXTRA CABINETS.

Depreciation (Physical, functional and external inadequacies, repairs needed, modernization, etc.): NO PHYSICAL CHANGE IS REQUIRED BY THIS REPORT'S VALUE CONCLUSION. MARKET APPEAL IS SUPPORTED BY THE HOME'S FUNCTIONAL UTILITY AND EXTERNAL LOCATIONAL FACTORS. THE PHYSICAL DEPRECIATION REFLECTS THE EFFECTIVE AGE ESTIMATE, BASED ON AREA SALES.

General market conditions and prevalence and impact in subject/market area regarding loan discounts, interest buydowns and concessions: THE MARKET IS CONSIDERED TO BE GENERALLY STABLE. LOAN DISCOUNTS, INTEREST RATE BUYDOWNS AND SALES CONCESSIONS ARE NOT PREVALENT IN THE CURRENT RESALE MARKET. PROMOTIONAL FINANCING CONCESSIONS BY DEVELOPERS/BUILDERS ARE COMMON.

Figure 3.   Appraisal 1. (*continued*)

UNIFORM RESIDENTIAL APPRAISAL REPORT   File No.

Valuation Section

Purpose of Appraisal is to estimate Market Value as defined in the Certification & Statement of Limiting Conditions.

COST APPROACH

BUILDING SKETCH (SHOW GROSS LIVING AREA ABOVE GRADE)
If for Freddie Mac or Fannie Mae, show only square foot calculations and cost approach comments in this space.

SEE SKETCH FOR MEASUREMENT ANALYSIS.
LIVING AREA: 2,119 SQUARE FEET

THE PROPERTY'S VALUE IS WELL SUPPORTED BY ITS
FUNCTIONAL UTILITY AND ITS LOCATION'S EXTERNAL
INFLUENCES. THE DEPRECIATION ESTIMATE REFLECTS
OBSERVED EFFECTIVE AGE, BASED ON AREA SALES.

THE APPRAISAL IS BASED ON A CASH OR EQUIVALENT
SALE AND NO PERSONAL PROPERTY IS INCLUDED IN THE
VALUATION. LAND VALUE IS BASED ON AREA LAND
SALES. THE LAND/VALUE RATIO OF THE SUBJECT
PROPERTY IS SUPPORTED BY THOSE FOR COMPARABLE
PROPERTIES.

ESTIMATED REPRODUCTION COST-NEW-OF IMPROVEMENTS:

Dwelling	2,119 Sq. Ft. @ $ 40.00	= $	84,760
ENTRY	60 Sq. Ft. @ $ 12.00	=	720
Extras		=	18,000
Special Energy Efficient Items INCLUDED		=	
Porches, Patios, etc. 458 SF @ $25		=	11,450
Garage/~~Carport~~ 525 Sq. Ft. @ $ 18.00		=	9,450
Total Estimated Cost New		= $	124,380

	Physical	Functional	External		
Less					
Depreciation	13M	N/A	N/A	= $	13,000
Depreciated Value of Improvements				= $	111,380
Site Imp. "as is" (driveway, landscaping, etc.)				= $	9,020
ESTIMATED SITE VALUE				= $	45,000
(If leasehold, show only leasehold value.)					165,400
INDICATED VALUE BY COST APPROACH				= $	

(Not Required by Freddie Mac and Fannie Mae)
Does property conform to applicable HUD/VA property standards? ☐ Yes ☐ No
If No, explain: _____

Construction Warranty ☐ Yes [X] No
Name of Warranty Program N/A
Warranty Coverage Expires N/A

SALES COMPARISON ANALYSIS

The undersigned has recited three recent sales of properties most similar and proximate to subject and has considered these in the market analysis. The description includes a dollar adjustment, reflecting market reaction to those items of significant variation between the subject and comparable properties. If a significant item in the comparable property is superior to, or more favorable than, the subject property, a minus (−) adjustment is made, thus reducing the indicated value of subject; if a significant item in the comparable is inferior to, or less favorable than, the subject property, a plus (+) adjustment is made, thus increasing the indicated value of the subject.

ITEM	SUBJECT	COMPARABLE NO. 1	+ (−) $ Adjustment	COMPARABLE NO. 2	+ (−) $ Adjustment	COMPARABLE NO. 3	+ (−) $ Adjustment
Address	456 CHERRY HILL ROAD	403 BENT TREE LANE		475 CHERRY HILL ROAD		191 FOREST TRAIL	
Proximity to Subject		1/4 MILE NW		SAME STREET		1 MILE NE	
Sales Price	$ 165,000	$160,000		$ 149,500		$149,000	
Price/Gross Liv. Area	$ 77.87	$ 75.65		$ 78.89		$ 86.78	
Data Source	LENDER	PUBLIC RECORDS		PUBLIC RECORDS		PUBLIC RECORDS	
VALUE ADJUSTMENTS	DESCRIPTION	DESCRIPTION	+ (−) $ Adjustment	DESCRIPTION	+ (−) $ Adjustment	DESCRIPTION	+ (−) $ Adjustment
Sales or Financing Concessions		CONV MTG		CONV MTG		CONV MTG	
Date of Sale/Time	CURRENT	1 MONTH AGO		2 MONTHS AGO		5 MONTHS AGO	
Location	GOOD	EQUAL		EQUAL		INFERIOR	+5,000
Site/View	13,907/AVG	14,200/EQUAL		11,370/INF	+5,000	10,000/INF	+7,100
Design and Appeal	RANCH/GOOD	RANCH/EQUAL		RANCH/EQUAL		RANCH/EQUAL	
Quality of Construction	AVG/ASPH R	AVG/ASPH R		AVG/TILE/SUP	−2,000	AVG/RANCH R	
Age	11	11		10		5	−3,000
Condition	GOOD	GOOD		GOOD		GOOD	
Above Grade Room Count	Total 7 / Bdrms 3 / Baths 2	Total 7 / Bdrms 3 / Baths 2		Total 7 / Bdrms 3 / Baths 2		Total 7 / Bdrms 3 / Baths 2	
Gross Living Area	2,119 Sq. Ft.	2,115 Sq. Ft.		1,895 Sq. Ft.		1,717 Sq. Ft.	
Basement & Finished Rooms Below Grade	NONE	NONE		NONE		NONE	
Functional Utility	GOOD	GOOD		GOOD		GOOD	
Heating/Cooling	FA/CENT	FA/CENT		FA/CENT		FA/CENT	
Garage/Carport	GARAGE/2	GARAGE/2		GARAGE/2		GARAGE/2/SM	+1,000
Porches, Patio, Pools, etc.	ENCL/PORCH CAGED POOL	EQUAL SMALLER	+4,000	SMALLER EQUAL	+5,000	SMALLER EQUAL	+5,000
Special Energy Efficient Items	H/C SYSTEM FANS	EQUAL EQUAL		EQUAL EQUAL		EQUAL EQUAL	
Fireplace(s)	STONE/1	NONE	+1,500	NONE	+1,500	EQUAL	
Other (e.g. kitchen equip., remodeling)	BUILT-INS KITCHEN	EQUAL		EQUAL		EQUAL	
Net Adj. (total)		[X] + ☐ − $ 5,500		[X] + ☐ − $ 9,500		[X] + ☐ − $ 15,100	
Indicated Value of Subject		$ 165,500		$ 159,000		$ 164,100	

Comments on Sales Comparison: ALL THREE SALES ARE LOCATED WITHIN THE SAME GENERAL AREA. SALE 1 WAS GIVEN THE MOST WEIGHT IN THE FINAL ANALYSIS BECAUSE IT REQUIRED THE FEWEST ADJUSTMENTS AND IS MOST SIMILAR OVERALL.

INDICATED VALUE BY SALES COMPARISON APPROACH .... $ 165,000

INDICATED VALUE BY INCOME APPROACH (If Applicable) Estimated Market Rent $ N/A /Mo. x Gross Rent Multiplier N/A = $

This appraisal is made [X] "as is" ☐ subject to the repairs, alterations, inspections or conditions listed below ☐ completion per plans and specifications.
Comments and Conditions of Appraisal: THE INCOME APPROACH IS NOT CONSIDERED APPLICABLE FOR PROPERTIES IN THIS AREA. THERE ARE NO SPECIAL FINANCING CONSIDERATIONS.

RECONCILIATION

Final Reconciliation: THE FINAL VALUE ESTIMATE IS BASED ON THE SALES COMPARISON APPROACH, AS THAT IS A REASONABLE AND SUPPORTABLE METHOD FOR THIS TYPE OF PROPERTY.

This appraisal is based upon the above requirements, the certification, contingent and limiting conditions, and Market Value definition that are stated in
☐ FmHA, HUD &/or VA instructions.
☐ Freddie Mac Form 439 (Rev. 7/86)/Fannie Mae Form 1004B (Rev. 7/86) filed with client _____ 19 ____ ☐ attached.
I (WE) ESTIMATE THE MARKET VALUE, AS DEFINED, OF THE SUBJECT PROPERTY AS OF SEPTEMBER 8 19 90 **to be $** 165,000
I (We) certify: that to the best of my (our) knowledge and belief the facts and data used herein are true and correct; that I (we) personally inspected the subject property, both inside and out, and have made an exterior inspection of all comparable sales cited in this report; and that I (we) have no undisclosed interest, present or prospective therein.

Appraiser(s) SIGNATURE *James Havlic*   Review Appraiser SIGNATURE *Todd Simpson*   ☐ Did [X] Did Not
NAME JAMES HAVLIC   (if applicable) NAME TODD SIMPSON   Inspect Property

Figure 3.   Appraisal 1. (*continued*)—Building Sketch

4564 Charing Cross Rd.

43

Cage

Pool

Cage

Poly pebble patio

39
Glassed in Porch
458#

14

10

Bronze "A" Frame Cage

17   4   22   4   21

BR

Kitchen

Living Room

Bath

25

46

Dining Room

FPL

BR

46

Foyer
12

Bath

5 Entry

Ldy. Clos.

6.5   20.5

6.5

Dressing Room

Master BR

60#

Garage
525#

21

CLOSET

17

21

27

Living Area #
4 X 22 =   88
6.5 X 6.5 =   42
21 X 46 =   906
12 X 29 =   348
25 X 27 =   675
TOTAL 2,1199#

Figure 3. Appraisal 1. (*continued*) — Neighborhood Map

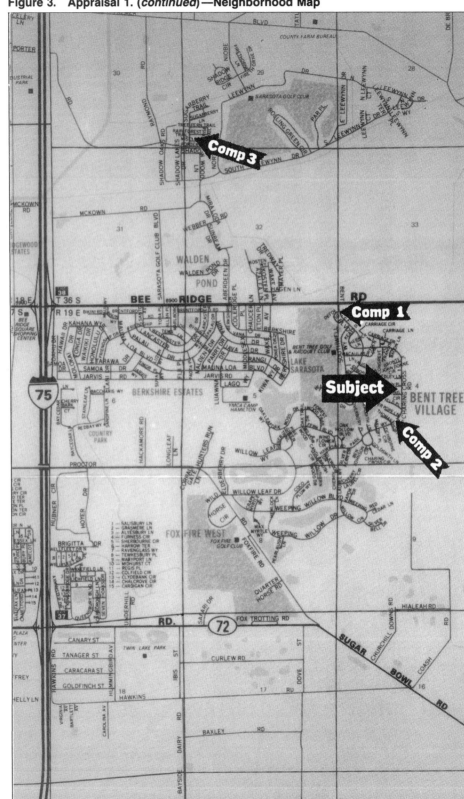

SOURCE: Map from the Sarasota Street Map © 1988 by Rand McNally R.L. 91-S-51. Reprinted with permission.

Figure 3. Appraisal 1. (*continued*)

Subject

Comparable 1.

Figure 3.   Appraisal 1. (*continued*)

Comparable 2.

Comparable 3.

PART THREE

The Uniform Residential Appraisal Report: A Closer View

Subject

Property Description & Analysis	**UNIFORM RESIDENTIAL APPRAISAL REPORT**		File No.		

SUBJECT					
Property Address			Census Tract	LENDER DISCRETIONARY USE	
City	County	State	Zip Code	Sale Price	$
Legal Description				Date	
Owner/Occupant			Map Reference	Mortgage Amount	$
Sale Price $	Date of Sale		PROPERTY RIGHTS APPRAISED	Mortgage Type	
Loan charges/concessions to be paid by seller $			☐ Fee Simple	Discount Points and Other Concessions	
R.E. Taxes $	Tax Year	HOA $/Mo.	☐ Leasehold	Paid by Seller	$
Lender/Client			☐ Condominium (HUD/VA)		
			☐ De Minimis PUD	Source	

Every appraisal begins in the same way. The appraiser defines the appraisal problem. Complete this section of the URAR form by following these steps:

- Give a complete legal description of the subject property.
- State the property rights being appraised.

File No.

The lender or agency involved may require that their file number be supplied in this space at the top right of each page of the form.

▶ **FmHA** Enter FmHA case number.
▶ **HUD/FHA** Enter FHA case number.

Property Address

Enter street address, if there is one, or rural route number. Enough information must be provided to locate the property.

▶ **FNMA** Use a complete property address. A post office box number is *not* acceptable. If the property has no house number, indicate the nearest intersection.

> ▶ **FmHA** Do *not* use a post office box number. If necessary, attach a map to the report showing the property location.

Census Tract

The United States is divided into numbered areas that are used for reference when census data are compiled. Enter the one- to six-digit census tract number. This number is found on the census tract map. If the property is within a rural area that does not have a designated tract number, enter N/A.

Census tract maps showing the tract numbers can be obtained from the Superintendent of Documents, Government Printing Office, Washington, DC 20402, (202) 783-3238, or the Data User Services Division, Customer Services (Publications), Bureau of the Census, Washington, DC 20233, (301) 763-4100.

For more complete identification, list the four-digit Standard Metropolitan Statistical Area (SMSA) number in this space, before the census tract number. SMSA numbers are available from regional offices of the Bureau of the Census.

City

Enter the name of the city within which the property is located or, if the property is outside the city limits, where the post office serving the property address is located.

County

Enter the name of the county within which the property is located. If the property is located in more than one county, all counties should be named.

State

Enter the full name or the two-letter postal abbreviation of the state within which the property is located. If the property is located in more than one state, all states should be named.

Zip Code

Enter the U.S. Postal Service five- or nine-digit delivery zone code.

Legal Description

Fill in the property description found in the grant deed to the present owner. If the deed in the owner's possession cannot be examined, examine a copy of it at the county recorder's office or office of register of deeds. If the legal description is lengthy, it may be included in a separate attachment.

> ▶ **FNMA** If the legal description is too long to fit the space on the form, include it as an addendum to the form *or* refer to the public records where the legal description can be found.
> ▶ **FmHA** Attach a full legal description of the property to the form, indicating any restrictions, easements or reservations.

▶ **RTC** The account officer should supply the appraiser with a copy of the property's legal description.

Owner/Occupant

The present legal owner of the property should always be identified. The borrower also can be identified here by adding the word BORROWER and that person's name. If the owner is not occupying the property, cross out the word "Occupant" on this line and enter the word OCCUPANT and that person's name on the last line of the *SUBJECT* section. If the property is vacant, note that fact.

Map Reference

Identify a commonly used map of the local area and enter the map reference points showing the location of the subject property. Attach a copy of the portion of the map showing the subject's location should be attached to the form as an addendum.

Sale Price $

If a sale of the property is pending enter the amount of the sale price stipulated in the contract of sale. If the sale price information comes from another source, identify that source. If the transaction is a property exchange, enter EXCHANGE. If the appraisal is being made as part of a loan refinancing, enter REFINANCE. If no sale or other transaction is pending, enter N/A or NONE.

▶ **FNMA** The lender must provide the appraiser with a copy of the sales contract and any other pertinent information known to the lender.

▶ **RTC** The appraisal is made assuming a sale on a cash basis *or*, if market conditions are such that there is a lack of comparable sales on a cash basis, the evaluation can be based on "typical terms" in the market area. If typical terms are assumed, they must be defined in the appraisal and their influence on market value (plus or minus) must be described and estimated. The appraiser may also make two separate valuations, one based on a cash basis sale and the other based on a sale on typical terms. RTC does not want "fire sale" or "liquidation value" appraisals.

Date of Sale

If a sale of the property is pending, enter the date on which the sale is to be closed. For any other transaction, enter N/A and the type of transaction; for example N/A *(REFINANCE)*. Alternatively, this line could be used to indicate the date of *appraisal*. If so, cross out the word "Sale" and enter APPRAISAL and the date.

Loan charges/concessions to be paid by seller $

The amount of any loan charges or other concessions to be paid by the seller should be entered here. This information will be revealed by inspecting the contract of sale, which the lender should provide to the appraiser.

If no loan charges or concessions to be paid by the seller are indicated by the contract of sale, then NONE (CONTRACT OF SALE) should be entered. If the appraiser's information comes from any other source (such as the broker, buyer, seller or lender), that source should be indicated.

▶ **FNMA** Enter the total dollar amount of any loan charges and/or concessions to be paid by the seller or any other party with a financial interest in the sale or financing of the subject property. The charges and/or concessions should be described briefly. If the appraisal is for purposes of a refinancing, that fact should be noted. Examples of loan charges and other concessions include:

- Settlement charges;
- Loan fees or charges;
- Discounts to the sale price;
- Payment of condominium or PUD fees;
- Interest rate buydowns or other below-market-rate financing;
- Refunds or credits;
- Absorption of monthly payments;
- Assignment of rent payments; and
- Nonrealty items included in the transaction.

▶ **VA** The appraiser is not required to investigate and complete this information but should supply it, if known, and its source. Otherwise enter NONE KNOWN.

R.E. Taxes $

Enter the total annual property tax due and whether the tax is paid on a current basis (for the current tax year) or in arrears (for the preceding tax year). If any amount is past due it should be entered with the notation PAST DUE. The tax amount can be found by examining the seller's tax bill or contacting the county tax assessor's or treasurer's office. It may also appear on the preliminary title report.

In some areas (such as California), property is reassessed for tax purposes at the time of sale. For California property enter the current total annual tax rate charged by the community in which the property is located. There will be very little difference among communities, however, because the base tax rate is set by state law.

▶ **RTC** Give the amount of annual property taxes and any past due taxes. Comment on the reasonableness of the taxes and, if they are high, explain their impact on appraised value.

Tax Year

Enter the tax year for which information is supplied.

HOA $/Mo.

If the property includes shared ownership of common areas under the authority of a homeowners' association, the amount charged per month for association fees (or one month's share of the amount charged for any other time period) should be entered here. Association fees typically are used to pay for landscaping and other exterior maintenance, upkeep of any shared buildings or other facilities (such as a clubhouse, swimming pool or tennis court) and administration expenses.

If the amount charged seems too high or too low for the area, note that fact.

Lender/Client

If the appraiser is performing the appraisal for a lender, enter the lender's name. If the appraiser is being paid by anyone else, indicate that person by name and status (such as OWNER or BUYER).

> ▸ **FmHA** If the report is to be used for loan-making purposes, enter the loan applicant's name. If the report is to be used for loan-servicing purposes, enter the borrower's name or advice number.
> ▸ **RTC** The appraisal may be used for multiple purposes, including bids at foreclosure sales, large protective advances and operating budgets as well as a property sale.

PROPERTY RIGHTS APPRAISED

Identify the property rights being appraised, as described below.

> ▸ **FmHA** Check the appropriate box.
> ▸ **FNMA** The URAR form can be used for single-family properties, including PUDs. FNMA has eliminated the *de minimis* PUD classification. A PUD unit can be appraised by using the URAR with the URAR PUD Addendum shown in Figure 4 or by using the Appraisal Report—Individual Condominium or PUD Unit (Form 1073). The URAR *cannot* be used for condominiums or cooperative projects. The property rights being appraised should be identified as either fee simple or leasehold.
> ▸ **VA** The URAR can be used for all property types. Always strike out the words "De Minimis," as this form can be used for any type of PUD. Condominium or PUD assessment fees, which must be reported, should be entered in the *COMMENTS* block of the *SITE* section.

Fee Simple

The highest right of ownership, also called *fee simple absolute*. Although most residential property is owned in fee simple, this does not mean that the property will be entirely free of easements, encroachments, deed reservations and restrictions, and the like. Any such encumbrance or reservation of an ownership right should be noted as specified on the appraisal form, in the *COMMENTS* block of the *SITE*

Figure 4. URAR PUD Addendum

URAR PUD ADDENDUM
INDIVIDUAL PLANNED UNIT DEVELOPMENT (PUD) UNIT
OR DE MINIMIS PUD UNIT
SUPPLEMENTAL PROJECT INFORMATION

Borrower/Client

Property Address

City   County   State   Zip

Lender

This Information is required when the appraiser uses the Uniform Residential Appraisal Report
(URAR) (FHLMC #70 - FNMA #1004) to appraise a PUD Unit or a De Minimis PUD Unit.
TO BE COMPLETED FOR ALL PUD AND DE MINIMIS PUD APPRAISALS

This appraisal is of an: _____ Individual PUD Unit   _____ Individual De Minimis PUD Unit

If completed: No. Phases _____   No. Units _____   No. Sold _____

If incomplete: Planned No. Phases _____   No. Units _____   No. Sold _____

Units in Subject Phase: Total _____   Completed _____   Sold _____   Rented _____

Approx. No. of Units for Sale: Subject Project _____   Subject Phase _____

Description of the common elements and recreational facilities: _____

Owners' association fees per month for the subject unit: $ _____

Utilities that are included in the owners' association fees:

_____ Water   _____ Gas   _____ Heat   _____ Others _____
_____ Hot Water   _____ Telephone   _____ Electricity   _____

Comment about whether the unit owners' association fees are reasonable in comparison to those for units in other projects of similar quality and design: _____

Comment about whether the project appears to be well-maintained: _____

The following information is a continuation of the sales comparison analysis presented in the attached URAR. The comparables used are the same as those used on the URAR. Adjustments made for the specific project information presented below are made in the same manner and are included in the total adjustments stated on the URAR.

	Subject	Comp. No. 1		Comp. No. 2		Comp. No. 3	
Project Name							
Item	Description	Description	+ Adj.	Description	+ Adj.	Description	+ Adj.
Common Elements and Recreational Facilities							
Mo. Assessment							
Number of Units in Project							
Leasehold/Fee							
Total Adjustment		$		$		$	

Comments on the analysis of common property, monthly assessment, and ownership rights. _____

Additional Comments: _____

APPRAISER(S)   REVIEW APPRAISER
Signature _____   (if applicable) Signature _____   ☐ Did
Name _____   Name _____   ☐ Did Not
                                                          Inspect Property

USF#04000   U.S. Forms Inc. 2 Central Square Grafton, MA 01519-0446 (508)839-4417 1-800-225-9583 section, or on the attached legal description. In oil states, conveyance of residential property with a reservation of mineral (oil and gas) rights in a former owner is common.

Leasehold

The right of one who has possession but not ownership. Leasehold interests in single-family residential real estate are rarely valued.

Condominium (HUD/VA)

Ownership of a defined airspace along with a share of common elements.

> ▶ **FNMA** Do not use the URAR form. Use Appraisal Report— Individual Condominium or PUD Unit (Form 1073) instead.

De Minimis PUD

This classification is no longer used. Cross out the words "De Minimis" if the property is a single-family residence in a planned unit development (PUD) that includes a shared interest in recreational or open space, clubhouse and sports or other facilities.

> ▶ **VA** You may use this form with *any* kind of PUD; strike out the words "De Minimis."

LENDER DISCRETIONARY USE

This section is completed by the lender, if there is one.

> ▶ **FmHA** Leave this section blank.
> ▶ **FNMA** This is the only section the appraiser does *not* complete. The lender should, but is not required to, complete this section following closing of the sale to provide information to comparable sales reporting services.
> ▶ **HUD/FHA** This section is to be completed by the field office or direct endorsement lender's underwriter after the purchaser has been approved and the case is ready for closing.
> ▶ **VA** This section is completed by the lender at the lender's discretion.

Sale Price $

Entered by lender.

Date

Entered by lender.

Mortgage Amount $

Entered by lender.

Mortgage Type

Entered by lender.

Discount Points and Other Concessions

Entered by lender.

Paid by Seller $

Entered by lender.

Source

Entered by lender.

► **Appraisal 1**

☐☐☐   **UNIFORM RESIDENTIAL APPRAISAL REPORT**   **File No.**
Property Description & Analysis   ☐☐☐

Property Address 456 CHERRY HILL ROAD	Census Tract 14

LENDER DISCRETIONARY USE
Sale Price $ _____

City SARASOTA County SARASOTA State FL Zip Code 34200	Date _____
Legal Description LOT 308 BENT TREE VILLAGE S/D, BK 12, PAGES 12-12 F	Mortgage Amount $ _____
Owner/Occupant SILAS REMBRANDT Map Reference G58	

PROPERTY RIGHTS APPRAISED — Mortgage Type

Sale Price $ 165,000   Date of Sale OCTOBER 15, 1990   [x] Fee Simple   Discount Points and Other Concessions

Loan charges/concessions to be paid by seller $ NONE   ☐ Leasehold   Paid by Seller $ _____

R.E. Taxes $ 1,123.73   Tax Year 1990-91   HOA $/Mo.   ☐ Condominium (HUD/VA)

Lender/Client MURPHY MORTGAGE CO., P.O. BOX 134   ☐ De Minimis PUD   Source

SERRA, FL 34224-1347

In Appraisal 1, the subject property is located at 456 Cherry Hill Road, Sarasota, Sarasota County, Florida. The census tract number is 14. The property's legal description is:

Lot 308, Bent Tree Village Subdivision, as recorded in Book 12, Pages 12-12 F of maps, Sarasota County, Florida

The owner and present occupant of the property is Silas Rembrandt. The map reference number is G58. The sale price of the property is $165,000, and the date of sale is October 15, 1990. There are no loan charges or concessions to be paid by the seller. The real estate taxes

for the tax year 1990–91 are $1,123.73. There are no homeowners' association dues on this property.

The appraisal is being performed for the Murphy Mortgage Company, P.O. Box 134, Serra, Florida 34224-1347, the buyer's lender. The subject property is a single-family detached residence in a *de minimis* planned unit development. There is a community-shared golf course, but membership is voluntary. There are homeowners' association dues of $100 per year to cover maintenance to the landscaped median down the main entrance road to the development. A fee simple interest in the property is being sold.

▶ Exercise: Appraisal 2

☐☐☐						☐☐☐

Property Description & Analysis **UNIFORM RESIDENTIAL APPRAISAL REPORT** **File No.**

Property Address	Census Tract	LENDER DISCRETIONARY USE
City	County	State	Zip Code	Sale Price $
Legal Description		Date
Owner/Occupant	Map Reference	Mortgage Amount $
Sale Price $	Date of Sale	PROPERTY RIGHTS APPRAISED	Mortgage Type
Loan charges/concessions to be paid by seller $	☐ Fee Simple	Discount Points and Other Concessions
R.E. Taxes $	Tax Year	HOA $/Mo.	☐ Leasehold	Paid by Seller $
Lender/Client	☐ Condominium (HUD/VA)	
	☐ De Minimis PUD	Source

Complete the blank URAR SUBJECT section provided above for Appraisal 2, using the following information. When you have finished, check your work against the completed Appraisal 2 in the Answer Key.

The subject property is a single-family detached residence located at 1053 Locust Lane, Pleasantown, Sunnyside County, Anystate. The census tract number is 9999. The property's legal description is:

Lot 5 of Block 32 of Pioneer Ranch Subdivision, as shown on page 997 of book 438, records of Sunnyside County.

Mildred and Frank Justice, a married couple, own and occupy the property, which includes no common areas. On September 15, 1991, they signed an Offer to Purchase and Receipt for Deposit made to them by Jack Morris and Hope Temple, a married couple. The sale price is $265,000. Property is assessed locally at a combined tax rate of .0145, which includes property, school and transportation district taxes typical for this metropolitan area. The current tax year is 1990–91 and no taxes are past due. There is no homeowners' association. This appraisal is being made at the request of the buyers' lender, State Savings Bank.

Neighborhood

					NEIGHBORHOOD ANALYSIS	Good	Avg.	Fair	Poor
LOCATION	☐ Urban	☐ Suburban	☐ Rural		Employment Stability	☐	☐	☐	☐
BUILT UP	☐ Over 75%	☐ 25-75%	☐ Under 25%		Convenience to Employment	☐	☐	☐	☐
GROWTH RATE	☐ Rapid	☐ Stable	☐ Slow		Convenience to Shopping	☐	☐	☐	☐
PROPERTY VALUES	☐ Increasing	☐ Stable	☐ Declining		Convenience to Schools	☐	☐	☐	☐
DEMAND/SUPPLY	☐ Shortage	☐ In Balance	☐ Over Supply		Adequacy of Public Transportation	☐	☐	☐	☐
MARKETING TIME	☐ Under 3 Mos.	☐ 3-6 Mos.	☐ Over 6 Mos.		Recreation Facilities	☐	☐	☐	☐

PRESENT LAND USE %	LAND USE CHANGE	PREDOMINANT OCCUPANCY	SINGLE FAMILY HOUSING PRICE $ (000) / AGE (yrs)						
Single Family ____	Not Likely ☐	Owner ☐		Adequacy of Utilities	☐	☐	☐	☐	
2-4 Family ____	Likely ☐	Tenant ☐		Property Compatibility	☐	☐	☐	☐	
Multi-family ____	In process ☐	Vacant (0-5%) ☐	Low	Protection from Detrimental Cond.	☐	☐	☐	☐	
Commercial ____	To: ____	Vacant (over 5%) ☐	High	Police & Fire Protection	☐	☐	☐	☐	
Industrial ____			Predominant	General Appearance of Properties	☐	☐	☐	☐	
Vacant ____			—	Appeal to Market	☐	☐	☐	☐	

Note: Race or the racial composition of the neighborhood are not considered reliable appraisal factors.
COMMENTS: _____

Study of the neighborhood is the starting point in gathering factual information, because anything that affects the neighborhood also affects the property being appraised. What exactly defines a *neighborhood?* In practice, it is the area within which any change has an immediate and direct influence on the value of the subject property.

Neighborhood boundaries are often established by natural barriers such as rivers, lakes and hills, or by man-made barriers such as streets, highways and rail lines. Boundaries also may be created by differences in land use, the income level of residents, the average value of homes, city limits, census tracts, political divisions, school districts and so on. The appraiser should understand the reasons for selecting neighborhood boundaries and be prepared to explain them in the report.

A residential neighborhood is constantly undergoing changes throughout its life cycle. A neighborhood's life cycle usually involves the following stages, varying only in intensity and duration:

1. Development and growth;
2. Stability;
3. Transition; and
4. Decline.

Because neighborhood analysis is so important, most appraisers include, as an addendum to the URAR, a *neighborhood map* showing neighborhood boundaries, the location of the subject property and the location of comparable properties used in the sales comparison approach. An example of a neighborhood map used in Appraisal 1 appears on page 24.

Complete this section of the URAR form by following the steps listed below.

- Define the local market area—the neighborhood—in terms of property supply and demand factors.
- Analyze present and likely future land uses.
- Describe available housing ownership and price levels.
- Grade neighborhood amenities.
- Comment on any other neighborhood factors likely to affect market value.

▶ **FNMA** A neighborhood analysis considers the influence of social, economic, government and environmental forces on property values in the subject neighborhood. Be specific and impartial in describing favorable or unfavorable factors. Avoid using subjective terms or phrases, such as "pride of ownership."

   The racial composition of a neighborhood is never a reliable appraisal factor. Fannie Mae does not designate certain areas as acceptable or unacceptable; that is, "red-line." Locational factors may be considered if based on a realistic perception of risk in a given neighborhood, but may not be based on improper factors such as race. Factors that serve as a "proxy for race" are "equally impermissible." Fannie Mae's guidelines are not intended to foster redlining in any form.

   In urban areas currently undergoing redevelopment, block-by-block underwriting and appraisal analysis are acceptable in considering either the block in which the subject property is located or facing blocks. The appraiser must demonstrate that local conditions support the appropriateness of the analysis used and that all essential factors have been considered.

LOCATION

Determine whether the subject property is in an *urban, suburban* or *rural* neighborhood and check the appropriate box.

▶ **FNMA** An *urban* location is one that relates to a *city; suburban* relates to the *area adjacent to a city;* and *rural* relates to the *country* or *anything beyond the suburban area.*

Fannie Mae purchases only those mortgages secured by property that is residential in nature. The determination of whether property is residential is based on consideration of the description of the subject property, zoning and present land use. Fannie Mae does not purchase mortgages on agricultural–type properties (such as farms, orchards or ranches), undeveloped land or land development–type properties.

The presence of significant outbuildings such as a silo, barn or other animal storage facility must be reviewed with great care by the lender, whether or not they contribute to appraised value, because they may indicate property that is agricultural in nature. On the other hand, outbuildings that are typical for residential properties in the area, such as a small barn or stable, and that are relatively insignificant in terms of their effect on property value, are acceptable.

All properties must be readily accessible by roads that meet local standards. All properties must have adequate utilities available and in service. Present or anticipated future uses of any adjoining property that may adversely affect the value or marketability of the subject property must be considered.

Properties in resort or vacation areas are acceptable only if they are suitable for year-round use. *Any property not suitable for year-round occupancy—regardless of location—is unacceptable.*

BUILT UP

This section indicates the percentage of *available* land in the neighborhood that has been improved. Land reserved for parks and other public uses is not included.

Over 75%

Check this box if more than 75% of the available land in the neighborhood has been improved.

25–75%

Check this box if between 25% and 75% of the available land in the neighborhood has been improved.

Under 25%

Check this box if less than 25% of the available land in the neighborhood has been improved.

If the "Under 25%" box is checked, the appraiser should comment on the reason for the low percentage of development and the neighborhood's future direction.

▶ **FNMA** Areas that are less than 25% developed are not acceptable for maximum financing.

In an area that is less than 25% developed, site values may not exceed 30% of total appraised value *unless* the higher site value is typical of comparable properties in the area. For example, if zoning, highest and best use and the present land use allow a two-acre lot size and this size is typical for the area, the site may warrant a higher proportion of total value.

GROWTH RATE

Indicate the rate of development within the subject neighborhood in relation to normal market factors. For example, a neighborhood that is 50% built up and is between three and five years old may be experiencing normal growth, but a 20-year-old neighborhood that is 50% built up may be suffering some form of stagnation.

A neighborhood's growth can be checked by contacting the local building department and asking for building permit statistics for the past several years and the year to date. Large numbers of permits can be translated into rapid growth.

Rapid

Check this box if the neighborhood is developing at a faster rate than are comparable neighborhoods.

Stable

Check this box if the neighborhood is developing at about the same rate as comparable neighborhoods, or if the neighborhood is fully developed.

Slow

Check this box if the neighborhood is developing at a slower rate than comparable neighborhoods.

If the *Slow* box is checked, the appraiser should explain the possible effect on the marketability and value of the subject property.

PROPERTY VALUES

The appraiser must indicate the current trend in market prices. Although some price fluctuations will be seasonal and are to be expected, year-to-year price changes for comparable properties should be charted to determine the overall trend of the market.

Note that, even though this category is described as PROPERTY VALUES, it refers to actual selling prices rather than estimated or appraised market values. Property sellers may feel they have "lost" value when a period of rapid appreciation is followed by a period of slower appreciation and high value expectations (asking prices) are not met, when in fact property values have increased overall though at a slower rate in some periods.

▸ **FNMA** Maximum financing is acceptable when property values are stable or increasing. If values are declining, comment on the reason for the decline and its effect on the property's marketability. Properties in such areas must be reviewed with great care. The reasons for a decline in values and the probability of its continuance are key considerations in the property's acceptability. The lender must not consider the use of maximum financing in any instance in which property values are declining.

Increasing

Check this box if property values have increased over the past year.

Stable

Check this box if property values have varied only slightly over the past year.

Declining

Check this box if property values have declined over the past year. Explain any decline in the *COMMENTS* part of this section.

▸ **HUD/FHA** When both the *Urban* and *Declining* boxes are checked, consider recommending that "the mortgage encumbering the property be insured pursuant to Section 223(e)."

DEMAND/SUPPLY

Property values will rise as demand increases and/or supply decreases. In the ideal market, supply and demand are in balance—there are enough home buyers relative to the number of houses on the market to keep prices stable. In reality, however, a perfect market is rare, and at any given time a neighborhood is likely to have a *seller's market* (not enough suitable, well-priced houses for sale to satisfy demand) or a *buyer's market* (many more houses for sale than demand warrants).

The demand/supply relationship in a neighborhood can be determined by analyzing the:

- Number of days houses have been on the market;
- Changes in sales prices over a period of time; and
- Number of sales versus the number of listings.

Shortage

Check this box if market data show a shortage of properties for sale, relative to demand.

In Balance

Check this box if market data show that demand/supply is in balance; that is, the number of sales has kept pace with the number of listings.

Over Supply

Check this box if the market data show an oversupply of properties for sale relative to demand.

If the *Over Supply* box is checked, comment on the reason for the excess and its probable effect on the value of the subject property.

> ▶ **FNMA** An oversupply of housing is undesirable, because it will result in property selling slowly. An oversupply may be neighborhoodwide or citywide. In either case, comment on the reason for the oversupply and its effect on property value.

A shortage of properties or a balance is preferred.

MARKETING TIME

Indicate the average time it takes to sell a reasonably priced property from the date it is first listed. The key phrase here is *reasonably priced*. An overpriced house may linger on the market indefinitely, undergoing an excruciating (to the seller) round of price reductions before finally attracting a buyer. On the other hand, an underpriced property may receive several purchase offers the first day it is listed. Neither situation may be an accurate reflection of the overall market.

A strong interrelationship exists among supply and demand, marketing time and property values. For example, a lengthy marketing time indicates a buyer's market (low demand and high supply) and often declining values. A relatively short marketing period suggests a seller's market (high demand and low supply), often resulting in stabilized to increasing property values.

Information relating to marketing time can be obtained from a local multiple listing service (MLS).

Under 3 Mos.

Check this box if the average property in the neighborhood sells in less than three months.

3–6 Mos.

Check this box if the average property in the neighborhood sells within three to six months.

Over 6 Mos.

Check this box if the average property in the neighborhood takes over six months to sell.

▶ **FNMA** When marketing time in a particular area is more than six months, comment on the reason why, as well as the effect the extended marketing period may have on the property's value.

PRESENT LAND USE %

Estimate the current use of available land in the subject neighborhood, in the categories listed. The total of all listed uses must equal 100%. If land in the neighborhood is used for purposes other than those indicated on the form, the appraiser should specify the property type and its percentage of use in the *COMMENTS* part of this section.

▶ **FmHA** Enter percentage of predominant use within the neighborhood. All figures should total 100%.

▶ **FNMA** Typically, dwellings best maintain their value when they are situated in neighborhoods that consist of other similar dwellings. Therefore, a single-family property in a neighborhood with apartments and commercial or industrial development may not have the stability required to sustain value over a long period of time. However, the negative impression of a property within a mixed-use neighborhood can be offset by factors that enhance the market value of the property through increased buyer demand. Typical enhancement factors include easy access to employment centers and a high level of community activity. Viable older neighborhoods frequently reflect a successful mix of commercial service uses such as grocery and other neighborhood stores or occasional multifamily properties.

Enter the relative percentages of the *developed* land uses listed on the form, rather than simply referring to the zoning classifications. Undeveloped land, regardless of zoning, should be reported as vacant.

Single Family

Estimate and record the percentage of land in the subject neighborhood used for single-family homes.

2–4 Family

Estimate and record the percentage of land in the subject neighborhood used for two- to four-family housing.

Multi-family

Estimate and record the percentage of land in the subject neighborhood used for properties that contain five or more units.

Commercial

Estimate and record the percentage of land in the subject neighborhood developed for businesses such as retail shops, office buildings, motels, hotels, theaters, restaurants and other commercial uses.

Industrial

Estimate and record the percentage of land in the subject neighborhood developed for factories, warehouses, utilities and other industrial uses.

Vacant

Estimate and record the percentage of vacant land in the subject neighborhood; that is, undeveloped land that otherwise is available for development.

> ▶ **FNMA** If there is a "significant" amount of vacant or undeveloped land in the neighborhood, comment on that fact in the *COMMENTS* part of this section.

LAND USE CHANGE

Indicate any ongoing or likely significant change in land use within the subject neighborhood. Explain in detail the impact of any such change on marketability and value in the *COMMENTS* Part of this section.

> ▶ **FmHA** Enter the potential for change in use within the neighborhood, within the next three to five years.
> ▶ **FNMA** To determine whether a neighborhood is undergoing transition, FNMA looks to present land use, predominant occupancy composition and the likelihood that either will change.

Not Likely

Check this box if it is unlikely that the neighborhood's land use will change.

Likely

Check this box if a change in the neighborhood's land use is likely, but no change has yet begun.

In process

Check this box if the neighborhood is currently changing to a new land use.

> ▶ **FNMA** A "neighborhood in transition" description must not be used to refer to the racial or ethnic composition—or the prospective racial or ethnic composition—of a neighborhood. ▶

The use of maximum financing must be carefully considered if the appraiser indicates that an area is undergoing transition that could have a negative impact on property value. For example, a neighborhood that is changing from a single-family use to a two- to four-family residential use could experience a negative effect on the marketability and values of properties in the neighborhood.

Properties also may change from owner-occupied to tenant-occupied, as commented on in the next part of this section.

To:

Indicate the new land-use pattern to which the neighborhood is changing; for example, from residential to commercial.

PREDOMINANT OCCUPANCY

Use this section of the URAR to report whether the majority of homes in the neighborhood are owner-occupied or tenant-occupied and the percentage that are vacant.

A high percentage of owner-occupancy tends to contribute to stable residential property values. The interest that homeowners have in protecting the value of their investment usually means they are more concerned than are tenants with keeping their homes in good repair, maintaining neat and attractive yards, participating in worthwhile community projects and seeing that zoning laws and deed restrictions are enforced.

Often there is a noticeable decline in prices when an area is in the process of transition from predominantly owner-occupied to predominantly tenant-occupied. Poorly maintained exteriors and grounds can be indicators of declining values.

> ▶ **FmHA** Enter the predominant occupancy in the neighborhood.
> ▶ **FNMA** Properties may change from owner-occupied to tenant-occupied, which can result in deterioration in the general appearance of the property and a consequent loss in value. Owner occupancy contributes greatly to the likelihood of long-term sustained value, because owners generally find it in their best interest to maintain their property. Although many tenants take excellent care of property, deterioration can occur. A high vacancy rate in the neighborhood must also be considered in terms of its long-range effect.
> ▶ **HUD/FHA** In addition to checking the box indicating *predominant occupancy*, show the *percentage* of homes that are owner-occupied and tenant-occupied.

Owner

Check this box if the homes in the subject property's neighborhood are predominantly owner-occupied.

▶ **HUD/FHA** Indicate the percentage of owner-occupied homes. Check the box if appropriate.

Tenant

Check this box if the homes in the subject property's neighborhood are predominantly tenant-occupied.

▶ **HUD/FHA** Indicate the percentage of tenant-occupied homes. Check the box if appropriate.

Vacant (0–5%)

Check this box if 5% or less of the homes in the neighborhood are vacant.

Vacant (over 5%)

Check this box if more than 5% of the homes in the neighborhood are vacant.

▶ **FmHA** "Vacant" refers to finished buildings. If the vacancy rate exceeds 10%, comment on the absorption potential, supply and demand factors.

SINGLE FAMILY HOUSING

Record the range of values and ages of neighborhood houses based on available market data. Isolated extremes at either end of the price or age range should be disregarded.

Price $ (000)

Enter the low and high values, excluding extremes.

▶ **FmHA** Enter the predominant low and high prices within the neighborhood, after excluding the extremes.

▶ **FNMA** A property with a sales price (or value) above the upper price range is considered an "overimprovement" for the neighborhood. An overimprovement may indicate that loan terms generally should be more conservative because the property may not be acceptable to typical purchasers. Property in an urban area that is being renovated should not be regarded as an overimprovement by the lender as long as market demand for such properties, as indicated by the existence of comparable properties, is strong.

A property with a sales price (or value) that is less than the lower price range is considered an "underimprovement."

Explain the effect on value of either overimprovement or underimprovement, as reflected in the *SALES COMPARISON ANALYSIS* adjustment grid on page 2 of the URAR.

AGE (yrs)

Enter the low and high numbers, excluding atypical extremes.

> ▶ **FNMA** Isolated high and low extremes should be excluded from the price or age range.

Predominant

Enter the most common or most frequently found price to the left, and the predominant age to the right.

> ▶ **FNMA** The predominant price can be stated as a single figure or, if more appropriate, as a range.
>
> The predominant age also can be recorded as a single figure or, if more appropriate, as a range.

NEIGHBORHOOD ANALYSIS   Good   Avg.   Fair   Poor

The desirability of the neighborhood, in terms of the amenities it offers residents, is very important. Is the neighborhood considered a good place to live? Support facilities such as schools, places of worship, transportation and shopping should be located conveniently for the residents of the neighborhood but not so close as to constitute a nuisance. One of the best protective measures against adverse influences is adequate zoning that is strictly enforced. Private restrictions requiring reasonable uniformity in the size and style of a house and its placement on the lot are effective controls if enforced by the community. Other features of a neighborhood that may contribute to its stability are good police and fire protection, opportunities for stable employment and attractive home sites.

The neighborhood analysis rating grid provides a list of items that are important to buyers in the marketplace. Each item should be compared with the same item in competing neighborhoods and rated as good, average, fair or poor. All *Fair* and *Poor* ratings must be fully explained in the *COMMENTS* part of this section or in an addendum.

> ▶ **FNMA** Comment on any rating of less than "Average," including the effect of the rating on the property's marketability and value.
>
> Explain any changes, either favorable or unfavorable, that have occurred or are occurring that will affect the marketability of neighborhood properties. There should be sufficient market demand in the neighborhood to support an active market for the subject property.
>
> A rating of *Good* indicates that the subject neighborhood is outstanding and superior in that respect to competing neighborhoods.
>
> A rating of *Average* indicates that the subject neighborhood is equal in that respect to the "norm" that is acceptable for competing neighborhoods.

A rating of *Fair* indicates that the subject neighborhood is inferior in the characteristic specified to what is considered acceptable in competing neighborhoods.

A rating of *Poor* indicates that the subject neighborhood is substantially inferior to—or in such small supply when compared to—competing neighborhoods with regard to the attribute mentioned that single-family property values are, or may be, affected adversely as a result.

All property amenities and services must be rated. If an amenity or service does not exist, it should be rated in comparison to whether competing neighborhoods offer that amenity or service. If an amenity is not offered and competing areas also do not offer it, then the *Average* rating would apply. An explanation of the rating would be appropriate, however, to adequately describe the subject neighborhood.

A lender should not offer maximum financing on any property that is not in a location offering at least average overall amenities, public services and property conditions.

▶ **HUD/FHA** Mark the most appropriate rating for each item listed.

Good indicates that the item or characteristic in the subject neighborhood is *superior* to the same characteristic found in a competing neighborhood.

Average indicates that the item or characteristic is *equal* to the same characteristic found in a competing neighborhood.

Fair indicates that the item or characteristic is *below* (inferior to) the same characteristic found in a competing neighborhood.

Poor indicates that the item or characteristic is in *small supply* or is *nonexistent* in the subject neighborhood but is found in a competing neighborhood.

▶ **VA** Explain only those items rated "Poor."

Employment Stability

Base your rating on the number of job opportunities and the variety and types of businesses and industries available to those living in the subject neighborhood. An area generally has greater employment stability if it has a diversity of businesses and industries rather than a single major industry or industries geared to the same economic cycles.

Convenience to Employment

Rate the distance and travel time required for neighborhood residents to get to their jobs. Availability, cost and convenience of public transportation should be considered as an alternative to private transportation.

Convenience to Shopping

Rate the neighborhood in terms of distance and travel time required for residents to get to both major and minor shopping areas. Availability, cost and convenience of public transportation should be considered as an alternative to private transportation.

Convenience to Schools

Rate the distance and travel time required for neighborhood residents to get to elementary and secondary schools. Quality of schools could also be noted, as this feature can vary tremendously from one district to another and can have a significant impact on property values.

Adequacy of Public Transportation

Determine and rate the types, quality, cost and convenience of public transportation servicing the subject neighborhood.

Recreation Facilities

Rate the number, types and quality of recreational facilities available to neighborhood residents. These include movie theaters, stadiums, parks, tennis courts, golf courses, swimming pools and health spas.

Adequacy of Utilities

Rate the quality, reliability and costs of utilities and other services available to the neighborhood. These include water, sewers, electricity, gas, telephone and garbage collection.

Property Compatibility

Many houses suffer a loss in value because they do not conform to the neighborhood in which they are located. Too much conformity, on the other hand, where all houses look the same, will also diminish value. Houses within a neighborhood should have enough variation in style and design to make the overall effect pleasing to the eye.

Typical factors to consider in this category include types of land uses prevalent in the neighborhood, lot sizes, and the degree of similarity among houses (style, age, size, quality and price range).

Protection from Detrimental Cond.

Smoke, fog, noxious fumes, radon contamination, use of asbestos-containing materials and urea formaldehyde insulation, and proximity to toxic waste dumps are just some of the environmental conditions that can threaten the health of neighborhood residents. The presence of such hazards also can have a significant negative effect on the value and marketability of property in the area.

> ▶ **FNMA** In July 1989, Fannie Mae provided lenders and appraisers with the following guideline regarding environmental hazards: "The typical residential appraiser is neither expected nor required to be an expert in the field of environmental hazards. However, the appraiser has a responsibility to note in the appraisal report, any adverse conditions that were observed during the inspection of the subject property, or information that he or she became aware of through normal research in performing an appraisal."

▶ **RTC** Note any potential environmental hazards. Examples include underground storage tanks, storage containers of known or unknown contents, evidence of waste disposal (such as sludge), paints, chemical residues, oil spillage, asbestos content in building material and the like.

Police & Fire Protection

Determine whether the neighborhood has adequate police and fire protection. Check also whether fire protection is provided by a full-time or a volunteer department. Volunteers have demonstrated exceptional skill in fighting fires, but a paid fire department usually is better equipped and more responsive to alarms. Insurance companies usually set lower rates for fire insurance where paid fire departments are located.

General Appearance of Properties

Naturally the neighborhood's general appearance is important. Well-kept properties usually reflect a strong neighborhood with stable or increasing values. Are yards well landscaped? Or filled with weeds? Are broken-down cars, bikes or appliances present in the yards? These can signal sloppy homeowners and lack of community concern. If city property is being appraised, are there vacant lots? Boarded-up stores? If so, how long have they been that way? They may indicate a neighborhood suffering economic as well as physical deterioration.

Check the outside appearance of houses. What condition are they in? Are the houses generally in good shape or falling apart? Do many need painting? Answers to such questions should tell much about the quality of the neighborhood—whether it is one of the best in the area or suffering from neglect.

▶ **FNMA** General appearance of the properties in the neighborhood is a key factor. Consider the extent to which the properties are receiving proper maintenance. Signs of maintenance and care usually reflect a strong neighborhood with stable or increasing values.

Appeal to Market

This rating is a summary of the overall attractiveness of the subject neighborhood. Typical characteristics to consider include natural scenic beauty, landscaping appeal, neighborhood design (the pattern of streets, parks and public areas, and the separation of commercial, industrial, multifamily and single-family residential areas), architectural appearance of houses, and the presence or lack of environmental hazards.

No one neighborhood will be perfect, but there will be many whose faults can be overlooked because their positive qualities overcome their liabilities.

▶ **FNMA** Essentially this is a summary rating of the extent to which all aspects of the neighborhood will appeal to the typical purchaser in the market. An individual property by itself cannot overcome a generally prevailing reluctance of the market to invest in a neighborhood. On the other hand, a relatively weak property in a strong and viable neighborhood is likely to sustain its value, although it still must be carefully analyzed.

Note: Race or the racial composition of the neighborhood are not considered reliable appraisal factors.

The neighborhood's racial composition must never be a factor in an appraisal.

COMMENTS:

Use this space to explain any of the responses in this section. If more space is needed, additional remarks can be supplied on an addendum attached to the appraisal report form. In addition, this *COMMENTS* section can be used to provide the client with a summary statement about the subject neighborhood.

▶ **FmHA** Summarize *NEIGHBORHOOD ANALYSIS* comments in this section. *All* items rated *Fair* or *Poor* must be explained.

▶ Appraisal 1

LOCATION		Urban	X	Suburban		Rural	NEIGHBORHOOD ANALYSIS	Good	Avg.	Fair	Poor
BUILT UP		Over 75%	X	25-75%		Under 25%	Employment Stability	X			
GROWTH RATE		Rapid	X	Stable		Slow	Convenience to Employment		X		
PROPERTY VALUES	x	Increasing		Stable		Declining	Convenience to Shopping		X		
DEMAND/SUPPLY		Shortage	X	In Balance		Over Supply	Convenience to Schools		X		
MARKETING TIME		Under 3 Mos.	X	3-6 Mos.		Over 6 Mos.	Adequacy of Public Transportation	X			

PRESENT LAND USE	%	LAND USE CHANGE		PREDOMINANT		SINGLE FAMILY HOUSING			Recreation Facilities	X			
						PRICE $ (000)		AGE (yrs)					
Single Family	75	Not Likely	X	OCCUPANCY					Adequacy of Utilities	X			
2-4 Family		Likely		Owner	X				Property Compatibility	X			
Multi-family	15	In process		Tenant		100 Low	NEW		Protection from Detrimental Cond.		X		
Commercial		To:		Vacant (0-5%)	X	800 High	15		Police & Fire Protection		X		
Industrial				Vacant (over 5%)		Predominant			General Appearance of Properties	X			
Vacant	10					200 —	8		Appeal to Market	X			

Note: Race or the racial composition of the neighborhood are not considered reliable appraisal factors.

COMMENTS: BENT TREE VILLAGE, A NEIGHBORHOOD OF UPSCALE RESIDENCES SURROUNDING COUNTRY CLUB FACILITIES. THE AREA HAS BEEN DEVELOPED AROUND A CHAMPIONSHIP GOLF COURSE WITH MOSTLY EXPENSIVE SINGLE-FAMILY RESIDENCES. CONVENIENCE TO INTERSTATE 75 IS GOOD, ALLOWING EASY ACCESS TO CENTERS OF EMPLOYMENT.

In Appraisal 1, the subject property is located in a desirable subdivision a few miles east of Sarasota, Florida. The 15-year-old neighborhood is 75% developed with single-family homes ranging in value from $100,000 to $800,000. Most are valued at $200,000, and virtually all are owner-occupied. Approximately 15% of the improved land contains multifamily dwellings and 10% of the parcels are undeveloped. The rate of development within the neighborhood is normal for the market area. Houses range in age from new to 15 years, with a predominant age of 8 years.

Employment stability in the subject neighborhood historically has been better than in competing areas. Convenience to employment, shopping and schools, as well as police and fire protection, are normal for the market area. However, recreational facilities and the quality, reliability and cost of utilities and other services available to the subject neighborhood are outstanding and superior to those found in competing neighborhoods.

The general appearance, compatibility and market appeal of properties in the subject neighborhood are clearly above average compared with those of competing areas. As a result there has been a steady demand for housing, with a continuing uptrend in values during the past several years. Most houses on the market are sold within three to six months.

▶ Exercise: Appraisal 2

NEIGHBORHOOD	LOCATION	☐ Urban	☐ Suburban	☐ Rural	NEIGHBORHOOD ANALYSIS	Good	Avg.	Fair	Poor
	BUILT UP	☐ Over 75%	☐ 25-75%	☐ Under 25%	Employment Stability	☐	☐	☐	☐
	GROWTH RATE	☐ Rapid	☐ Stable	☐ Slow	Convenience to Employment	☐	☐	☐	☐
	PROPERTY VALUES	☐ Increasing	☐ Stable	☐ Declining	Convenience to Shopping	☐	☐	☐	☐
	DEMAND/SUPPLY	☐ Shortage	☐ In Balance	☐ Over Supply	Convenience to Schools	☐	☐	☐	☐
	MARKETING TIME	☐ Under 3 Mos.	☐ 3-6 Mos.	☐ Over 6 Mos.	Adequacy of Public Transportation	☐	☐	☐	☐

PRESENT LAND USE	%	LAND USE CHANGE	PREDOMINANT OCCUPANCY	SINGLE FAMILY HOUSING PRICE $ (000) AGE (yrs)	Recreation Facilities	☐	☐	☐	☐
Single Family	___	Not Likely ☐			Adequacy of Utilities	☐	☐	☐	☐
2-4 Family	___	Likely ☐	Owner ☐		Property Compatibility	☐	☐	☐	☐
Multi-family	___	In process ☐	Tenant ☐	Low	Protection from Detrimental Cond.	☐	☐	☐	☐
Commercial	___	To: _____	Vacant (0-5%) ☐	High	Police & Fire Protection	☐	☐	☐	☐
Industrial	___		Vacant (over 5%) ☐	Predominant	General Appearance of Properties	☐	☐	☐	☐
Vacant				—	Appeal to Market	☐	☐	☐	☐

Note: Race or the racial composition of the neighborhood are not considered reliable appraisal factors.

COMMENTS: _____

Complete the blank URAR *NEIGHBORHOOD* section provided above for Appraisal 2, using the following information. When you have finished, check your work against the completed Appraisal 2 in the Answer Key.

The subject property is located in a suburban subdivision 10 miles from the downtown shopping and business areas of a medium-sized city. The 29-year-old neighborhood is 98% developed with about 200 single-family homes currently ranging in value from $225,000 to $295,000. Although there is no construction at present, building permits already issued indicate that the subdivision should be fully developed within 12 to 18 months.

Market analysis shows that the residents of the subject neighborhood are mostly executives, salespeople and owners and officers of small businesses. The average home price is about $260,000, with 95% of homes owner-occupied and few or no vacancies among the rental units. The majority of homes are about 20 years old, but they range in age from 1 to 29 years. There have been few houses for sale in the subdivision and demand is high, creating a seller's market. Most houses on the market are sold within 30 to 60 days.

Good public transportation is available to the subject neighborhood. There is a regional shopping mall about two miles away, with national chains, local businesses, a bowling center, restaurants, banking facilities and movie theaters. A public golf course is located about five miles away. The neighborhood is within walking distance of public grade schools; a good public high school is a little over two miles away; various places of worship are located within one mile. Electricity, gas, water, and sanitary and storm sewers are available as public services.

Except for the general appearance of properties and market appeal, which are above average, all other subject neighborhood amenities are on a par with those in competing areas.

Site

Dimensions						Topography		/
Site Area			Corner Lot			Size		
Zoning Classification			Zoning Compliance			Shape		
HIGHEST & BEST USE: Present Use			Other Use			Drainage		
UTILITIES	Public	Other	SITE IMPROVEMENTS	Type	Public	Private	View	
Electricity	☐		Street		☐	☐	Landscaping	
Gas	☐		Curb/Gutter		☐	☐	Driveway	
Water	☐		Sidewalk		☐	☐	Apparent Easements	
Sanitary Sewer	☐		Street Lights		☐	☐	FEMA Flood Hazard Yes*	No
Storm Sewer			Alley		☐	☐	FEMA* Map/Zone	
COMMENTS (Apparent adverse easements, encroachments, special assessments, slide areas, etc.):								

The appraiser must adequately describe the property that is the subject of the appraisal, starting with the subject site. To do so the appraiser must:

- Give the dimensions and topography of the site.
- Specify site improvements other than structures.
- Note whether the property is in a flood hazard zone and whether there are any encumbrances on the property or other adverse influences (unstable soil for example).

Dimensions

Give the perimeter measurements, in feet, of the parcel being appraised.

> ▶ **HUD/FHA** List all dimensions of the site. If the site has an irregular shape, enter the boundary dimensions; for example, 85′ × 150′ × 195′ × 250′.

Site Area

Enter the total square footage of land area included in the parcel. If the site is more than 1 acre, the area can be given in acres and fractions of an acre; for example, 6½ acres.

▶ **FmHA** Enter site dimensions. If the site is irregular, enter total square footage. If the site contains more than one acre, enter the number of acres.

▶ **HUD/FHA** Enter area in square feet or in acres.

Corner Lot

If the site is considered a corner (bordered by two streets) enter YES. If not enter NO.

In the past a corner lot was considered desirable and thus more valuable because typically it was larger, allowed more attractive landscaping and views than "inside" lots and benefited from the privacy afforded by sharing only two lot lines with neighbors. Now that smaller lot sizes are prevalent, there may be no size advantage to a corner location, and there may be an increase in noise as well as loss of privacy due to the extra street exposure. In any event, if the site is a corner the appraiser should note any effect on value in the market area.

▶ **HUD/FHA** Enter YES or NO.

Zoning Classification

Enter the zoning code and category title designated by the local zoning authority to show the permitted property use(s). Most municipal and county zoning districts use letter and number codes as well as short identifying labels, such as R-1 RESIDENTIAL/SINGLE-FAMILY. If the area is not zoned enter N/A.

In areas that do not have zoning, limitations on property use similar to those imposed by zoning are brought about by the use of *conditions, covenants and restrictions (CC&Rs)* in deeds. CC&Rs also are frequently used in subdivisions so that architectural and property maintenance standards are met to ensure property values. The existence of any such deed restrictions, and the property's conformity with them, should be noted in the *COMMENTS* section in this part of the form.

Note also that other kinds of zones frequently overlay property use zones. Some of these are mentioned later, in the discussion of the *COMMENTS* section for this part of the URAR.

▶ **FNMA** Give the zoning code for the area in which the property is located and a brief explanation of what the code stands for; for example, R-1 SINGLE-FAMILY.

▶ **HUD/FHA** Enter the zoning type by both the abbreviation and descriptive label, such as R-1 RESIDENTIAL/SINGLE-FAMILY.

Use the designation HISTORIC, if applicable. If the property use is nonconforming enter NONCONFORMING and whether the use is a legal one that has been approved by the local zoning authority.

Always determine whether current property use is in compliance with zoning regulations.

Zoning Compliance

If the property represents a legally permitted use in conformance with the applicable zoning, enter YES. If the property use is not in conformance with the applicable zoning but has been legally permitted by a zoning variance or special use permit issued to the property owner, enter LEGAL NONCONFORMING and explain the special circumstances in the *COMMENTS* section in this part of the form.

A property use also can be a legal nonconforming one if it is "grandfathered in" at the time of a change in zoning classification. For example, an older residential area, because of its proximity to a growing downtown commercial district, may be rezoned for commercial use, yet the existing single-family residences will be allowed to remain.

If the property use is not in conformance with the zoning code and has not been legally sanctioned by a zoning variance, special use permit or other means, enter NO and explain your response in the *COMMENTS* section in this part of the form.

Always take into account the effect on value of an illegal or nonconforming use as well as a prospective change of use.

▶ **FNMA** If the property improvements do not reflect a legal conforming use of the land, as permitted by the applicable zoning, the appraiser should so state. Fannie Mae *will not* purchase a mortgage secured by property that is not a legally permissible use of the land. On the other hand, Fannie Mae *will* purchase a mortgage secured by property that is a legal but nonconforming use of the land, as long as the impact on property value and marketability of the nonconforming use is reflected in the appraiser's estimate of value.

▶ **HUD/FHA** Enter YES or NO/LEGAL NONCONFORMING USE, as appropriate. A legal nonconforming use requires some explanation, either in the *COMMENTS* part of this section or in an addendum.

HIGHEST AND BEST USE:

The highest and best use of property is that *legally permitted* use that is *physically possible, financially feasible* and *economically desirable* (the most profitable alternative).

A study of the highest and best use for commercially zoned property may be many pages long, analyzing and comparing potential property uses. For residential appraisals, considerations of property use usually take into account whether the present structures are typical of the neighborhood and whether market demand is such that the site is more valuable with the improvements than without them.

As a practical matter, zoning and other restraints usually simplify analysis of highest and best use for residential property.

Of greater concern is the residence in an area that has been zoned or rezoned for nonresidential use. If the structure fronts on a major roadway and is zoned commercial, its highest and best use may be a commercial use. The extent to which the area is already devoted to commercial use, the ease with which the existing improvements can be converted to a potential new use and the demand for that kind of commercial space must all be considered in the determination.

▸ **FNMA** The highest and best use of a site is that reasonable and probable use that supports the highest present value on the effective date of the appraisal. A highest and best use must meet four criteria:

1. The use must be legally permitted.
2. The use must be financially feasible.
3. The use must be physically possible.
4. The use must provide more profit than any other use of the site would generate.

Present Use

Answer the question: "Is the property, with its present improvements, being put to its highest and best use?" The answer will be either *YES* or *NO*.

If the current use of the property is its highest and best use, no further information need be supplied. If the present use of the property is not its highest and best use, however, a brief statement of what the highest and best use would be must be provided in the next space.

▸ **FNMA** The URAR highest and best use analysis is not the type of strict analysis that considers the subject site as if vacant. Consider the site *as improved*, unless it is financially feasible to renovate the existing dwelling or remove it and build a new one. If the appraiser's comparable sales analysis indicates that the property is reasonably typical of the area and compatible with market demand, the only determination to be made is whether the site is more valuable with the existing improvements or without them.

▸ **HUD/FHA** Consider the highest and best use of the site *in relation to the neighborhood.* If the site's present use is not its highest and best use, enter NO and explain your answer in the *COMMENTS* part of this section.

Other Use

If the subject property already represents its highest and best use, enter N/A here. If this is not the case, state the property's highest and best use here. Your opinion should be justified by a brief description of your analysis and conclusions in the *COMMENTS* section below or in an addendum.

Note that, for most purposes, including mortgage loan origination and secondary market sales, property and improvements used to secure a loan *must* represent the property's highest and best use. If your analysis indicates otherwise, your client should be informed immediately, before you proceed any further with the appraisal.

▸ **FNMA** If the current improvements do not represent the highest and best use of the site, FNMA will *not* purchase a mortgage secured by the subject property.

▸ **HUD/FHA** If the present use is not the site's highest and best use, indicate the use that would be the site's highest and best use. Explain your response in the *COMMENTS* part of this section.

UTILITIES

To be considered suitable for building purposes, a site must have certain utilities available to it. Electricity can be supplied by a variety of sources, including private generator. Gas is desirable in addition to electricity in most areas as a lower-cost or more-efficient alternative to electricity for cooking, heating and other household purposes. There must be a source of water. Sewage must be disposed of in a legally permitted, safe and hygienic way. Areas of high-density development or particular geologic features, such as bedrock close to the surface that inhibits water absorption, usually have storm sewers to decrease the risk of flooding.

▸ **FmHA** Identify utilities available for use to the site.

▸ **FNMA** To qualify for maximum financing, the site should have utilities that meet community standards and are accepted generally by area residents.

The appraiser must comment on any effect on market value created by environmental hazards or any other condition affecting well, septic or public water facilities.

Public

Check this box if the listed utility is available to the subject property from a public source.

▸ **HUD/FHA** Public utilities are those provided by a governnment.

Other

If the listed utility is available to the subject property from a source other than a public one, whether on or off the site, indicate its ownership and (if it is not on the subject site) its location. For example, if the only water supply is a private on-site water well, enter **PRIVATE WELL**.

▶ **HUD/FHA** A utility may be provided by an individual and/or community system, rather than a government. If this is the case, indicate here how service is provided.

Electricity

Check the box if electricity is available to the subject property from a public source. Enter any private source, such as an on-site generator, if applicable.

▶ **HUD/FHA** Indicate whether electricity is underground.

Gas

Check the box if natural gas for cooking and/or heating is available to the subject property from a public source. Enter any private source, such as propane stored in an on-site tank.

Water

Check the box if water is available to the subject property from a public source. Enter any private source.

▶ **FNMA** If public water facilities are not available, a community or private well must be available and utilized by the subject property. A private well, if any, must be located on the subject site. If a private community facility is used, the owners of the subject property must have the right to access the system's facilities, which must be viable on an ongoing basis.

Sanitary Sewer

Check the box if a sanitary sewer is available to the subject property from a public source. Enter any nonpublic community or private septic system.

▶ **FNMA** If public sewer facilities are not available, a community or private septic system must be available and utilized by the subject property. A private septic system, if any, must be located on the subject site. If a private community septic system is used, the owners of the subject property must have the right to access the system's facilities, which must be viable on an ongoing basis.

Storm Sewer

Check the box if a storm sewer is available to the subject property from a public source, or indicate any private arrangement.

SITE IMPROVEMENTS

In this section, you will indicate the kinds of improvements that have been made to make the site more suitable for development.

▶ **FmHA** Indicate site improvements.

▶ **FNMA** To qualify for maximum financing, the site should have street improvements that conform to those of the market area.

Type

Enter the construction material used in any of the listed improvements on or adjacent to the subject property.

▶ **HUD/FHA** Enter YES or NO, describe the improvement briefly and check the appropriate box. For example, for *Street*, you might enter ASPHALT and check *Public.* An important consideration also to note here is whether there is year-round maintenance of an improvement.

Public

An improvement is considered public if it is made and maintained at public expense.

▶ **HUD/FHA** Check this box if applicable. "Public" refers to a government that can regulate use; it does not refer to a homeowners' association.

Private

An improvement is considered private if it is made or maintained at the expense of the property owner, either individually or as part of a homeowners' association.

▶ **HUD/FHA** Check this box if applicable and indicate whether there is year-round maintenance of the improvement.

Street

Indicate the material used to pave the street on which the property is located and whether the street is public or private.

▶ **FNMA** The property should front on a publicly dedicated and maintained street that meets community standards. If the street does not meet community standards, comment in this section on the impact on the property's marketability and value.

If the street is privately owned, whether by a community or one or more homeowners, a legally enforceable maintenance agreement should be in effect, and the street should meet community standards. If there is no agreement and/or the street does not meet community standards, comment on the resulting impact on the property's marketability and value.

Curb/Gutter

If the property has curbs and gutters, indicate the construction material used and whether the curbs and gutters are considered public or private property. If there are no curbs and gutters, enter NONE.

▶ **FNMA** If curbs and gutters are typical of other properties in the community, they should be present in the subject site. If the subject does not conform to other properties in the area, comment on the effect on marketability and value of the absence of these features.

Sidewalk

If sidewalks are present, indicate the paving material used and whether the sidewalks are considered public or private. (Note that the local governing authority may consider the sidewalks a public right-of-way, yet require the adjacent private property owner to maintain them.) If there are no sidewalks, enter NONE.

▶ **FNMA** If sidewalks typically are found in the community, they should be present in the subject site. If the subject does not conform to other properties in the area, comment on the effect on marketability and value of the absence of this feature.

Street Lights

If there are street lights in the vicinity, indicate what kind they are and whether they are public or private. If there are no street lights, enter NONE.

▶ **FNMA** If street lights are typically found on or near other properties in the community, they should be present on or in the immediate vicinity of the subject site. If the subject does not conform to other properties in the community, comment on the effect on marketability and value of the absence of this feature.

Alley

If the property is bordered on any side by an alley, enter the type of paving material used. If there is no alley, enter NONE.

▶ **FNMA** If other properties in the area typically have access to an alley, the subject should have access to an alley. If the subject does not conform to other properties in the area, comment on the effect on marketability and value of the absence of this feature.

Topography

The general contour of the land and the approximate degree of any incline or decline from street level should be noted; for example, LEVEL or 30% DOWNHILL GRADE. If the site's topography is such that it should be valued lower than other properties in the neighborhood (because of increased construction costs or decreased utility, for instance), explain the effect on value in the *COMMENTS* section below.

▶ **FNMA** For the property to qualify for maximum financing, the site's topography should be conforming and acceptable in the market area.

▶ **HUD/FHA** Indicate the site's topography, such as level, sloped and so on.

Size

Note how the site compares in size to other properties in the neighborhood; for example, TYPICAL or OVERSIZED. Any difference that affects value should be explained below in the *COMMENTS* section.

▶ **FNMA** For the property to qualify for maximum financing, the site's size should be conforming and acceptable in the market area.

▶ **HUD/FHA** Describe the subject site in relation to other properties in the neighborhood; for example, TYPICAL, SMALL or LARGE.

Shape

Enter the shape of the perimeter of the site; for example, SQUARE or RECTANGULAR. If the site's value is affected by its irregular or atypical shape, provide the reason(s) for the effect on value in the *COMMENTS* section below.

▶ **FNMA** For the property to qualify for maximum financing, the site's shape should be conforming and acceptable in the market area.

▶ **HUD/FHA** Enter the site's configuration; for example, TRIANGULAR, SQUARE or RECTANGULAR.

Drainage

The site should have natural drainage channels or storm sewers for water flow. Water should not be allowed to collect at the base of the house. Basement or crawl space dampness or water marks on foundation walls or supports may indicate poor drainage. A house on a steep downhill slope may need a special underground channel (a "french drain") to carry water around the foundation. Once installed, drains may need to be cleaned out occasionally. Heavy, bushy growth around the base of a house may clog underground drains with roots and keep water from flowing freely.

▶ **FmHA** Indicate conditions observed.

▶ **FNMA** Drainage must be away from improvements so that water does not collect in or around them.

▶ **HUD/FHA** Indicate whether existing drainage is adequate or inadequate. If inadequate, explain and specify necessary corrective measures, if feasible.

View

Describe the kind of views seen from the interior of the house. The topography of the land and design of the house will determine the views. A house with views that are unobstructed because there are no nearby structures or because the house is on a hill, will be valued higher than houses that do not share these amenities. The value of the view will be the premium paid in the area for that kind of property.

A house built around an atrium or with walled patios or garden areas, will have interior views. If comparable properties have similar views, there will be no detrimental effect on value.

- ▶ **FmHA** Indicate conditions observed.
- ▶ **FNMA** For the property to qualify for maximum financing, the site's amenities should be conforming and acceptable in the market area.
- ▶ **HUD/FHA** Briefly describe the view from the property. Identify a view that has a significant positive or negative influence on value as being average, superior or inferior to other local sites; for example, MOUNTAINS—AVERAGE.

Landscaping

If the property is not landscaped, enter NONE. If the property is landscaped, describe the type of landscaping (such as LAWN, MATURE, EXTENSIVE or OVERGROWN) and the quality of landscaping in terms of the standard in the neighborhood. For example, an unadorned lawn may be described as LAWN—GOOD in an area of modestly priced and unpretentious homes. The same landscaping in an area of extensively landscaped luxury homes might be considered only fair. Any significant differences between the subject and other properties in the area should be noted below in the *COMMENTS* section.

Landscaping that does not generally conform to the style most commonly found in the area may result in a loss in value if the property is seen as undesirable because of unattractiveness or lack of utility. A cactus garden may be entirely appropriate in Phoenix, Arizona, for instance, but inappropriate in Portland, Oregon.

- ▶ **FmHA** Indicate conditions observed.
- ▶ **HUD/FHA** Indicate whether landscaping is adequate or inadequate as compared with other properties in the neighborhood.

Driveway

If the property has a driveway, enter the type of paving. If the property has no driveway, enter NONE.

- ▶ **FmHA** Indicate conditions observed.
- ▶ **HUD/FHA** Enter type of driveway paving, such as CONCRETE, ASPHALT or GRAVEL.

Apparent Easements

Note any easements that are visible or discovered by inspection of the property; for instance, a shared road or the presence of a utility pole. Common easements also include underground utility lines, such as those for electricity, telephone and cable television transmission. Also note any easements that may not be visible but are listed in the preliminary title report.

▶ **FmHA** Indicate conditions observed.

▶ **HUD/FHA** If there appears to be an easement, check to make sure.

FEMA Flood Hazard

The Federal Emergency Management Agency (FEMA) has identified flood hazard areas throughout the United States. Check the local Flood Insurance Rate Map (FIRM) to determine whether the subject property is located in a flood hazard area.

▶ **FNMA** Indicate whether the property is in a FEMA flood hazard area. Flood hazard area maps can be obtained from FEMA at 1-800-638-6620 (continental U.S.), 1-800-492-6605 (Maryland) or 1-800-638-6831 (Alaska, Hawaii, Puerto Rico and the Virgin Islands). Written requests (required for more than five maps) can be made to Federal Emergency Management Agency, Flood Map Distribution Center, 6930 (A-F) San Tomas Road, Baltimore, MD 21227-6227.

▶ **HUD/FHA** If any part of the subject property is within a Special Flood Hazard Area, check *Yes;* otherwise, check *No.*

Yes*

Check this response if *any* part of the subject site is located in a flood hazard area. If part of the site is located in a flood hazard area but the improvements are located outside the flood hazard area, explain that fact in the *COMMENTS* part of this section.

▶ **FNMA** Check this response if the property is located in a FEMA flood hazard area. Flood insurance is required if the property *improvements* are located in a special flood hazard area (zones A, AO, AH, A1-30, A-99, V or V1-30). If part of the property is located in a flood hazard area but the improvements are not, flood insurance is not required.

No

If no part of the subject site is located in a flood hazard area, check this response.

▶ **FNMA** Check this response if the property is *not* located in a FEMA flood hazard area.

FEMA* Map/Zone

If any part of the subject site is located in a flood hazard area, indicate the map number on which the site can be found and the flood zone number in which it is located.

▶ **FNMA** If the subject property is located in a flood hazard area, provide the map or community panel number and specific flood zone on the appraisal report.

▶ **HUD/FHA** If the previous response was *Yes,* enter the FEMA map and zone number. Properties within zones A *and* V require flood insurance because these zones are designated by FEMA as Special Flood Hazard Areas. Properties within zones B or C do not require flood insurance as they are not Special Flood Hazard Areas.

▸ **VA** If the property is located in a special flood hazard area, provide the map number and designated zone.

COMMENTS (Apparent adverse easements, encroachments, special assessments, slide areas, etc.):

This is the space in which to explain any responses in this section. If more space is needed, additional remarks can be supplied on an addendum attached to the appraisal report form.

As noted above, under *Zoning Classification*, a variety of zones frequently overlay property use zones. In California, for instance, property located within one-quarter of a mile of an active earthquake fault may fall within a *special studies zone* and require special approval before a building permit is issued. The fact that property is located within such a zone must be disclosed to a prospective buyer of the property by the agent representing the seller, or by the seller if there is no agent. The California Division of Mines and Geology has maps available showing the location of the special studies zones throughout the state. California also recognizes and has special permit requirements for property located within *coastal zones*, which generally include all property from the Pacific coast inland about 1,000 yards.

A frequently used property classification throughout the country is the *Historic District* designation, which may affect the potential use of the property, particularly in terms of additions to or remodeling of the existing structure(s).

Any designation that has the potential to affect property value should be mentioned and analyzed by the appraiser.

▸ **FmHA** Enter comments as appropriate to the site.

▸ **FNMA** Because amenities, easements and encroachments may affect the property's marketability, you must comment on them if the site is not typical for the neighborhood.

▶ Appraisal 1

Dimensions	125 x 180 x 58 x 139			Topography	LEVEL
Site Area	13,907.50 SF	Corner Lot	NO	Size	13,907.50/TYPICAL
Zoning Classification	RSF-1/PUD (RES.)	Zoning Compliance	YES	Shape	IRREGULAR
HIGHEST & BEST USE: Present Use	YES	Other Use		Drainage	ADEQUATE

UTILITIES	Public	Other	SITE IMPROVEMENTS	Type	Public	Private	View	INTERIOR-PATIO-ATRIUM
Electricity	X	FPL	Street	ASPHALT	X		Landscaping	GOOD/TYPICAL
Gas			Curb/Gutter	CONCRETE	X		Driveway	POLYPEBBLE
Water	X	S'EAST	Sidewalk	NONE			Apparent Easements	NORMAL UTILITIES
Sanitary Sewer	X	S'EAST	Street Lights	NONE			FEMA Flood Hazard	Yes* No "C"
Storm Sewer	X	COUNTY	Alley	NONE			FEMA* Map/Zone	1251440170 5-84

COMMENTS (Apparent adverse easements, encroachments, special assessments, slide areas, etc.): NO ADVERSE INFLUENCES, EASEMENTS, OR ENCROACHMENTS VISIBLE ON THE PROPERTY. SITE IMPROVEMENTS ARE ADEQUATE AND THE SITE GRADE PERMITS ADEQUATE DRAINAGE AWAY FROM THE HOME'S FOUNDATION.

In Appraisal 1, the subject site is 125' by 180' by 58' by 139', for a total square footage of 13,907.50. The property is not a corner lot and is classified RSF-1/PUD, a residential use. The property as improved is in compliance with the zoning requirements and represents the highest and best use of the site.

The property has electricity, water, and sanitary and storm sewers, all on public lines. There is no gas line available, however. The street is asphalt, with concrete curbs and gutters, all publicly maintained. There are no sidewalks, street lights or alleys in this subdivision.

The subject site is level and rectangular, though irregularly shaped. It has adequate drainage. Views from the house are of interior patio and atrium areas. Landscaping is good and typical of this area. The driveway has a polypebble finish. Only normal utility easements are apparent. The property is located in FEMA zone C, as indicated on map 1251440170 of 5-84.

No adverse influences, easements or encroachments are visible on the property. Site improvements are adequate, and the site grade permits adequate drainage away from the home's foundation.

▶ Exercise: Appraisal 2

SITE							
Dimensions				Topography			
Site Area			Corner Lot	Size			
Zoning Classification			Zoning Compliance	Shape			
HIGHEST & BEST USE: Present Use			Other Use	Drainage			

UTILITIES	Public	Other	SITE IMPROVEMENTS	Type	Public	Private
Electricity	☐		Street		☐	☐
Gas	☐		Curb/Gutter		☐	☐
Water	☐		Sidewalk		☐	☐
Sanitary Sewer	☐		Street Lights		☐	☐
Storm Sewer	☐		Alley		☐	☐

View	
Landscaping	
Driveway	
Apparent Easements	
FEMA Flood Hazard	Yes* ___ No ___
FEMA* Map/Zone	

COMMENTS (Apparent adverse easements, encroachments, special assessments, slide areas, etc.):

Complete the blank URAR *SITE* section provided above for Appraisal 2, using the following information. When you have finished, check your work against the completed Appraisal 2 in the Answer Key.

The subject property is a rectangle, 75 feet (street frontage) by 150 feet, typical of the area, and is not located on a corner. The property is in compliance with its zoning classification of SF-1, Single-Family Residential, and represents the highest and best use of the site.

Electricity, gas, water, sanitary sewer and storm sewer are available as public services. The public street is asphalt paved with concrete curbs and gutters. There is no sidewalk or alley. Public street lights are mercury vapor.

The site is gently rolling, with the house built on the highest part of the lot, so that the property is well drained away from the house. There is a view of the surrounding hills, typical of this area. Landscaping is of a good-quality xeriscape (low-water usage) type now favored in this area, with mature evergreen plantings and ground covers. The driveway is concrete. There are no apparent easements other than underground utility lines. The property is not located in a FEMA flood hazard zone.

SECTION 4

Improvements

GENERAL DESCRIPTION	EXTERIOR DESCRIPTION	FOUNDATION	BASEMENT	INSULATION
Units	Foundation	Slab	Area Sq. Ft.	Roof ☐
Stories	Exterior Walls	Crawl Space	% Finished	Ceiling ☐
Type (Det./Att.)	Roof Surface	Basement	Ceiling	Walls ☐
Design (Style)	Gutters & Dwnspts.	Sump Pump	Walls	Floor ☐
Existing	Window Type	Dampness	Floor	None ☐
Proposed	Storm Sash	Settlement	Outside Entry	Adequacy ☐
Under Construction	Screens	Infestation		Energy Efficient Items:
Age (Yrs.)	Manufactured House			
Effective Age (Yrs.)				

Quality of construction and materials, as well as design, condition, utility and physical characteristics of improvements, combine to influence demand and therefore the marketability and value of a property. A detailed and accurate description of the subject structure is essential to any valuation assignment—especially in selecting "comps" (comparable properties) for the Sales Comparison Approach and in calculating reproduction or replacement cost and depreciation for the Cost Approach. The appraiser must:

• Describe the style, age and condition of existing or incomplete property improvements.
• Describe the exterior features of improvements.
• List the type of foundation and any evidence of deterioration or infestation.
• Itemize the basement finishing materials.
• Indicate the type of insulation and any special energy-efficient items used.

GENERAL DESCRIPTION

The style, size and age of improvements are listed in this part.

Units

Enter the *number* of units contained in the subject dwelling. Both Fannie Mae and Freddie Mac generally allow use of the URAR for *one-unit* properties *only*. Fannie Mae does allow the URAR to be used for homes with "in-law" or small rental units, if the property is not in an area zoned for multifamily residences. (In such cases, zoning typically is R-1, with a variance for the rental unit.) FHA and VA allow the URAR to be used for properties with up to *four* units.

> ▶ **FNMA** Fannie Mae does not specify minimum size or living area requirements for properties. However, dwelling units of any type should contain sufficient living area to be acceptable to typical purchasers or tenants in the subject market area. There should be comparables of similar size to the subject property to support the general acceptability of a particular property type.

> ▶ **HUD/FHA** Enter the number of units being valued, up to four units.

Stories

Enter the number of *above-grade* floors of finished living area.

> ▶ **HUD/FHA** Enter the number of stories above grade. Do *not* include any basement areas.

Type (Det./Att.)

Determine whether the subject dwelling is *detached* (free-standing) or *attached* (shares at least one common wall with another structure) and enter the appropriate abbreviation.

> ▶ **HUD/FHA** Enter DET. (detached), S/D (semidetached) or R (row).

Design (Style)

Enter the name of the architectural design or style of the subject dwelling using terminology common to the area. For example, the structure may be identified by one of the traditional style designations, such as Tudor, Spanish Colonial, Colonial American, Georgian, Victorian, or by house type, such as ranch, Cape Cod, two-story, split-level and raised ranch.

> ▶ **HUD/FHA** Briefly describe the building style using local custom terminology. Some examples are Cape Cod, bilevel, split-level, split-foyer, town house and so on. Do *not* use a builder's model name.

Existing

Enter YES if you are appraising a fully built structure. Otherwise, enter NO or N/A.

▸ **HUD/FHA** Enter YES or NO.

Proposed

Enter YES if you are appraising a proposed structure. Otherwise enter NO or N/A.

▸ **HUD/FHA** Enter YES or NO.

Under Construction

Enter YES if you are appraising a structure under construction. Otherwise enter NO or N/A.

Note: If you are appraising a proposed structure or one that is under construction, indicate the plans and specifications used in the appraisal in the *COMMENTS* section or in an addendum to the URAR.

▸ **HUD/FHA** Enter YES or NO. A YES requires plans and specs for the appraiser to review. If the construction is the rehabilitation of an existing structure, enter REHAB instead of YES or NO.

Age (Yrs.)

Enter the *actual* (chronological) age of the subject dwelling.

▸ **FNMA** In general a property should be within the general age range of the neighborhood. This will be the usual case, simply because most neighborhoods are developed over a relatively short time span. A property outside the general age range will require special consideration.

Unless there is strong evidence of long-term neighborhood stability, a new dwelling in an old neighborhood will carry some marginal risk. Conversely, an old dwelling in a newly developed area is generally acceptable if renovation will result in its conforming with the neighborhood.

Older properties in neighborhoods where the improvements have been maintained in a way that sustains the properties' values are acceptable for maximum financing. Because of their location, these properties frequently will have enough advantages over newer properties in outlying areas to create equal or greater market demand. Certain older properties also may be in demand because of their unique architectural design or other factors.

▸ **HUD/FHA** Enter actual age. Constructions records (if available) may be helpful.

Effective Age (Yrs.)

Enter the subject dwelling's *effective age*—its age in years indicated by the condition and utility of the structure. A building's effective age may or may not coincide with its chronological age. If a building has had better-than-average maintenance, is superior in quality and design or there is a scarcity of such buildings in the market, its effective age may be less than its actual age. A 50-year-old house, for example, may have an effective age of only 25 years because of rehabilitation, modernization or strong market demand. On the other hand, a poorly constructed house that has been inadequately maintained may have an effective age greater than its actual age.

▶ **FNMA** The relationship between the actual and effective ages of the property is a good indication of its condition. A property that has been well maintained generally will have an effective age somewhat lower than its actual age. On the other hand, properties that have an effective age higher than their actual age probably have not been well maintained or may have a particular physical problem. In such cases, in its review of the appraisal the lender must pay particular attention to the condition of the subject property.

FNMA does not place a restriction on the age of eligible dwellings. Consequently mortgages on older dwellings that meet our general requirements are acceptable. The improvements for all properties must be of the quality and condition that will meet local building codes and must be acceptable to typical purchasers in the subject market area.

▶ **HUD/FHA** Enter effective age, if appropriate. Estimation of effective age is a subjective judgment of the appraiser. It may be preferable to give a range of years.

A difference between actual and effective ages typically is caused by a level of maintenance or remodeling that may be below or above average. Significant differences between the actual and effective ages should be noted.

EXTERIOR DESCRIPTION

Examine and describe the exterior of the subject dwelling.

Foundation

Enter the type of material used for the foundation. Foundations are constructed of cut stone, stone and brick, concrete block or poured concrete. Poured concrete is the most common foundation material because of its strength and resistance to moisture.

▶ **HUD/FHA** Enter the type of construction, such as poured concrete, concrete block or wood.

Exterior Walls

Enter the type of wall construction (such as wood-frame or masonry) and siding materials used to form the exterior walls of the house.

Wood-frame construction is by far the type most frequently used in building single-family houses. Many different types of exterior siding are used as coverings over the house frame. Wood shingles, wood clapboard, aluminum, vinyl, brick veneer and stucco are the most often seen. Sometimes wood panels, asbestos-cement shingles and asphalt shingles are used on the exterior walls of homes. Siding materials are meant to make the walls weather tight and to create an attractive facade.

▶ **HUD/FHA** Enter the type of construction material. Examples include aluminum, wood siding, brick veneer, porcelain, log or stucco. If a combination of materials has been used, show the predominant material first.

Roof Surface

Enter the type of material used to cover the roof of the house. Common materials include asphalt shingles (with a base mat of cellulose or fiberglass), wood shingles and shakes, clay and concrete tile, slate and metal.

▶ **HUD/FHA** Enter the type of roof material, such as composition, wood, slate or tile.

Gutters & Dwnspts.

Enter the type of material used for gutters along the roof edges and downspouts leading from the gutters to a drainage area. Aluminum and vinyl gutters are now the most common kind as they require virtually no maintenance. Galvanized metal gutters must be kept painted inside and out. Although seldom seen today, wood gutters were once the standard.

▶ **HUD/FHA** Enter the type of gutters and downspouts, if any, such as galvanized, aluminum, wood or plastic. If only part of the house has gutters and downspouts, state where they are located. If there are no gutters or downspouts, enter NONE.

Window Type

Enter the predominant window type found in the house and indicate the window frame material used (wood, aluminum, vinyl, and so on). Common window types are described in Figure 5.

▶ **HUD/FHA** Describe the type of window, such as double-hung, casement or sliding. Identify the construction type, such as aluminum, wood or vinyl.

Storm Sash

Storm sashes (also called storm windows) provide good insulation and can save on fuel costs.

* Enter YES if all windows have storm sashes.
* Enter NO if none of the windows have storm sashes.
* Enter PARTIAL if some windows have storm sashes.

Figure 5.   Common Window Types

Double-Hung

The double-hung window has both an upper and lower sash that slides vertically along separate tracks. This arrangement allows cool air to come in at the bottom and warm air to go out through the top.

Horizontal Sliding

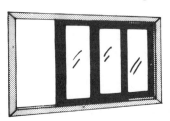

The horizontal sliding window moves back and forth on tracks. As with the double-hung type, only 50 percent of this window can be opened for fresh air.

Casement

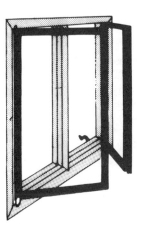

Casement windows are hinged at the side and open outward. One advantage of the casement window is that the entire window can be opened for ventilation.

Figure 5. Common Window Types (*continued*)

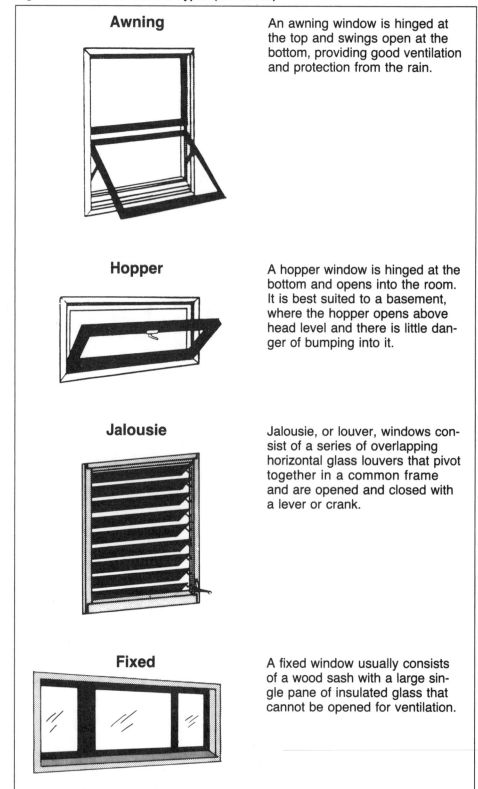

Awning

An awning window is hinged at the top and swings open at the bottom, providing good ventilation and protection from the rain.

Hopper

A hopper window is hinged at the bottom and opens into the room. It is best suited to a basement, where the hopper opens above head level and there is little danger of bumping into it.

Jalousie

Jalousie, or louver, windows consist of a series of overlapping horizontal glass louvers that pivot together in a common frame and are opened and closed with a lever or crank.

Fixed

A fixed window usually consists of a wood sash with a large single pane of insulated glass that cannot be opened for ventilation.

SOURCE: William L. Ventolo, Jr., *The Complete Home Inspection Kit* (Chicago: Dearborn Financial Publishing, Inc., 1990), 67.

▶ **HUD/FHA** Describe the combination or style of storm sash.

Screens

All windows that open should have screens.

* Enter YES if all windows have screens.
* Enter NO if none of the windows have screens.
* Enter PARTIAL if some windows have screens.

▶ **HUD/FHA** Enter YES or NO. If the use is only partial, state the window location where screens are used.

Manufactured House

Enter YES if the subject is a manufactured house. Enter NO or N/A if the subject is not a manufactured house.

There are four basic types of manufactured housing, each characterized by the extent of assemblage completed in the factory.

1. *Mobile home.* This is the most complete and least expensive of manufactured houses, needing only to be anchored to a foundation and connected to utilities.
2. *Modular house.* This comes from the factory in single or multiple room sections, which are then fitted together at the construction site.
3. *Panelized house.* At the factory, entire wall units, complete with electrical and plumbing installations, are constructed and transported to the site where final assembly takes place.
4. *Precut house.* As the name implies, materials are delivered to the construction site already cut and ready to assemble.

▶ **FNMA** If applicable, consider the specific eligibility criteria for mortgages secured by manufactured (or factory-built) housing units and adequately address them in the appraisal report.

A manufactured housing unit must be legally classified as real estate, must be permanently affixed to a foundation and must assume the characteristics of site-built housing. It must also have been built under the Federal Home Construction and Safety Standards established by HUD in June 1976. Other factory-built housing—such as prefabricated, panelized, modular, or sectional—needs to assume the characteristics of site-built housing and to meet local zoning and building codes.

There are no minimum requirements for width, size or roof pitch for manufactured housing units. Each unit must have sufficient square footage and room dimensions to be acceptable to typical purchasers in the subject market area. The wheels, axles and trailer hitches must be removed when the unit is placed on its permanent site. Both perimeter and pier foundations are required to have footings that are located below the frost line. When piers are used, they must be placed where the unit manufacturer recommends. Anchors must be provided if state law requires them. The foundation system must have been designed by an engineer to meet the soil conditions of the site.

You must address both the marketability and comparability of manufactured housing units. The materials and construction of the improvements must be acceptable in the subject market area. You should also comment on the sufficiency of the unit's living area, interior room size, storage, adequacy of room pitch and overhangs and the compatibility of the exterior finish. In addition, you must address the marketability and value of manufactured housing units in the subject market area in comparison to the marketability of site-built housing in the area.

Single-width manufactured housing units must be located in a Fannie Mae–approved project. A multiwidth unit may be located on an individual lot or in any project (although in certain areas the Fannie Mae regional office may require subdivision approval for units located on individual lots).

Use similar manufactured housing units as comparable sales, that is, compare single-width units to single-width units and multiwidth units to multiwidth units. If comparable sales of similar units are not available, you may use site-built housing as comparable sales, as long as you explain why you are doing so. If there is a preference for site-built housing in the subject market area, you must adjust the site-built comparables to reflect the market's reaction to manufactured housing units.

If the subject property is another kind of factory-built housing, use sales of similar factory-built housing as comparables if they are available. If they are not available, you may use sales of comparable site-built housing, as long as you provide an explanation for doing so and make appropriate adjustments if there is a market preference for site-built housing.

▶ **HUD/FHA** For mobile homes, enter MH; for modular homes, enter MOD.

FOUNDATION

The type of foundation construction and any evidence of water, settlement or insect infestation damage is entered in this part.

Slab

Enter YES if the house rests on a concrete slab foundation. Otherwise, enter NO.

Slab construction consists of a poured concrete foundation that rests on a footing and has a slab of concrete flooring, usually four inches thick.

▶ **HUD/FHA** Enter YES or NO.

Crawl Space

Enter YES if the house has a crawl space. If it does not, enter NO.

Many houses do not have basements but are built over an excavation. The space between the ground and the floor of the house is the crawl space. The minimum depth of such space should be 24 inches under the floor joists to allow access to the underfloor by crawling (hence the name).

▶ **HUD/FHA** Enter YES or NO. If there is a partial crawl space, include the percentage of floor area covered.

Basement

Enter YES if the house has a basement. If it does not enter NO.

The number of new houses with basements has declined steadily, particularly in the warmer areas of the United States. This is due in part to lower construction costs of houses without basements and an apparent decrease in the need for the basement space.

Note: If more than one type of foundation is found in a single house, enter the *percentage* of floor area covered by each type. For example, if the foundation is one-half basement and one-half crawl space, enter YES (or PARTIAL)—50% on both the *Basement* and *Crawl Space* lines.

▶ **HUD/FHA** Enter FULL, PARTIAL or NONE, as appropriate.

Sump Pump

Enter YES if the house has a sump pump in the basement. If it does not, enter NO.

A sump pump to drain any accumulation of water from the basement can be a critical feature in an area with a high water table or one that is otherwise prone to flooding.

▶ **HUD/FHA** Enter YES or NO.

Dampness

Enter YES if the basement shows signs of dampness. If it does not, enter NO.

Wet basements can cause extensive damage. Cement flaking from walls and dark stains on the ceiling and walls are common signs of leaks and seepage. Look also for mildew and dry rot in the basement ceiling beams and structure. Check the condition of the exterior foundation walls around the house. Are there cracks and signs of water penetration? A damp basement can have a significant effect on both marketability and value. Correcting a wet basement condition is often expensive and sometimes impossible if the house was not built properly.

A vapor barrier, one of the best features of today's well-built houses, protects basements from water damage. It is usually a thick polyethylene sheet laid on the earth underneath the house. In slab construction, the barrier is between the concrete floor and the layer of gravel spread over the ground. Although the barrier is completely hidden in slab or basement houses, it should be visible in crawl spaces. Clay drain tiles laid along the outer base of the foundation wall leading away from the house are another protection against basement water.

Note: If you answer YES on the *Dampness* line, give your opinion of its effect on value in the *COMMENTS* section or in an addendum to the URAR. If the problem appears serious, you may need to consult a professional inspector or contractor.

▶ **HUD/FHA** Enter YES or NO.

Settlement

Enter YES if you see signs of settlement. If you do not, enter NO.

If there appears to be a settlement problem, you should comment on its seriousness and probable effect on value; however, you are not expected to perform an engineer's function. A recommendation that the client consult a structural engineer to determine the extent of any settlement damage, whether the problem can be cured and what the work will cost, may need to be included in the *Comments and Conditions of Appraisal* section on page 2. If necessary, the appraisal report can be made subject to the client obtaining and reviewing a structural engineer's report.

A basement is always the lowest level of a house and is usually left unfinished by the builder. If the basement has not been finished, the exposed foundation walls can tell a lot about the structural soundness of the house. For example, look for curves or bows in the walls. They might indicate excessive weight being applied in that area. Small hairline cracks in foundation walls, the result of years of settling and shrinking, ordinarily do not pose a structural threat. On the other hand, cracks that are wider at the top than the bottom, called V-cracks, are cause for alarm. V-cracks are signs that point to a settlement problem.

▶ **HUD/FHA** Enter YES or NO. Check for cracks.

Infestation

Enter YES if there are signs of insect infestation. If none are apparent, enter NO.

The earth is infested with termites and other insects that are very destructive to wood. Before the slab for the foundation is poured, the ground should be chemically treated to poison termites and thus prevent them from coming up through or around the foundation and into the wooden structure. Chemical treatment of lumber used for sills and beams and installation of metal termite shields also provide protection.

If a home is infested, termite control and repair by the owner should be included in the terms of the purchase. In some areas, notably

California, any corrective work must be completed before a conventional loan will be granted. Be sure to check out the local practice.

▶ **FNMA** If you indicate that there is evidence of dampness, wood-boring insects, or settlement, comment on the effect on the subject property's marketability and value in an addendum. The lender must either provide satisfactory evidence that the condition was corrected or submit a professionally prepared report indicating that, based on an inspection of the property, the condition does not pose any threat of structural damage to the improvements.

▶ **HUD/FHA** Enter YES or NONE APPARENT. Look for all types of insects and damage. If there is any question, require a termite inspection.

BASEMENT

Complete this part only if the subject house has a basement. If the house does *not* have a basement, enter N/A in the blank space at the top of this part.

Area Sq. Ft.
Enter the gross basement area in square feet.

▶ **HUD/FHA** Enter the number of square feet.

% Finished
Calculate and enter the percentage of total basement area that has been finished—that is, converted into usable living space. Enter 0% if the basement is totally unfinished.

▶ **HUD/FHA** Enter the percentage of basement square footage (the figure entered on the line above) that is finished.

Ceiling
Enter the type of material used to finish the basement ceiling. Enter N/A if the basement is unfinished.

▶ **HUD/FHA** Enter material type.

Walls
Enter the type of material used to finish the basement walls. Enter N/A if the basement is unfinished.

▶ **HUD/FHA** Enter material type.

Floor
Enter the type of material used to finish the basement floor. Note if any part of the floor is dirt. Enter N/A if the basement is unfinished.

▶ **HUD/FHA** Enter the floor type. Comment if any part of the floor is dirt.

Outside Entry

Enter YES if the basement has an outside entrance, and indicate whether the entry is at ground level. Enter NO if no outside entry or access is available.

Ground-level access to the basement usually makes it more valuable as living space.

The blank lines at the bottom of this part can be used for any additional information or explanation about the basement area.

▶ **HUD/FHA** Enter YES or NO. If YES, indicate the type of entry.

INSULATION

The amount of insulation a home should have depends on the climate, the cost of fuel and a family's comfort needs. In general, however, homes with electric heat require more insulation than homes for which heat is supplied by gas or oil, and more insulation is needed in homes with air-conditioning. Each climatic area makes different energy demands on a house. Homes in very warm or very cold climates need more insulation than homes in temperate climates.

The effectiveness of insulating materials is related not only to thickness but also to resistance to heat flow. This rating is known as the *R-value. R* stands for *resistance* to heat flow. The *higher* the R-value rating of insulation, the better it will resist heat loss and heat gain. In general, one inch of insulating material equals approximately 3½ Rs (for example, six inches of insulation would equal R-21). The exact calculation depends on the type of insulation.

Figure 6 shows the areas of a home where insulation is required.

▶ **FNMA** Indicate the "R" value for insulation and comment on the adequacy of the insulation.

Roof

Ceiling

Walls

Floor

Place an x in these boxes, as appropriate, if you are positive there is insulation in these areas. On the line next to each box, enter the R-value and/or the type of insulation used (such as batts or blankets, loose or blown fill, and rigid board), if known. If the owner says the house has insulation but you can't personally verify its existence,

Figure 6.   Areas of a House Requiring Insulation

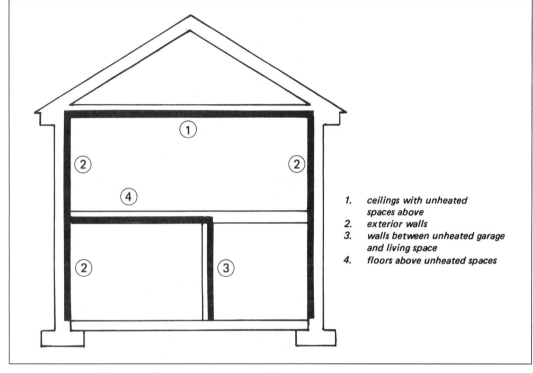

1. ceilings with unheated
    spaces above
2. exterior walls
3. walls between unheated garage
    and living space
4. floors above unheated spaces

SOURCE: William L. Ventolo, Jr. *The Complete Home Inspection Kit* (Dearborn Financial Publishing, Inc., 1990), 128.

mark X in the appropriate box(es); then enter AS PER OWNER on the line next to each box.

▶ **HUD/FHA** Make every effort to determine the type of insulation and R-factor. If the existence of insulation cannot be determined, enter UNKNOWN. Do not guess.

On the line next to each box, enter one of the following: G (good), A (average), F (fair), P (poor) or U (undetermined).

Enter an X or (√) in the box to denote the existence of insulation if the feature was verified. For example, Walls A, (X) would be the completed entry to indicate that wall insulation was verified and judged to be average.

None

Place an X in this box only if you are sure the house is *not* insulated. If you cannot determine the existence of insulation, enter UNKNOWN on the line next to the *None* box.

Adequacy

Place an X in this box if the type and amount of insulation appear typical for the subject area; then indicate AVG (average) on the line next to the box.

If in your opinion insulation in the subject house is better than or inferior to other homes in the market area, enter **GOOD**, **FAIR** or **POOR** on the *Adequacy* line as appropriate.

Energy Efficient Items:

Do any property features, besides insulation, contribute to the energy efficiency of the home? Such items include fans, fireplace inserts, low-emissivity (low-E) glass, active or passive solar-heating systems, and high-efficiency furnaces and water heaters.

▶ **FNMA** An energy-efficient property is one that uses cost-effective design, materials, equipment and site orientation to conserve nonrenewable fuels. Special energy-saving items should be recognized in the appraisal process. The nature of these items and their contribution to value will vary throughout the country because of differing climatic conditions and utility costs.

You will also list energy-efficient items in the *SALES COMPARISON ANALYSIS* grid on page 2 and note the overall contribution of these items to the market value of the subject property.

▶ **HUD/FHA** Identify any special energy-efficient items such as extra insulation, attic vents, heat pump or design of home (such as solar or earth sheltered).

▶ Appraisal 1

GENERAL DESCRIPTION		EXTERIOR DESCRIPTION		FOUNDATION		BASEMENT	N/A	INSULATION		
Units	1	Foundation	CONCRETE	Slab	YES	Area Sq. Ft.		Roof		☐
Stories	1	Exterior Walls	CEDAR/STUCCO	Crawl Space	N/A	% Finished		Ceiling	R-38	X
Type (Det./Att.)	DET.	Roof Surface	ASPH SHGLS	Basement	N/A	Ceiling		Walls	R-22	X
Design (Style)	RANCH	Gutters & Dwnspts.	ALUMINUM	Sump Pump	N/A	Walls		Floor		☐
Existing	YES	Window Type	ALUMINUM	Dampness	N/A	Floor		None		☐
Proposed	N/A	Storm Sash	N/A	Settlement	NO	Outside Entry		Adequacy	G	X
Under Construction	N/A	Screens	YES	Infestation	NO			Energy Efficient Items:		
Age (Yrs.)	11	Manufactured House	N/A				FANS,	FIREPLACE,		
Effective Age (Yrs.)	5-7							H/C SYSTEM		

In Appraisal 1, the subject property is an 11-year-old, single-family ranch with an effective age estimated at five to seven years. The house has a concrete slab foundation with no apparent settlement or infestation problems.

The roof is covered by heavyweight, top-grade asphalt shingles. Maintenance-free aluminum gutters are pitched toward the downspouts so that rainwater can drain away properly. The exterior siding is a combination of cedar and stucco. Window frames are made of aluminum; all windows have screens.

The original contractor, who continues to build houses in the area, has verified that the subject has batt insulation in all ceilings and walls with R-values of 38 and 22 respectively—considered above average for the market area. Energy-efficient items include fans in every room, a fireplace and a high-efficiency heating and cooling system.

▶ Exercise: Appraisal 2

IMPROVEMENTS	GENERAL DESCRIPTION		EXTERIOR DESCRIPTION		FOUNDATION		BASEMENT		INSULATION		
	Units	___	Foundation	___	Slab	___	Area Sq. Ft.	___	Roof	___	☐
	Stories	___	Exterior Walls	___	Crawl Space	___	% Finished	___	Ceiling	___	☐
	Type (Det./Att.)	___	Roof Surface	___	Basement	___	Ceiling	___	Walls	___	☐
	Design (Style)	___	Gutters & Dwnspts.	___	Sump Pump	___	Walls	___	Floor	___	☐
	Existing	___	Window Type	___	Dampness	___	Floor	___	None	___	☐
	Proposed	___	Storm Sash	___	Settlement	___	Outside Entry	___	Adequacy	___	☐
	Under Construction	___	Screens	___	Infestation	___			Energy Efficient Items:		
	Age (Yrs.)	___	Manufactured House	___							
	Effective Age (Yrs.)	___									

Complete the blank URAR *IMPROVEMENTS* section provided above for Appraisal 2, using the following information. When you have finished, check your work against the completed Appraisal 2 in the Answer Key.

The subject property is an 18-year-old, one-story detached ranch-style house with a finished basement area of approximately 1,000 square feet. The remaining foundation is a concrete slab. Effective age is estimated to be the same as actual age, primarily due to lack of preventive maintenance.

The wood-frame house, which was built on-site, has plywood siding with brick veneer trim and a wood shingle roof. Gutters and downspouts are made of aluminum. The wood-framed double-hung windows have thermopane glass and aluminum combination storms and screens.

There are no signs of dampness or smells of mildew in the basement, which has a sump pump and is entered from the kitchen. There is no evidence of settlement in the walls or floor. The ceilings and floors in the rest of the house seem plumb, square and level.

The basement is nicely finished with an acoustic tile ceiling, wood-paneled walls and vinyl tile flooring over a plywood subfloor. There are no visible signs of termites or other wood-boring insects. In fact, a recent professional termite inspection proved negative.

Insulation is about average for the subject area—R-19 within the walls and R-33 in the ceilings, as shown in the building plans provided by the homeowner. There are no energy-efficient items within the home.

Room List

ROOMS	Foyer	Living	Dining	Kitchen	Den	Family Rm.	Rec. Rm.	Bedrooms	# Baths	Laundry	Other	Area Sq. Ft.
Basement												
Level 1												
Level 2												

Finished area **above** grade contains: Rooms;   Bedroom(s);   Bath(s);   Square Feet of Gross Living Area

The *ROOM LIST* section of the URAR form indicates the number of rooms in the subject property, their use and the total number of square feet of living space.

Information provided in the *ROOM LIST* section also will be used in the *SALES COMPARISON ANALYSIS* on page 2. Because the subject property is the standard by which comparable properties are selected and evaluated, the same criteria used to determine room count and above-grade square footage for the subject also must be applied to the comps. For example, if the foyer is not included in the subject's room count, it should not be included in comp room counts.

In the same manner, if a finished attic is part of the subject's GLA (gross living area), the same kind of improvement either should be part of the GLA of comparable properties or otherwise reflected in the adjustment process. If the appraiser concludes that the bottom level of a split-level subject is below grade, the bottom level of similar comparables also must be treated as below grade. The key words in a room count are *accuracy* and *consistency*.

To develop accurate room information for a subject structure:

* Indicate the number and type of rooms found on each level.
* Calculate the total square footage of each level, including the basement.
* Include the total number of rooms *above grade, excluding* areas such as foyers, baths, attics and laundry rooms.

- List the total bedroom count.
- List the total bath count.
- Include the total *above-grade* living area.

ROOMS

Indicate the number of each type of room listed that is found on the separate levels of the house, including the basement. If the subject does not contain a listed room type, leave that space blank. If the subject contains a room type that is *not* listed (such as an attic), enter that room type by name in the space under the heading *Other*.

Figure 7, from the *HUD Minimum Property Standards* for a single-family residence, can be used as a guideline for minimum room sizes.

▶ **FNMA** Fannie Mae does not specify minimum size or living area requirements for properties; however, dwelling units of any type should contain sufficient living area to be acceptable to typical purchasers or tenants in the subject market area. Comparables should be similar in size to the subject property to support the general acceptability of a particular property type.

▶ **HUD/FHA** Questions concerning *room design* and *count* should reflect local custom.

The room count typically includes a living room (LR), dining room (DR), kitchen (KT), den (DN), recreation room (REC) and bedroom (BR). In completing this section, enter the *number* of each room type on each level. DO NOT enter the dimensions.

Typically the foyer, bath, and laundry room are not counted as rooms. A room is a *livable area* with a *specific use*.

Basement

Enter the number of each room type found in a *finished* basement. For example, if the basement area has been made into a recreation room, enter 1 in the space under *Rec. Rm.*

Calculate and enter *total* square footage (last column) of the basement area, whether finished or unfinished. This figure should match

Figure 7. Minimum Room Sizes

Name of Space	Living Unit with 1 BR (sq. ft.)	Living Unit with 2 BR (sq. ft.)	Living Unit with 3 BR (sq. ft.)	Living Unit with 4 BR (sq. ft.)	Least Dimension
Living Room	160	160	170	180	11' 0"
Dining Room	80	80	95	110	8' 0"
BR (Primary)	120	120	120	120	9' 4"
BR (Secondary)	—	80	80	80	8' 4"
Total BR Area	120	200	280	360	

the one entered in the *Basement* space of the *IMPROVEMENTS* section of the URAR.

Note: Square footage calculations must be based on *outside* dimensions.

> ▸ **HUD/FHA** The basement generally is *completely below* the grade (ground level). This is NOT counted in the finished gross living area at the grade level.

Level 1

Enter the number of each room type found on the first level of the subject structure. Then calculate and record the total square footage of "Level 1" in the *Area Sq. Ft.* column.

> ▸ **HUD/FHA** Level 1 includes all finished living area at grade level.

Level 2

Enter the number of each room type found on the second level of the subject structure. Then calculate and record the total square footage of "Level 2" in the *Area Sq. Ft.* column.

The blank line under "Level 2" can be used to insert a living level not listed on the form; for example, a third story.

> ▸ **HUD/FHA** Level 2 includes all finished area above the first level.

Foyer

The foyer is the entrance area, which may be set off by full or partial walls and a distinctive floor finish, such as ceramic tile. Smaller homes may not have a separate foyer.

> ▸ **HUD/FHA** The foyer is the entrance hall of a house.

Living

The formal living room, usually located adjacent to the foyer or front entry, has diminished in importance as the family room and the large "country kitchen" have gained popularity.

Dining

The formal dining area has made a comeback over the past decade as entertaining at home has found new favor. In many homes, rooms have been "opened up," that is, made to appear larger by elimination of dividing walls between different living areas. This is frequently the case with the living room and dining room. The typical *L*-shaped living/dining area should count as *two* rooms, if one of these conditions is met:

- The dining area is as large as a typical dining room in the subject market; or
- The addition of a hypothetical wall would convert the dining area into a room with the same or greater utility and with the same or more convenience.

▶ **HUD/FHA** Depending on its size, an L-shaped dining area off the kitchen may or may not be counted as a room. A simple test is to insert a hypothetical wall to separate the two combined areas. If residents could utilize the resulting two rooms with the same or more utility and without increased inconvenience, the room count should be two. If the hypothetical wall would result in a lack of utility and increased inconvenience, the room count should be one.

Kitchen

Kitchen specifications should meet at least the minimal level of acceptance in the subject market. Usually this will include room for major appliances, as well as a separate work surface and eating area. The kitchen space may be large enough to encompass a separate sitting area as well, perhaps with a fireplace and room for an entertainment center. This "great room" concept is reminiscent of colonial days, when a single room provided for all living functions. A separate sitting area would qualify for treatment as a separate room if it met the criteria described above for treatment of an *L*-shaped living/dining area. In other words, would the two separate areas have the same utility and convenience, even if a wall was between them?

Den

The concept of a "den" for private adult work and relaxation is somewhat dated, having been replaced by the "home office." In many homes this is simply a bedroom used as a study or work space.

Family Rm.

The family room is an informal living space, usually near or adjacent to the kitchen, and often serving as the TV entertainment center.

Rec. Rm.

The recreation, or "rec," room is an even more informal area. It may be a finished basement area and typically may include indoor sports equipment, such as a pool table.

Bedrooms

A bedroom will have a closet and should not serve as a corridor to any other room.

Baths

The number of bathrooms are counted as follows:

- *1*—Full bath with toilet, sink and tub
- *¾*—Three-quarter bath with toilet, sink and shower (in some areas, may be considered full bath)
- *½*—Half-bath with toilet and sink
- *¼*—Quarter-bath with toilet only (illegal in some areas)

A room with a sink or shower only is classified as a washroom or shower room, as appropriate, and should be listed by name in the *Other* column.

Laundry

This should not be counted as a separate room area unless it is within the house; that is, a garage laundry area is not counted.

Other

Enter interior living spaces not listed in another category; for example, a special-purpose room, such as a breakfast room or sunroom.

Area Sq. Ft.

Enter the square footage of each level of living space.

▶ **HUD/FHA** Calculate the overall square footage of each level from the exterior dimensions of the structure.

Finished area ABOVE grade contains:

Indicate the *finished* area of the subject structure that is *above grade*—number of rooms, number of bedrooms, number of baths and square feet of living area.

- *Below grade:* Finished living area about four feet below exterior grade; for example, the below-grade-level finished space in a bilevel, split-level, trilevel and so on.
- *Basement:* Generally considered fully below exterior grade and *not* counted as gross living area (GLA), even if finished.
  Exception: The lower level of a house built into a hillside or cliff, provided it has windows and a quality of finish equal to or better than the rest of the house.
- *Above grade:* All portions of the finished living area at or above exterior grade; for example, space in a ranch, 1½ story (Cape Cod), two-story colonial and so on.
- *Attic:* An attic should be included in the GLA only if the following conditions are met:
  1. The quality of finish is equal to that found in other finished areas of the house.
  2. The area is heated.
  3. The ceiling is five feet or more in height.
  4. The space contains windows that provide light and air equal to that available in the other finished areas of the house.

▶ **FNMA** Fannie Mae considers a level to be below grade if any portion of it is below grade, regardless of the quality of its finish or the window area of the room. Therefore a walk-out basement with finished rooms would *not* be included in the above-grade room count.

Nevertheless, rooms not included in the above-grade room count may add substantially to the value of the property, particularly if the quality of the finish is high. For that reason, report the basement or other partially below-grade areas separately and make appropriate adjustments for them on the *Basement & Finished Rooms Below Grade* line in the *SALES COMPARISON ANALYSIS* grid. To ensure consistency in the sales comparison analysis, compare above-grade areas to above-grade areas and below-grade areas to below-grade areas. However, if it becomes necessary to deviate from this approach because of the style of the subject property or of any comparables, explain the reason for the deviation and clearly describe the comparisons being made.

Rooms;

Enter the total number of rooms *above* grade. Areas such as foyers, baths, unfinished attics and laundry rooms are normally *not* included in this count.

Bedroom(s);

Enter the total number of bedrooms *above* grade.

Bath(s);

Enter the total number of bathrooms *above* grade.

Square Feet of Gross Living Area

Calculate and record the total square feet of living area *above* grade. Figure 8 describes how gross living area (GLA) is measured.

▶ **HUD/FHA** Enter the total square footage *above grade.*

In general a room totally underground is not as valuable as one above ground.

Figure 8.   Calculating Living Area

The living area of a house is the area enclosed by the outside dimensions of the heated and air-conditioned portions of the house. This excludes basements (even if finished and heated), open porches, garages, unfinished attics and so on.

When measuring a house in preparation for calculating the living area, follow these steps:

1. Draw a sketch of the foundation.
2. Measure *all* outside walls.
3. If the house has an attached garage, treat the inside garage walls that are common to the house as outside walls of the house.
4. Measure the garage.
5. Round off all measurements to the nearest half-foot (for example, 32'4" becomes 32½') for ease of calculating.
6. Before leaving the house, check to see that net dimensions of opposite sides are equal. If they are not, remeasure.
7. Section off the sketch into rectangles.
8. Calculate the area of each rectangle.
9. Add up the areas, being careful to *subtract* the area of the garage, *if necessary.*
10. Before leaving the house, *always* recheck all dimensions.

▶ Appraisal 1

ROOMS	Foyer	Living	Dining	Kitchen	Den	Family Rm.	Rec. Rm.	Bedrooms	# Baths	Laundry	Other	Area Sq. Ft.
Basement											ENCL.	
Level 1	1	1	1	1				3	2	1	PORCH	2,119
Level 2												

Finished area **above** grade contains: 7 Rooms;   3 Bedroom(s);   2 Bath(s);   2,119 Square Feet of Gross Living Area

In Appraisal 1, the subject property is a single-family, ranch-style home. It contains a foyer, three bedrooms, two baths, kitchen, living room, dining room, laundry room and glassed-in porch area with carpet, ceiling fans and its own heating and air-conditioning system.

Gross area, based on outside dimensions, is 2,644 square feet—including a 21′ × 25′ garage.

▶ Exercise: Appraisal 2

ROOMS	Foyer	Living	Dining	Kitchen	Den	Family Rm.	Rec. Rm.	Bedrooms	# Baths	Laundry	Other	Area Sq. Ft.
Basement												
Level 1												
Level 2												

Finished area **above** grade contains: Rooms;   Bedroom(s);   Bath(s);   Square Feet of Gross Living Area

Complete the blank URAR *ROOM LIST* section provided above for Appraisal 2, using the following information. When you have finished, check your work against the completed Appraisal 2 in the Answer Key.

The subject property is a one-story house with a 1,000-square-foot finished basement, which is used as a recreation room.

The house contains the following above-grade rooms: foyer, living room, dining room, kitchen, family room, four bedrooms and two baths (each with toilet, sink and tub/shower); total area is 1,980 square feet.

Interior

SURFACES	Materials/Condition	HEATING		KITCHEN EQUIP.		ATTIC		IMPROVEMENT ANALYSIS	Good	Avg.	Fair	Poor
Floors		Type		Refrigerator		None		Quality of Construction				
Walls		Fuel		Range/Oven		Stairs		Condition of Improvements				
Trim/Finish		Condition		Disposal		Drop Stair		Room Sizes/Layout				
Bath Floor		Adequacy		Dishwasher		Scuttle		Closets and Storage				
Bath Wainscot		COOLING		Fan/Hood		Floor		Energy Efficiency				
Doors		Central		Compactor		Heated		Plumbing-Adequacy & Condition				
		Other		Washer/Dryer		Finished		Electrical-Adequacy & Condition				
		Condition		Microwave				Kitchen Cabinets-Adequacy & Cond.				
Fireplace(s)	#	Adequacy		Intercom				Compatibility to Neighborhood				
								Appeal & Marketability				
								Estimated Remaining Economic Life			Yrs.	
								Estimated Remaining Physical Life			Yrs.	

The *INTERIOR* section of the URAR is used to record information about the type, quality and condition of interior surface materials and equipment used throughout the house.

SURFACES

Interior surface finishes include all wall and floor coverings. Unusual ceiling coverings or treatment (such as cove moldings or acoustic tile) should be noted on one of the lines under the listing "Doors."

Materials/Condition

For each item in this block:

• Identify the type of material that covers each surface; and
• Rate (good, average, fair or poor) the quality of materials, workmanship and condition of the finished surfaces in terms of the standard in the neighborhood.

For example, an entry of **WD/CPT/CT/AVG** means *wood* floors, *carpeting*, *ceramic tile* floors, and a rating of *average*.

Ratings of **FAIR** and **POOR** must be explained in the *COMMENTS* section at the bottom of Page 1 or in an addendum.

▶ **VA** Comment only on items rated *POOR.*

Floors

Enter the type of materials used for floors; enter **GOOD, AVG, FAIR** or **POOR**, as appropriate.

Common floor coverings include wall-to-wall carpeting, vinyl tile, vinyl sheet goods (often called linoleum) and hard surfaces such as wood, slate, brick, marble, terrazzo, stone and ceramic tile.

Walls

Enter the types of wall finish found throughout the interior of the house; enter **GOOD, AVG, FAIR** or **POOR**.

Most interior wall surfaces are covered with wallboard (also called plasterboard, sheetrock or drywall), plaster, prefinished paneling or solid wood paneling. Decorative finishes include paint, wallpaper or wallcoverings such as vinyl, suede, silk, foil, burlap and cork.

Trim/Finish

Enter the type of material used for trim; enter **GOOD, AVG, FAIR** or **POOR**.

Also called *molding*, trim usually describes the pieces used to finish walls around openings, at corners and where two different materials meet. Most interior trim is made of Ponderosa pine or Idaho white pine. Trim for painting is milled from pine, gum, poplar and similar woods; trim for staining comes from a decorative hardwood such as oak, walnut, chestnut, birch or mahogany. Hardboard and vinyl moldings are the latest substitutes for wood.

Bath Floor

Enter the type of material used for bathroom floors; enter **GOOD, AVG, FAIR** or **POOR**.

Ceramic tile and vinyl tile and sheeting continue to be the most popular bathroom floor coverings, but other materials such as carpeting, marble, hardwood, rubber and asphalt tile also are used.

Bath Wainscot

Enter the type of material used for bathroom wainscoting; enter **GOOD, AVG, FAIR** or **POOR**.

Wainscoting is the lower part of a wall that is finished differently from the wall above. Materials used on shower walls and around tubs and sinks include ceramic tile, plastic tile, fiberglass and other synthetic water-resistant coverings.

Doors

Indicate the kinds of doors found throughout the house; enter GOOD, AVG, FAIR or POOR.

Wood doors are available in solid wood (plank), veneer over solid wood or veneer over a hollow core. Solid cores generally are preferred for exterior doors because they provide better heat and sound insulation and are more resistant to warping. Hollow-core doors, about a third as heavy as the solid-core type, are used for interior locations where heat and sound insulation are not as critical.

Steel and *aluminum* doors are not solid metal but have a lighter inner core of wood, wood and foam or rigid foam. The aluminum or steel exterior surface comes primed or with a baked-enamel finish, is weather resistant and doesn't swell or shrink. It's also fire retardant.

Sliding glass doors have one or more panels that slide in a frame of metal or wood. The panels may hold either single or insulating glass depending on the local climate. Some glass doors provide self-storing screens in a separate track of the door frame.

Typical entries for *Doors* might be:

- EXT/WD/SC/GOOD for *exterior* doors, *wood, solid core* and a rating of *good;* or
- INT/WD/HC/AVG for *interior* doors, *wood, hollow core* and a rating of *average.*

Fireplace(s)

Indicate type (such as built-in masonry or freestanding metal), location and number of fireplaces; enter GOOD, AVG, FAIR or POOR. If the subject has no fireplace, enter NONE.

Today's furnaces and heat pumps do a good job of meeting our physical heating needs but provide little emotional satisfaction. That's where the fireplace comes in. There's nothing quite like the pleasure of watching crackling flames on a cold winter night.

Most fireplaces are constructed of brick or stone and have a single opening with a damper and hearth. A masonry fireplace (brick, stone or similar material) is expensive to build and normally is used less than any other feature of a house, even in cold climates. It is not too efficient either, because much of the heat goes up the chimney instead of into the room. Despite these negatives, many buyers are willing to pay extra for a home with a fireplace, even in climates where a fireplace is hardly a necessity.

Sample entries for a fireplace are BRICK/LR/GOOD *(brick, living room, good),* STONE/FR/AVG *(stone, family room, average),* METAL/FS/MBR/FAIR *(metal, freestanding, master bedroom, fair).*

Note: Fireplaces are assumed to be wood-burning unless otherwise stated.

HEATING

Heating systems fall into two basic categories, *central* heating and *space* heating. They draw their heat from one of four sources: warm air, hot water, steam and the sun. The systems are powered by gas, oil, electricity or solid fuels such as coal and wood.

Central Heating Systems. There are three basic central heating systems: *warm-air, hot-water* and *steam.*

In a *warm-air* system, a furnace heats air that is then distributed to the rooms in the house via ducts. The older gravity-type warm-air heating system operates on the principle that lighter warm air rises and heavier cold air sinks. The modern version, a *forced* warm-air system, operates on the same principle but adds a fan or blower to increase air movement. The blower forces the air through the ducts so that heat arrives more quickly to all areas of the house. Most homes today have blower-forced warm-air heating systems with continuous air circulation.

A *hot-water* system operates on the principle of circulation and recirculation of heated water. Water heated in the boiler is pumped through the pipes to the radiators where heat is distributed into the rooms. As the water cools it returns to the boiler to start the cycle over again.

Unlike a warm-air system that uses a furnace to heat air, a *steam* system uses a boiler to generate steam. Water in the boiler is heated until steam forms. The steam circulates through the pipes (without the aid of a pump) until it reaches the radiators in the rooms. Air in the radiators is expelled through air vents. As the steam cools, it turns back into water and returns to the boiler.

Although steam systems are no longer installed in new construction, they are still found in older homes.

Space Heating Systems. Space heaters are the simplest and least expensive of all heating devices. In this category are stoves, circulatory heaters, unit heaters, floor heaters, wall heaters and resistance heaters. In northern climates, central heating systems are sometimes supplemented with space heaters in entryways, glassed-in porches, bathrooms and unheated garages used as workshops.

Solar Heating. Most solar heating units suitable for residential use operate by gathering the heat from the sun's rays with one or more *solar collectors.* Water or air is forced through a series of pipes in the solar collector to be heated by the sun's rays. The hot air or water is then stored in a heavily insulated storage tank until it is needed to heat the house.

Solar heating systems do have drawbacks. They are more expensive than conventional heating systems, and if local utility costs are low enough, the addition of a solar system to an existing house may be impractical. The heat production of a solar system is limited by both storage capacity and the need for good (sunny) weather, which means that most such systems must have an independent heating unit for backup.

Heat Pump. A *heat pump* is an electrically powered unit that provides both heating in winter and cooling in summer. It is actually an air-conditioning system that is used in reverse during the winter.

The most commonly used residential-size heat pump takes heat from the outdoor air in winter (sometimes water is used) and pumps it indoors. In summer the cycle is reversed—warm air is taken out of the house.

Heat pumps are most efficient in mild climates where temperatures do not drop below 30° for any length of time. In northern climates auxiliary heat boosters may be added to the indoor unit. Under normal weather conditions these heat boosters do not operate. When necessary, they turn on to make up the difference in temperature and reduce the strain on the heat pump.

As is true with any air-conditioning system, the heat pump's compressor/condenser is mounted outside the house, and the evaporator is inside.

Type

Enter the type of heating system found in the house; for example, blower-forced warm-air, heat pump, hot water, steam.

Fuel

Indicate whether the heating system is powered by gas, oil, electricity, coal, wood or solar energy.

Condition

Enter GOOD, AVG, FAIR or POOR as appropriate. If you rate the condition of the heating system as fair or poor, explain your reasons in the *COMMENTS* section on page 1 or in an addendum.

Adequacy

Rate the heating system in terms of its effectiveness. Enter ADEQUATE or INADEQUATE. If you judge the heating system as inadequate, explain.

Poor heating often is caused by:

* Insufficient insulation or weatherproofing in a house;
* Poor design and installation of the air-duct system;
* Systems that need cleaning and adjustments; or
* Heating units that are too small for the house.

COOLING

Central Forced-Air System. In areas of the country where summer temperatures warrant, new homes typically are centrally air-conditioned. In other areas, new homes may be prepared ("prepped") for air-conditioning by installation of a compatible forced-air heating system.

Air-conditioning units are rated either in BTUs or in tons. Twelve thousand BTUs are the equivalent of a one-ton capacity. In general a house normally requires 1 ton of cooling capacity for every 600 feet of air-conditioned space. Thus an 1,800-square-foot house would require a 3-ton system.

Most central forced-air systems operate on gas or electricity, although some use oil for fuel. Some types have the heating and cooling apparatus in two separate units with the condenser/compressor located outside the house and the remaining parts (evaporator, coil, blower and controls) located either in the attic or in the furnace area. Less-expensive central forced-air systems have the heating and cooling systems built into a single unit.

Most warm-air furnaces today are designed so that a cooling unit can be added at a later time. All types can use the same ducts, blowers and filters whether they are heating or cooling the house.

Room Air Conditioners. In some northern areas where the number of hot, humid days doesn't warrant the cost of installing central air-conditioning, room air conditioners provide low-cost summer comfort. These units contain a compact compression cooling system. The condenser faces outdoors and removes the heat from the high-pressure hot gas. The evaporator faces the room, and a blower cools the room by drawing room air over the cold evaporator coils.

Central

Enter YES if the subject house has central air-conditioning. If it does not, enter NO.

Other

If the subject has central air, leave this line blank. If the subject does *not* have central air, enter the type of air-conditioning system it does have, if any. If ROOM AIR CONDITIONER or some other cooling system is entered on this line, indicate also the number of units contained in the house.

Remember: Tangible items not permanently attached to real estate, and thus not considered fixtures, are classified as *personal property* and usually are not included in an appraisal of the real property. A window air-conditioner, for example, would ordinarily be considered personal property, but if a hole were cut in a wall expressly for the installation of the air-conditioner, the unit would probably be considered part of the real estate.

Condition

Enter GOOD, AVG, FAIR or POOR. If you rate the condition of the cooling system as fair or poor, explain your reasons in the *COMMENTS* section on page 1 or in an addendum.

Adequacy

Rate the cooling system in terms of its effectiveness. Enter ADE-QUATE or INADEQUATE, as appropriate. If you judge the cooling system as inadequate, explain.

Poor cooling often is caused by:

- Insufficient insulation or weatherproofing in a house;
- Poor design and installation of the air-duct system;
- Systems that need cleaning and adjustments; or
- Cooling units that are too small for the house.

KITCHEN EQUIP.

In this section of the URAR, you will identify those appliances or other items of equipment in the subject kitchen that are considered *fixtures*. A *fixture* is something that was once personal property but has since been installed or attached to the land or building in a permanent manner; that is, it cannot be removed easily or without damaging the building. A fixture is regarded by law as part of the real estate and must be included in the valuation process.

Mark x in the box beside each *built-in* appliance or other item of equipment that is considered a *fixture*. These must be included in your estimate of market value.

If the appliance or item of equipment is *personal property*, enter P in the appropriate box or boxes. The value of personal property is *not* included in your estimate of market value.

If the subject kitchen does *not* have an appliance or other item of equipment listed, leave that box *blank*.

Note: Some lines in this section list two different items; for example *FAN/HOOD*. If the subject kitchen has one item but not the other, cross out the missing item and mark the box.

Refrigerator

Enter x if present as a fixture, P if personal property.

Range/Oven

Enter x if present as a fixture, P if personal property.

Disposal

Enter x if present as a fixture, P if personal property.

Dishwasher

Enter x if present as a fixture, P if personal property.

Fan/Hood

Enter x if present as a fixture, P if personal property.

Compactor

Enter x if present as a fixture, P if personal property.

Washer/Dryer

Enter x if present as a fixture, P if personal property.

Microwave

Enter x if present as a fixture, P if personal property.

Intercom

Enter x if present as a fixture, P if personal property.

ATTIC

Complete this section only if the subject house has an attic. If the house does *not* have an attic, mark x in the *None* box and leave the rest of the section blank.

The attic is the area located between the rafters and the ceiling joists. If the subject has an attic, specify type of access, whether it has a floor and whether it is heated or finished. Enter any additional features of the attic space in the blank lines following *Finished.*

None

Enter x in this box if the house does not have an attic.

Stairs

Enter x in this box if there are permanent or fixed stairs leading to the attic.

Drop Stair

Enter x in this box if access is gained by pulling down a folding ladder or staircase hidden in the ceiling below the attic floor.

Scuttle

Enter x in this box if entry is through a covered opening in the ceiling.

Floor

Enter x in this box if the attic has a floor.

Heated

Enter x in this box if the attic is heated.

Finished

Enter x in this box if the attic has finished floors, walls and ceiling.

Note: Attic space that warrants above-grade living area consideration should be included in the *ROOM LIST* section.

▶ **HUD/FHA** Additional space such as an attic or room above the garage should be described in terms of how it actually can be used. The essential question is whether it can be included in the above-grade living area.

IMPROVEMENT ANALYSIS

The rating grid in this section provides a list of items that are important to buyers in the marketplace. Each feature of the subject property should be compared with the same feature found in competing properties in the neighborhood and rated as *GOOD, AVG, FAIR* or *POOR*. All fair and poor ratings must be fully explained in the *COMMENTS* section on page 1 or in an addendum to satisfy Fannie Mae, Freddie Mac and HUD requirements. The VA requires an explanation only for items marked *POOR*.

Keep in mind that it is not the appraiser's task to perform a detailed inspection of plumbing (including septic) and electrical systems. The appraiser can only note whether they appear to be functioning properly. If the condition of either system cannot be verified, the appraiser should note that fact and recommend the client obtain further reports from appropriate sources, as the client deems necessary.

▶ **FNMA** Report the condition of the improvements in factual, specific terms. Any condition that may affect the value or marketability of the subject property must be reported to ensure that the property is adequately described. The use of ratings does not preclude you from reporting the detrimental condition of improvements even if that condition is also typical for competing properties. For instance, if a property is characterized by deferred maintenance or a lack of updating, you should note that fact even if the same condition applies to competing properties in the neighborhood.

Good

Enter x if the subject's improvement is better than that of other properties in the neighborhood.

Avg.

Enter x if the subject's improvement is typical of properties in the neighborhood.

Fair

Enter x if the subject's improvement is of slightly poorer quality than that of other properties in the neighborhood.

▶ **FNMA** A less-than-average rating indicates that the rated item is inferior to that of competing properties in the subject market area and will probably meet buyer resistance. A *fair* rating will make a property ineligible for maximum financing. Comment on the reasons for the rating and its effect on the subject's marketability and value.

Poor

Enter x if the subject's improvement is of markedly poorer quality than that of other properties in the neighborhood.

▶ **FNMA** A less-than-average rating indicates that the rated item is inferior to that of competing properties in the subject market area and will probably meet buyer resistance. A *poor* rating will make a property ineligible for maximum financing. Comment on the reasons for the rating and its effect on the subject's marketability and value.

Quality of Construction

Enter x for good, average, fair or poor, considering the quality of workmanship and the quality and durability of the materials used in the construction of the subject dwelling.

Condition of Improvements

Enter x for good, average, fair or poor, considering the overall condition of improvements.

Is the subject well maintained or are there signs of neglect? With a little attention at the appropriate time, a house will last for decades, even centuries. Are there signs of physical deterioration (the effects of ordinary wear and tear and the action of the elements)?

Room Sizes/Layout

Enter x for good, average, fair or poor.

Size and location of rooms have a substantial bearing on livability. Ideally, every house should have three clear-cut zones to accommodate the three main kinds of activities: working, sleeping and living. The *work zone* includes the kitchen, laundry area and perhaps a workshop; the *living zone* contains the living, dining and family rooms; the *sleeping zone* contains the bedrooms. Each zone should be separate from the others so that activities in one do not interfere with those in another.

Good interior zoning takes into consideration:

- Halls, stairways and entries—efficient and convenient channeling of household traffic;
- Kitchen—access to garage and dining areas;
- Laundry—convenience to bedrooms;
- Living room—view and winter sunlight;
- Family room—far from bedrooms for noise control;

- Dining room—adjacent to kitchen;
- Bedrooms—away from noisy areas and public view;
- Bathrooms—one for every two adults and every three children, with toilet and lavatory on every floor;
- Storage space—a closet for every resident, plus linen closet and large-item storage; and
- Garage—close to kitchen, without blocking light or views.

▶ **FNMA** Dwellings with unusual layouts, peculiar floor plans, or inadequate equipment or amenities generally have limited market appeal and should not be considered for maximum financing. A review of the room list and floor plan for the dwelling unit may indicate an unusual layout; for example, bedrooms on a level with no bath, or a kitchen on a level different from the dining room. If you indicate that such inadequacies result in market resistance to the property, you should make appropriate adjustments to reflect this in the overall analysis. On the other hand, if market acceptance can be demonstrated through the use of comparable sales with the same inadequacies, no adjustments are required.

Closets and Storage

Enter x for good, average, fair or poor.

Check the adequacy and convenience of closets and other storage space throughout the house, including general-purpose space to store tools, seasonal clothes and all the things people collect over time. Keep in mind that the amount of storage space in a house plays a very important part in the buying decision of the majority of home shoppers.

Energy Efficiency

Enter x for good, average, fair or poor.

Energy-efficient homes have the potential to provide comfort and convenience using far less energy than do conventional houses.

In checking for energy efficiency, consider the following:

- Insulation R-values;
- Weatherstripping and caulking;
- Window locations;
- Special window glass, such as low-E;
- Heating and cooling equipment size, performance, efficiency and location;
- Fireplace design;
- Orientation of the house on the site;
- Active and/or passive solar systems;
- Ductwork length and insulation;
- Energy efficiency of water-heating system;
- Landscape design;
- Attic and other fans;
- Storm windows and doors;

- Performance efficiency of fixtures, including kitchen appliances such as a built-in dishwasher; and
- Equipment maintenance.

Plumbing-Adequacy & Condition

Enter x for good, average, fair or poor. If *adequacy* and *condition* are rated differently, specify which rating applies to each factor. Remember that the appraiser is not rating the actual condition of the system, only reporting its *observable* condition.

The plumbing system in a house is actually a number of separate systems, each with a special function.

- The *water-supply system* brings water to the house from a well or city main and distributes hot and cold water through two sets of pipes.
- The *drainage system* collects waste and used water from fixtures and carries it away to a central point for disposal outside the house.
- The *vent piping system* carries out of the house all sewer gases that develop in drainage lines. It also equalizes air pressure within the waste system so that waste will flow away and not back up into fixtures.
- The *waste-collecting system* is needed only when the main waste drain in the house is lower than sewer level under the street or when the house has more than one drainage system.
- The *house connection pipe system* is the waste connection from the house to the city sewer line, to a septic tank or to some other waste-disposal facility.

In evaluating the plumbing, check:

- Type of materials used for piping (copper is best, iron or steel is worst);
- Pipes for signs of leaks and corrosion;
- Drainage;
- Water pressure;
- Water heater;
- Septic system (if there is one);
- Well (if there is one);
- Number, style, quality and condition of plumbing fixtures;
- Fixtures for proper venting;
- Fixtures for shutoff valves; and
- Overall performance of system.

Electrical-Adequacy & Condition

Enter x for good, average, fair or poor.

If *adequacy* and *condition* are rated differently, specify which rating applies to each factor. Remember that the appraiser is not rating the actual condition of the system, only reporting its *observable* condition.

The electrical system is evaluated in terms of three key characteristics:

1. *Safety.* The system must meet all National Electrical Code (NEC) requirements; each major appliance should have its own circuit, and lighting circuits should be isolated from electrical equipment that causes fluctuations in voltage.
2. *Capacity.* The system must meet the home's existing needs and have the capacity to accommodate room additions and new appliances.
3. *Convenience.* Switches, lights and outlets should be sufficient in number and located so that occupants need not walk in the dark or use extension cords.

In evaluating the electrical system, check:

* Service drop (two-wire or three-wire);
* Service panel (fused or circuit-breaker type);
* Wiring;
* Main disconnect switch;
* Ampere service capacity (minimum of 100 amperes);
* Number of electrical outlets per room;
* Number of light switches per room; and
* Adequacy and style of lighting fixtures.

Kitchen Cabinets-Adequacy & Cond.

Enter x for good, average, fair or poor. If *adequacy* and *condition* are rated differently, specify which rating applies to each factor.

Check the kitchen cabinets for quality of construction. Open the doors and drawers of all units to check for size and condition. Note inoperable doors or drawers and any missing hardware. Check that wall units and floor units are properly mounted and secured. Check also the adequacy of base and wall cabinet storage space, counter space, lighting and placement of counter space.

Compatibility to Neighborhood

Enter x for good, average, fair or poor. Compare the subject property to competing properties in the neighborhood in terms of age, type, design, size and construction of materials.

> ▶ **FNMA** Improvements should conform generally to the neighborhood in terms of age, type, design and materials used for their construction. If there is market resistance to a property because its improvements are incompatible with the neighborhood or with the requirements of the competitive market—because of remaining economic life; adequacy of plumbing, heating or electrical services; design; quality; size; condition; or any other reason directly related to market demand—the lender should underwrite the loan more carefully and, if appropriate, require more conservative mortgage terms. However, the lender should be aware that many older neighborhoods have favorable heterogeneity in architectural styles, land use and age of housing. For example, older

neighborhoods are especially likely to have been developed through custom building; such variety may be a positive marketing factor.

In the appraisal and underwriting process, special consideration must be given to properties that represent special or unique housing for the subject neighborhood. For example, nontraditional housing types—such as earth houses, geodesic domes, log houses and the like—or housing that is atypical for the neighborhood—such as a contemporary dwelling in a housing market that consists of colonial dwellings—must be reviewed with care. In addition, for the property to be eligible for maximum financing, you must be able to establish that an active, viable market exists. If there is limited evidence of market acceptance, the lender must require more conservative mortgage terms. However, if you are not able to find any evidence of market acceptance, and the characteristics of the property are so significant or so unique that you cannot establish a reliable estimate of market value, Fannie Mae will not accept the property as security for a mortgage.

FNMA does not specify minimum size or living area requirements for properties. However, dwelling units of any type should contain sufficient living area to be acceptable to typical purchasers or tenants in the subject market area. Comparables should be similar in size to the subject property to support the general acceptability of a particular property type.

Appeal & Marketability

Enter x for good, average, fair or poor.

Compare the subject to competing properties in terms of quality of construction and materials, design, physical characteristics, livability and overall appeal to the typical buyer. Consider the following:

* Type and style of architecture;
* Size—area, number of rooms;
* Types of rooms and layout;
* Quality of construction and materials;
* Age and condition—effective age;
* Number of bedrooms and baths;
* Master suite and master bath concept; and
* Special features—fireplaces, pool, greenhouse, wood deck, for example.

Estimated Remaining Economic Life _____ Yrs.

Record your estimate of *remaining economic life*, the estimated period of time during which improvements continue to contribute to property value. This estimate must necessarily be based largely on experience and judgment, that is, knowing what evidence to look for and how to apply it. The assumption should not always be that the improvements will continue to deteriorate at their present rate. Rehabilitation, modernization or remodeling can extend the life of the improvements; lack of normal maintenance can shorten economic life. Changing economic conditions and the attitudes and reactions of typical buyers of competitive properties also affect remaining economic life.

Note: Remaining economic life can be recorded as a single figure or as a range in years, if more appropriate.

▸ **FNMA** The remaining economic life of a property is the estimated period over which the improvements will continue to contribute to the value of the property, or the estimated period in which the improvements increase the value of the property above that for the vacant site. Four basic forces influence real property values: social standards, economic factors, government controls and environmental conditions. Because these forces may result in a change in the improvements' contribution to value, estimating the remaining economic life of a property can be difficult. Therefore, you should emphasize the overall quality and design of the improvements and the attitudes of typical purchasers in the subject market area. You may state the remaining economic life as a single figure or as a range (if that is more appropriate).

Generally the mortgage term should not exceed the appraiser's estimate of the remaining economic life for the subject property. However, a remaining economic life that is less than the term of the mortgage may be acceptable if the improvements represent a fairly typical residential property for the neighborhood, rather than a speculative land or land development–type property. In such cases, the reason for the shorter remaining economic life must be the result of economic factors (which would increase the value of the site), rather than the result of the physical deterioration or condition of the improvements. Fannie Mae will not purchase any mortgage secured by a property that does not have a minimum remaining economic life that is equal to at least one-half the mortgage term.

▸ **HUD/FHA** "Enter the number of years the property is expected to remain competitive in the market. You should use 40 years unless an obvious and verifiable pressure exists which can be conclusively shown to render the remaining economic life to be less than 40 years."

Estimated Remaining Physical Life _____ Yrs.

Record your estimate of the time period over which improvements may be expected to remain in existence, assuming normal maintenance. Physical life may be greater than or equal to—but never less than—a property's economic life.

Fannie Mae and Freddie Mac do not require an estimate of remaining physical life, but VA and FHA do. If physical life projections are not required, enter N/A on this line.

▸ **FNMA** Because the URAR form was designed to meet the needs of several different user groups, it also includes a space for inserting the property's estimated remaining physical life. The remaining physical life of a property is the estimated period over which improvements will physically last if they receive normal maintenance. For mortgages that will be sold to Fannie Mae, you do not need to report the remaining physical life and N/A may be inserted in that space. If you do report the remaining physical life, the lender need not consider it, because any related property deficiencies will be discussed in the URAR sections that address economic life, improvement analysis and comments on the property's condition.

▶ **HUD/FHA** Complete this entry only if the property is located in a 223(e) area in which economic life is waived and physical life is used instead.

▶ Appraisal 1

SURFACES	Materials/Condition	HEATING		KITCHEN EQUIP.		ATTIC		IMPROVEMENT ANALYSIS	Good	Avg.	Fair	Poor
Floors	WD/CPT/G	Type	FA/CENT	Refrigerator	P	None		Quality of Construction		X		
Walls	DRYWALL/WP/A	Fuel	ELECT	Range/Oven	X	Stairs		Condition of Improvements	X			
Trim/Finish	WD/A	Condition	GOOD	Disposal	X	Drop Stair	X	Room Sizes/Layout	X			
Bath Floor	CT/A	Adequacy	ADEQ	Dishwasher	X	Scuttle		Closets and Storage	X			
Bath Wainscot	CT/A	COOLING		Fan/Hood	X	Floor		Energy Efficiency	X			
Doors	INT/HC/G	Central	YES	Compactor	X	Heated		Plumbing-Adequacy & Condition	X			
	EXT/WD/SC/GLASS/G	Other		Washer/Dryer		Finished		Electrical-Adequacy & Condition	X			
		Condition	GOOD	Microwave	P			Kitchen Cabinets-Adequacy & Cond.	X			
Fireplace(s)	STONE/FR/G # 1	Adequacy	ADEQ	Intercom				Compatibility to Neighborhood	X			
								Appeal & Marketability	X			

Estimated Remaining Economic Life   53-55 Yrs.
Estimated Remaining Physical Life   55-60 Yrs.

In Appraisal 1, the subject property has good market appeal and compatibility within the neighborhood. Although quality of construction and workmanship are typical of competing properties, all other interior features are rated above average—including room sizes and layout, closets and storage, kitchen cabinets, plumbing and fixtures, electrical system and overall energy efficiency.

The attic is unfinished with drop-down stairs. The house has an energy-efficient central forced-air heating and cooling system fueled by electricity. The system is in good shape with adequate output.

It is the appraiser's opinion that the remaining economic life of the property is between 53 and 55 years.

Additional data on interior improvements include the following:

- Quality parquet floors in kitchen, dining room, foyer and hallways—good condition;
- Ceramic tile floor and wainscoting in bathrooms—average condition;
- Finished oak flooring covered with quality wall-to-wall carpeting in other rooms—good condition;
- Ponderosa pine trim throughout—average condition;
- Stone, wood-burning fireplace in family room—good condition;
- Wall covering of drywall, taped and painted or papered—average condition;
- Exterior doors of veneer over solid wood and sliding glass—interior doors of veneer over a hollow core—good condition;
- Kitchen built-ins—oven and range, dishwasher, garbage disposal, trash compactor and hood-type exhaust fan;
- Other appliances—refrigerator and microwave oven; and
- Energy-efficient items (in addition to the heating and cooling system) including fans, fireplace, water heater and insulated ducts.

▶ **Exercise: Appraisal 2**

INTERIOR			HEATING		KITCHEN EQUIP.		ATTIC		IMPROVEMENT ANALYSIS	Good	Avg.	Fair	Poor
SURFACES	Materials/Condition		Type		Refrigerator	☐	None	☐	Quality of Construction	☐	☐	☐	☐
Floors			Fuel		Range/Oven	☐	Stairs	☐	Condition of Improvements	☐	☐	☐	☐
Walls			Condition		Disposal	☐	Drop Stair	☐	Room Sizes/Layout	☐	☐	☐	☐
Trim/Finish			Adequacy		Dishwasher	☐	Scuttle	☐	Closets and Storage	☐	☐	☐	☐
Bath Floor			COOLING		Fan/Hood	☐	Floor	☐	Energy Efficiency	☐	☐	☐	☐
Bath Wainscot			Central		Compactor	☐	Heated	☐	Plumbing-Adequacy & Condition	☐	☐	☐	☐
Doors			Other		Washer/Dryer	☐	Finished	☐	Electrical-Adequacy & Condition	☐	☐	☐	☐
			Condition		Microwave	☐			Kitchen Cabinets-Adequacy & Cond.	☐	☐	☐	☐
Fireplace(s)	#		Adequacy		Intercom	☐			Compatibility to Neighborhood	☐	☐	☐	☐
									Appeal & Marketability	☐	☐	☐	☐
									Estimated Remaining Economic Life				Yrs.
									Estimated Remaining Physical Life				Yrs.

Complete the blank URAR *INTERIOR* section for Appraisal 2, using the following information. When you have finished, check your work against the completed Appraisal 2 in the Answer Key.

The subject property has wall-to-wall carpeting throughout the above-grade living area, except for vinyl sheet tile flooring in the kitchen and baths. All wall surfaces are painted drywall, with stained and varnished pine trim. All interior doors are hollow-core mahogany, stained and varnished. There is a masonry fireplace in the family room. All interior surfaces are in average condition.

The heating and cooling systems are gas-fired forced-air with central air-conditioning. They are in average condition and are adequate for a home of this size.

The kitchen has built-in stove, range top, fan/hood, dishwasher and garbage disposal. The refrigerator is the personal property of the owners and is not included in the sale. There is no trash compactor, microwave or intercom. There is no attic.

Overall, the construction quality of the home's interior is average, as is its condition. Because the subject is part of a subdivision built primarily by the same builder, room sizes and layout vary little throughout the neighborhood. Closets and other storage spaces are typically adequate. The home is also typical of the neighborhood in having no special energy-efficient items. Plumbing and electrical systems, in this home as in others in the neighborhood, are adequate for residents' demands. Kitchen cabinets are standard-grade oak, with a stained and varnished finish.

The home is compatible with its neighborhood, having average appeal and marketability. Its estimated remaining economic life is 32 years, as is its estimated remaining physical life.

Autos

AUTOS	CAR STORAGE:	Garage		Attached		Adequate		House Entry	
	No. Cars ___	Carport		Detached		Inadequate		Outside Entry	
	Condition ___	None		Built-In		Electric Door		Basement Entry	

Complete the *AUTOS* section only if the subject has a completely or partially enclosed automobile parking space—a garage or carport. If the dwelling does not have a garage or carport, mark the *None* box and leave the rest of this section blank.

CAR STORAGE:

Garage

Mark this box if the subject property has a garage.

Carport

Mark this box if the subject property has a carport.

None

If this box is marked, give your opinion of its effect on the marketability and value of the house, either in the *COMMENTS* section or in an addendum.

No. Cars

Enter the number of cars the garage or carport can hold.

Condition

Enter GOOD, AVG, FAIR or POOR as appropriate. If you rate the condition of the garage or carport as fair or poor, explain your reasons in the *COMMENTS* section or in an addendum.

Attached

Mark this box if the garage or carport is attached to (shares at least one common wall with) the house.

Detached

Mark this box if the garage or carport shares no common wall with the house.

Built-In

Mark this box if the garage is built in; that is, it shares at least one common wall with the house and its ceiling is the floor of another part of the house.

Adequate

Mark this box if the garage or carport meets neighborhood standards. Base your judgment on:

* Type of car storage predominant in the area;
* Number of cars that typically can be stored; and
* Size of the typical structure.

Inadequate

Mark this box if the garage or carport is below neighborhood standards and explain why in the *COMMENTS* section or in an addendum.

Electric Door

Mark this box if the garage has an electric door opener.

House Entry

Mark this box if one can enter the house from inside the garage or carport.

Outside Entry

Mark this box if there is an outside entrance to the garage or carport other than the overhead door or car entrance.

Basement Entry

Mark this box if one can enter the basement of the house from the garage or carport.

▶ Appraisal 1

AUTOS	CAR STORAGE:		Garage	X	Attached		Adequate	X	House Entry	X	
	No. Cars	2	Carport		Detached		Inadequate		Outside Entry	X	
	Condition	GOOD	None		Built-In	X	Electric Door	X	Basement Entry		

In Appraisal 1, the subject property has a 21′ × 25′ two-car garage (typical for the area) in better-than-average condition. The garage has an electric door opener, and the garage ceiling forms the floor of the attic above. The garage can be entered from the outside through the overhead door on the street side and through a solid wood door on the north wall. The back wall, common to both the house and the garage, has a fire-retardant steel door leading into the house.

▶ Exercise: Appraisal 2

AUTOS	CAR STORAGE:		Garage		Attached		Adequate		House Entry		
	No. Cars		Carport		Detached		Inadequate		Outside Entry		
	Condition		None		Built-In		Electric Door		Basement Entry		

Complete the blank URAR *AUTOS* section provided above for Appraisal 2, using the following information. When you have finished, you can check your work against the completed Appraisal 2 in the Answer Key.

The subject property has a two-car detached garage with an electric double garage door opener and separate side entrance. The wood-frame structure is typical of the neighborhood and is in average condition.

Comments

COMMENTS	**Additional features:** _____
	_____
	Depreciation (Physical, functional and external inadequacies, repairs needed, modernization, etc.): _____
	_____
	_____
	General market conditions and prevalence and impact in subject/market area regarding loan discounts, interest buydowns and concessions: _____
	_____
	_____

Freddie Mac Form 70   10/86   (10 ch.)   U.S. Forms Inc., 2 Central Square, Grafton, MA 01519-0446, 1-800-225-9583   Fannie Mae Form 1004   10/86

The *COMMENTS* section provides space for the appraiser to:

- List features of the subject property not reported elsewhere on the form;
- Explain any physical, functional or external inadequacies of the subject;
- Comment on general market conditions affecting values within the subject market area; and
- Comment on any special financing considerations affecting market value.

This is also the space in which the appraiser can explain any responses entered on page 1 of the URAR. If more space is needed, additional remarks can be supplied in an addendum attached to the form.

Additional features

Enter here any features of the subject property not previously described, such as a wet bar, skylight, workshop, swimming pool, hot tub, sauna, greenhouse, fence, patio, deck, unusual landscaping, island kitchen, security device, and so on.

Depreciation (Physical, functional and external inadequacies, repairs needed, modernization, etc.):

Indicate whether the subject structure suffers from any form of depreciation and what corrective action, if any, needs to be taken.

Depreciation is an economic effect caused by physical deterioration, functional obsolescence, external obsolescence or a combination of these.

As they age, most structures suffer some value-reducing effects on their physical qualities, resulting from ordinary use, disintegration and action of the elements. The degree to which a structure is subject to deterioration depends mainly on the quality of materials and workmanship that were put into it and the degree to which the structure has been maintained. Deterioration may be normal or minor in a well-constructed, well-maintained house. However, in a poorly constructed, poorly maintained house, deterioration will occur much more rapidly, often resulting in serious damage to walls, foundations, roof or floor construction.

The effects of deterioration may be a leaky roof, internal water damage, corroded plumbing lines, cracked plaster, peeling paint, worn flooring, broken steps and numerous other physical deficiencies that make the property less desirable to potential buyers.

Functional depreciation may stem from either a deficiency within the property (such as poor traffic patterns, inferior design, inefficient room layout or outmoded style) or a superadequacy (overimprovement, such as excessive quality or size of building components and equipment in a moderately priced neighborhood).

External depreciation is a loss in value due to factors outside the property boundaries. Typical causes are:

* Population movements that either *reduce* the total number of people available to buy property or *replace* higher-economic-level buyers with those on a lower economic level;
* Growth of industrial and commercial areas that, in the absence of adequate zoning, encroach on residential areas;
* Proximity to airports with their noise and danger potential;
* Nuisances and hazards such as excessive noise, smoke and traffic;
* Excessive real estate taxes and assessments; and
* Deterioration in quality and accessibility of schools, shopping and community facilities.

Note: Comments should be consistent with the information on depreciation given in the *COST APPROACH* section on page 2 of the URAR.

General market conditions and prevalence and impact in subject/ market area regarding loan discounts, interest buydowns and concessions:

Describe any influences or conditions outside the subject property that may have a negative or positive effect on its value. For example, what is the current and anticipated supply and demand situation for housing in the market area? Are any special financing arrangements prevalent in the market area that would cause the transaction price of one property to differ from that of an identical property? For example, the buyer of a comparable property may have assumed an existing mortgage at a favorable interest rate. Or a seller may have arranged a buydown, paying cash to the lender so that a mortgage could be offered at an interest rate lower than the prevailing market rate. In either case, the buyer probably paid a higher price for the property to obtain below-market financing. On the other hand, interest rates at above-market levels often result in lower sales prices.

▶ **FNMA** Address any needed repairs or any physical, functional or external inadequacies in the *COMMENTS* section. Include comments related to general market conditions in the subject market area in the space provided for that purpose.

▶ **HUD/FHA** Explain financing concessions for the subject and the market area. Also explain whether the subject is consistent with or different from the market area in that regard.

▶ **VA** Fee appraisers *must* report here the *existence* or *nonexistence* of sales or financing incentives or concessions in the subject market area and make a statement regarding their effect, if any, on the sales prices of comparable homes. This must be done in each and every case, proposed or existing. The appraiser is not required to investigate incentives or concessions involving the subject property. Statements in this section must be consistent with those in the *SALES COMPARISON ANALYSIS* section on page 2.

▶ **Appraisal 1**

COMMENTS

Additional features: FRONT ENTRY PORCH, DRIVE AND WALK PAVED WITH POLYPEBBLE, REAR POOL WITH BRONZE CAGE AND POLYPEBBLE DECK, GLASSED-IN PORCH AREA WITH CARPET AND CEILING FANS, ROOF VENTS, WOOD FENCING, ISLAND KITCHEN WITH EXTRA CABINETS.

Depreciation (Physical, functional and external inadequacies, repairs needed, modernization, etc.): NO PHYSICAL CHANGE IS REQUIRED BY THIS REPORT'S VALUE CONCLUSION. MARKET APPEAL IS SUPPORTED BY THE HOME'S FUNCTIONAL UTILITY AND EXTERNAL LOCATIONAL FACTORS. THE PHYSICAL DEPRECIATION REFLECTS THE EFFECTIVE AGE ESTIMATE, BASED ON AREA SALES.

General market conditions and prevalence and impact in subject/market area regarding loan discounts, interest buydowns and concessions: THE MARKET IS CONSIDERED TO BE GENERALLY STABLE. LOAN DISCOUNTS, INTEREST RATE BUYDOWNS AND SALES CONCESSIONS ARE NOT PREVALENT IN THE CURRENT RESALE MARKET. PROMOTIONAL FINANCING CONCESSIONS BY DEVELOPERS/BUILDERS ARE COMMON.

In Appraisal 1, the subject property contains many special features. These include front entry porch, drive and walk paved with polypebble, rear pool with bronze cage and polypebble deck, glassed-in porch area with carpet and ceiling fans, roof vents, wood fencing and island kitchen with extra cabinets.

No physical change is required by this report's value conclusion. Market appeal is supported by the home's functional utility and external locational factors. The physical depreciation reflects the effective age estimate, based on area sales.

The market is considered generally stable. Loan discounts, interest rate buydowns and sales concessions are not prevalent in the current resale market. Promotional financing concessions by developers/builders are common, however.

▶ **Exercise: Appraisal 2**

COMMENTS

Additional features: _____

Depreciation (Physical, functional and external inadequacies, repairs needed, modernization, etc.): _____

General market conditions and prevalence and impact in subject/market area regarding loan discounts, interest buydowns and concessions: _____

Complete the blank URAR *COMMENTS* section provided above for Appraisal 2, using the following information. When you have finished, you can check your work against the completed Appraisal 2 in the Answer Key.

Additional features of this property include rear wood deck, ceiling fan in the kitchen and skylight in the master bath. Overall, the subject house is in average condition with normal wear and tear. However, one side of the roof shows excessive wear and should be replaced. No unusual functional obsolescence or external inadequacies were observed.

The current housing market is active and reflects a strong local economy. Typical financing in the area is through conventional mortgages. No loan discounts, interest buydowns or sales concessions were found for the subject or for comparable sales in this market; thus, financing adjustments are not required.

Purpose of Appraisal

Valuation Section   **UNIFORM RESIDENTIAL APPRAISAL REPORT**   File No.

Purpose of Appraisal is to estimate Market Value as defined in the Certification & Statement of Limiting Conditions.

The appraiser's purpose in making the appraisal must be known. It is also necessary to state the conditions under which the appraisal is being performed. The appraiser must:

* State the purpose of the appraisal.
* State the terms under which the appraisal has been performed.
* State any limiting conditions on the appraisal valuation.

The most common way (for most government agencies the *only* way) in which to present the information listed above is to append to the URAR report a copy of the form that appears in Figure 9. The form is explained below.

Definition of Market Value

Most residential appraisals are conducted to determine the subject property's market value. This definition uses a "most probable price" standard for the market value estimate. Market value is the value the property is likely to achieve in an arm's-length transaction occurring on the open market. Market value is *not* the highest price possible under the most favorable circumstances.

> ▶ **RTC** Market value is the most probable price a property should bring in a competitive and open market under all conditions requisite to a fair sale, with buyer and seller each acting prudently and knowledgeably, and assuming the price is not affected by undue stimulus. Implicit in this definition is consummation of a

Figure 9. Definition of Market Value, Certification and Statement of Limiting Conditions

DEFINITION OF MARKET VALUE: The most probable price which a property should bring in a competitive and open market under all conditions requisite to a fair sale, the buyer and seller, each acting prudently, knowledgeably and assuming the price is not affected by undue stimulus. Implicit in this definition is the consummation of a sale as of a specified date and the passing of title from seller to buyer under conditions whereby: (1) buyer and seller are typically motivated; (2) both parties are well informed or well advised, and each acting in what he considers his own best interest; (3) a reasonable time is allowed for exposure in the open market; (4) payment is made in terms of cash in U.S. dollars or in terms of financial arrangements comparable thereto; and (5) the price represents the normal consideration for the property sold unaffected by special or creative financing or sales concessions* granted by anyone associated with the sale.

* Adjustments to the comparables must be made for special or creative financing or sales concessions. No adjustments are necessary for those costs which are normally paid by sellers as a result of tradition or law in a market area; these costs are readily identifiable since the seller pays these costs in virtually all sales transactions. Special or creative financing adjustments can be made to the comparable property by comparisons to financing terms offered by a third party institutional lender that is not already involved in the property or transaction. Any adjustment should not be calculated on a mechanical dollar for dollar cost of the financing or concession but the dollar amount of any adjustment should approximate the market's reaction to the financing or concessions based on the appraiser's judgment.

CERTIFICATION AND STATEMENT OF LIMITING CONDITIONS

CERTIFICATION: The Appraiser certifies and agrees that:

1. The Appraiser has no present or contemplated future interest in the property appraised; and neither the employment to make the appraisal, nor the compensation for it, is contingent upon the appraised value of the property.

2. The Appraiser has no personal interest in or bias with respect to the subject matter of the appraisal report or the participants to the sale. The "Estimate of Market Value" in the appraisal report is not based in whole or in part upon the race, color, or national origin of the prospective owners or occupants of the property appraised, or upon the race, color or national origin of the present owners or occupants of the properties in the vicinity of the property appraised.

3. The Appraiser has personally inspected the property, both inside and out, and has made an exterior inspection of all comparable sales listed in the report. To the best of the Appraiser's knowledge and belief, all statements and information in this report are true and correct, and the Appraiser has not knowingly withheld any significant information.

4. All contingent and limiting conditions are contained herein (imposed by the terms of the assignment or by the undersigned affecting the analyses, opinions, and conclusions contained in the report).

5. This appraisal report has been made in conformity with and is subject to the requirements of the Code of Professional Ethics and Standards of Professional Conduct of the appraisal organizations with which the Appraiser is affiliated.

6. All conclusions and opinions concerning the real estate that are set forth in the appraisal report were prepared by the Appraiser whose signature appears on the appraisal report, unless indicated as "Review Appraiser." No change of any item in the appraisal report shall be made by anyone other than the Appraiser, and the Appraiser shall have no responsibility for any such unauthorized change.

CONTINGENT AND LIMITING CONDITIONS: The certification of the Appraiser appearing in the appraisal report is subject to the following conditions and to such other specific and limiting conditions as are set forth by the Appraiser in the report.

1. The Appraiser assumes no responsibility for matters of a legal nature affecting the property appraised or the title thereto, nor does the Appraiser render any opinion as to the title, which is assumed to be good and marketable. The property is appraised as though under responsible ownership.

2. Any sketch in the report may show approximate dimensions and is included to assist the reader in visualizing the property. The Appraiser has made no survey of the property.

3. The Appraiser is not required to give testimony or appear in court because of having made the appraisal with reference to the property in question, unless arrangements have been previously made therefor.

4. Any distribution of the valuation in the report between land and improvements applies only under the existing program of utilization. The separate valuations for land and building must not be used in conjunction with any other appraisal and are invalid if so used.

5. The Appraiser assumes that there are no hidden or unapparent conditions of the property, subsoil, or structures, which would render it more or less valuable. The Appraiser assumes no responsibility for such conditions, or for engineering which might be required to discover such factors.

6. Information, estimates, and opinions furnished to the Appraiser, and contained in the report, were obtained from sources considered reliable and believed to be true and correct. However, no responsibility for accuracy of such items furnished the Appraiser can be assumed by the Appraiser.

7. Disclosure of the contents of the appraisal report is governed by the Bylaws and Regulations of the professional appraisal organizations with which the Appraiser is affiliated.

8. Neither all, nor any part of the content of the report, or copy thereof (including conclusions as to the property value, the identity of the Appraiser, professional designations, reference to any professional appraisal organizations, or the firm with which the Appraiser is connected), shall be used for any purposes by anyone but the client specified in the report, the borrower if appraisal fee paid by same, the mortgagee or its successors and assigns, mortgage insurers, consultants, professional appraisal organizations, any state or federally approved financial institution, any department, agency, or instrumentality of the United States or any state or the District of Columbia, without the previous written consent of the Appraiser; nor shall it be conveyed by anyone to the public through advertising, public relations, news, sales, or other media, without the written consent and approval of the Appraiser.

9. On all appraisals, subject to satisfactory completion, repairs, or alterations, the appraisal report and value conclusion are contingent upon completion of the improvements in a workmanlike manner.

Date: _____   Appraiser(s) _____

FREDDIE MAC
FORM 439   JUL 86   U.S. Forms Inc., 2 Central Sq., Grafton, MA 01519-0446   1-800-225-9583   1-839-4417   FANNIE MAE
USF 00600   FORM 1004B   JUL 86

sale as of a specified date and passing of title from seller to buyer under conditions whereby:

- Buyer and seller are typically motivated;
- Both parties are well informed or well advised, and each is acting in what he or she considers his or her own best interest;
- Payment is made in terms of cash in U.S. dollars or in terms of financial arrangements comparable to cash; and
- The price represents the normal consideration for the property sold, unaffected by special or creative financing or sales concessions granted by anyone associated with the sale.

Certification

As an appraiser, you certify that you have no present or contemplated future interest in the property being appraised and that the appraisal has been performed without racial or other bias toward the prospective owners or occupants of the property or the present owners or occupants of properties in the neighborhood. You certify that you have personally inspected the property and followed the Code of Professional Ethics and Standards of Professional Conduct of the appraisal organizations with which you are affiliated. There must be no limiting conditions to the appraisal beyond what is stated on this page.

Contingent and Limiting Conditions

As an appraiser, you make no legal judgments concerning the property, particularly about the condition of its title, which is assumed to be good and marketable. You are not expected to make a formal survey of the property being appraised and property dimensions presented in the report are approximate only. Unless otherwise agreed, you will not be required to testify in court concerning the appraisal. The separate valuations of land and improvements using the cost approach are valid only for the property's present utilization. You assume there are no hidden property defects that would affect the estimate of value. While you make use of information, estimates and opinions taken from a variety of sources that you consider reliable, you take no responsibility for the accuracy of such information. Disclosure of the contents of the appraisal report is governed by the rules of the appraisal organization to which you belong. Limitations on use of the appraisal report are stated. If the appraisal is subject to the completion, repair or altering of property improvements, you must assume that all work will be performed in a workmanlike manner.

Date

The date of appraisal.

Appraiser(s)

Your signature as the appraiser making the estimate of value.

Cost Approach

<table>
<tr>
<td colspan="2">BUILDING SKETCH (SHOW GROSS LIVING AREA ABOVE GRADE)
If for Freddie Mac or Fannie Mae, show only square foot calculations and cost approach comments in this space</td>
<td colspan="4">ESTIMATED REPRODUCTION COST-NEW-OF IMPROVEMENTS:</td>
</tr>
</table>

BUILDING SKETCH (SHOW GROSS LIVING AREA ABOVE GRADE)	ESTIMATED REPRODUCTION COST-NEW-OF IMPROVEMENTS:
If for Freddie Mac or Fannie Mae, show only square foot calculations and cost approach comments in this space	Dwelling _____ Sq. Ft. @ $ _____ = $ _____
	_____ Sq. Ft. @ $ _____ = _____
	Extras _____ = _____
	_____ = _____
	Special Energy Efficient Items _____ = _____
	Porches, Patios, etc. _____ = _____
	Garage/Carport _____ Sq. Ft. @ $ _____ = _____
	Total Estimated Cost New .... = $ _____
	Physical | Functional | External
	Less
	Depreciation _____ | _____ | _____ = $ _____
	Depreciated Value of Improvements .... = $ _____
	Site Imp. "as is" (driveway, landscaping, etc.) = $ _____
	ESTIMATED SITE VALUE .... = $ _____
	(If leasehold, show only leasehold value.)
	INDICATED VALUE BY COST APPROACH .... = $ _____
(Not Required by Freddie Mac and Fannie Mae)	Construction Warranty [ ] Yes [ ] No
Does property conform to applicable HUD/VA property standards? [ ] Yes [ ] No	Name of Warranty Program _____
If No, explain: _____	Warranty Coverage Expires _____

An appraiser makes use of construction costs to determine value by the cost approach. The formula for the cost approach is:

$$\begin{array}{c}\text{Reproduction or}\\\text{Replacement Cost}\\\text{of Improvement(s)}\end{array} - \begin{array}{c}\text{Accrued}\\\text{Depreciation}\end{array} + \text{Site Value} = \text{Property Value}$$

First the appraiser estimates the present *reproduction cost* to construct a duplicate of all the improvements on the subject property. If the improvements would be impossible or impractical to duplicate, the appraiser estimates *replacement cost*, the cost of constructing improvements with the same functional utility. The appraiser next reduces the estimated present construction cost by the loss in value the subject property has undergone due to depreciation since it was first constructed. The appraiser then adds to the depreciated cost

124

estimate the estimated value of the subject site. The resulting figure is the property's indicated value by the cost approach.

Virtually every appraisal reported on the URAR form will include a cost approach analysis. The appraiser must provide the figures used to determine the estimate of value by the cost approach. The analysis will require the appraiser to:

- Compute the area of all property improvements.
- Estimate the reproduction cost of all improvements.
- Estimate the amount by which the improvements have depreciated.
- Estimate land value.
- Add land value to depreciated cost to find the indicated value.

▶ **FNMA** Fannie Mae will not accept appraisals that rely *solely* on the cost approach as an indicator of market value.

In the cost approach the indicated value of a property is reached by estimating the reproduction cost of new improvements, subtracting the amount of depreciation of the improvements from all causes and adding an estimate of the value of the site as if it were vacant and available to be developed to its highest and best use.

The cost approach to value assumes that a potential purchaser will consider building a substitute residence that has the same use as the property that is being appraised. This approach, then, measures value as a cost of production. The reliability of the cost approach depends on valid reproduction cost estimates, proper depreciation estimates and an accurate site value. As the effective age of a property increases, the reliability of the cost approach may decrease because the depreciation estimates may be subjective.

Usually the cost approach is a good indicator of value in appraising newer or renovated properties that are one- to four-family residences or units in PUD or *de minimis* PUD projects.

You do not have to consider the cost approach when appraising units in condominium and cooperative projects, because such units are integral parts of the total project, and the cost approach generally is impractical for determining the value of any given unit.

BUILDING SKETCH

This space will be used to show either a rough drawing of the perimeter of the subject structure(s), with dimensions given in feet, *or* the measurement calculations indicating the total square footage of the structure along with any comments you feel are necessary to explain how the cost approach was applied. The alternative you use will be determined by the agency for whom the appraisal is prepared.

Comments on such items as the source of cost data, types of depreciation found and how the site value was derived can be included here or in an addendum, as space constraints permit. What is important is that you explain any significant factors affecting value. For instance, deductions for depreciation other than general wear and tear should be separately itemized. Items of functional or external obsolescence should be listed and explained.

▶ **FmHA** Leave blank. Complete this information on the reverse side of the Marshall and Swift Form 1007: "Square Foot Appraisal Form," shown in Figure 10. ATTACH A RECENT PHOTOGRAPH OF THE EXISTING HOME IN THIS SECTION.

▶ **HUD/FHA** There should be a building sketch that includes all exterior dimensions of the house as well as patios, porches, garages, breezeways and other "offsets." If there is a patio, indicate whether it has a roof by entering COVERED or UNCOVERED.

▶ **VA** A building sketch should be made only if necessary to illustrate unique features of the subject, the presence of functional obsolescence or other special property characteristics.

ESTIMATED REPRODUCTION COST – NEW – OF IMPROVEMENTS:

Estimate the cost to construct the subject improvements at current market prices. All building components should be comparable in kind and quality to those used in the subject. If duplication of improvements, particularly in older structures, would be impossible or impractical (as may be the case with the elaborate exterior and interior trim work found in many Victorian-era homes), estimate the cost of a functionally identical replacement.

Cost-estimating services, such as Boekh and Marshall and Swift, provide construction cost data that cover a wide range of property improvements in specific parts of the country, updated frequently to reflect current market conditions. Local builder surveys, used in conjunction with information from a cost-estimating service, help appraisers stay up to date on construction cost variables.

▶ **FNMA** The reproduction cost estimate should reflect the cost of construction based on current prices of producing a replica of the property being appraised, including all of its positive and negative characteristics. Although construction materials used for the estimate should be as similar as possible to those used for the subject property, they do not have to be identical.

▶ **HUD/FHA** You do not need to complete this section, *except* for the estimated value of the *site*. If the subject property is proposed construction, or was constructed less than one year ago, complete and attach Marshall and Swift Form 1007 (Figure 10), in conformance with Deputy Assistant Secretary Nistler's Memorandum of Instructions dated December 17, 1985.

Figure 10.   Marshall and Swift form 1007: "Square Foot Appraisal Form"

SQUARE FOOT APPRAISAL FORM
For use with the RESIDENTIAL COST HANDBOOK

Appraisal for _____   Property owner _____

Address _____

Appraiser _____   Date _____

TYPE		QUALITY		STYLE		EXTERIOR WALLS		GARAGE TYPE	
Single Family	☒	Low	☐	No. Stories One		Hardboard/Plywood	☐	Detached	☐
Multiple	☐	Fair	☐	Bi-level	☐	Stucco	☒	Attached	☒
Town House	☐	Average	☐	Split Level	☐	Siding or Shingle	☐	Built-In	☐
Row House	☐	Good	☒	1½ story - Fin.	☐	Masonry Veneer	☐	Subterranean	☐
Manufactured		Very Good	☐	1½ story - Unf.	☐	Common Brick	☐	Carport	☐
House	☐	Excellent	☐	2½ story - Fin.	☐	Face Brick or Stone	☐	Garage Area	

FLOOR AREA   **BASEMENT AREA**   2½ story - Unf. ☐   Concrete Block ☐   560 Sq. Ft.

1st 2,388 Sq. Ft.   Unf. _____   End Row ☐   **MANUFACTURED**   **BALCONY AREA**

2nd _____   Fin. _____   Inside Row ☐   Alum., Ribbed ☐

3rd _____   **NUMBER OF PLUMBING**   Lap Siding ☐   **PORCH BRZWY. AREA**

Total 2,388 Sq. Ft.   Fixtures 13   **NUMBER OF MULTIPLE**   Hardboard ☐   (a) 233 Sq. Ft.

Rough-in 1   **UNITS** _____   Plywood ☐   (b) _____

	Quan.	Cost	+ −	Extension
1. COMPUTE RESIDENCE BASIC COST: Floor area x selected sq. ft. cost	2,388	$34.40		$ 82,147
2. SQUARE FOOT ADJUSTMENTS:			+ −	
3. Roofing Wood Shingle (Base)				
4. Subfloor Concrete Slab	2,388	1.89	−	⟨4,513⟩
5. Floor Cover 80% Carpet @$2.23 = $1.78 20% Res. @ $1.93 = $.39	2,388	2.17	+	5,182
6. Plaster Interior				
7. Heating/Cooling Warm and Cooled Air (Mild Climate)	2,388	.65	+	1,552
8. Energy Adjustment /Insulation: Mild Climate	2,388	.19	−	⟨454⟩
9. Foundation				
10. LUMP SUM ADJUSTMENTS:				
11. Plumbing 11 Fixt + 1 R.I (Base) 2 Additional Fixtures	2	755	+	1,510
12. Fireplaces Double, One Story	1	2,900	+	2,900
13. Built-in Appliances R/O @$835 RH & F @$230 Dishwasher @$510	1	1,575	+	1,575
14. Miscellaneous (Dormers) Garbage Disposal @$205, Exh. Fan @$110	1	315	+	315
15. SUBTOTAL ADJ. RESIDENCE COST: Line 1 plus or minus Lines 2-14				$90,214
16. BASEMENT, UNFINISHED				
17. Add for basement interior finish				
18. Add for basement outside entrance				
19. Add for basement garage: Single ☐ Double ☐				
20. PORCH/BREEZEWAY, describe Open/Slab @$2.02 & Roof @$5.50	233	7.52	+	1,752
21. & Ceiling @$1.52	233	1.52	+	354
22. SUBTOTAL RESIDENCE COST: Total of Lines 15-21				$92,320
23. GARAGE OR CARPORT - sq. ft. area x selected sq. ft. cost Use 600 Sq. Ft. Cost	560	$13.06	+	7,313
24. Miscellaneous (roofing adjustment) Attached Garage −Deduct for com wall	28	5,335	−	1,494
25. SUBTOTAL GARAGE COST: Line 23 plus or minus Line 24				⟨5,819⟩
26. SUBTOTAL OF ALL BUILDING IMPROVEMENTS: Sum of Lines 22 and 25				$98,139
27. Current Cost Multiplier 1.03 x Local Multiplier 1.05 1.03 x 1.05 = 1.082			X	
28. REPLACEMENT COST NEW: Line 26 x 27 98,139 x 1.082				$106,186
29. Depreciation: Age _____ Condition _____ Deduction _____ % of Line 28 _____				
30. Depreciated cost of building improvements: Line 28 less Line 29				
31. Yard improvements cost: List, total, apply local multiplier and depreciate on reverse side				
32. Landscaping cost: List and compute on reverse side				
33. Lot or land value				
34. **TOTAL INDICATED VALUE:** Total of Lines 30-33				

FORM 1007   *See back of page for sketch and computations*

Dwelling

Enter the number of square feet of living space of the home. Be sure to measure square footage based on the form of measurement assumed by the cost service from which you receive cost data. Then enter the current construction cost per square foot of living space for a comparable new structure. Finally, multiply the number of square feet by the cost per square foot to determine a dollar value for the improvement.

A second line is provided for calculating the cost of any areas or improvements (basement space or a secondary living structure, such as a guest house) not included in the figure derived on the first line.

Extras

Describe any special property features not included in the base cost per square foot and provide a current construction cost estimate of that feature. Such items might include an extra bathroom, built-ins, special finishing materials or other "upgrades."

Special Energy Efficient Items

Identify and enter the current construction cost of any energy-efficient item, such as a solar hot-water system.

Porches, Patios, etc.

Describe porch, deck, patio or other exterior space by type and square footage and provide a current construction cost; for example, 500 SQ. FT. DECK = $5,000.

Garage/Carport

If the property has a garage or carport, cross out the inapplicable word and enter the square footage of garage or carport space, the current construction cost per square foot of similar space and the dollar figure derived by multiplying those two figures.

Total Estimated Cost New

Add all the dollar amounts recorded in this column up to this point and enter the total here.

Less Depreciation

Unless you are appraising a brand new property with no evidence of any form of physical, functional or external deterioration, you will have to compute the amount by which the subject improvements have been reduced in value due to these factors. All property will physically deteriorate over time and may also suffer a loss in value due to changing market demands or the influence of economic factors or nearby land uses. In the 1980s, economic factors propelled property values in some parts of the country from all-time highs to dramatic lows over just a few years. It is the appraiser's task to stay abreast of market conditions and their causes, so that they be reflected where appropriate in the estimate of appraised value.

While there is not room here for a thorough analysis of each form of depreciation, the Fannie Mae requirements that follow provide a useful overview. Remember that, if a dollar amount for depreciation is recorded at the right, it must be broken down into the various depreciation categories to which it applies.

▶ **FNMA** You must consider each of the three principal types of depreciation—physical, functional and external.

Physical depreciation, traditionally referred to as *physical deterioration*, is a loss in value caused by deterioration in the physical condition of the improvements. Physical deterioration is classified as curable or incurable. *Curable* physical deterioration refers to items of deferred maintenance that are relatively easily and economically accomplished (for example painting or repairing a broken stair rail). Items of *incurable* physical deterioration are impractical to correct because the cost to cure would not add commensurate value to the property; an example is extensive water damage to rafters and interior walls due to a roof that should have been replaced 10 years ago.

Functional depreciation, traditionally referred to as *functional obsolescence*, is a loss in value caused by defects in the design of a structure. Design elements that may cause a degree of functional obsolescence include inadequacies in architectural style, floor plan, sizes and types of rooms and style of fixtures. Functional obsolescence is caused by changing market preferences, as in the case of a home with a bedroom on a level that has no bathroom, and is generally incurable. An outmoded fixture, such as a wall-hung kitchen sink, is an example of curable functional obsolescence.

External depreciation, traditionally referred to as *economic obsolescence*, is a loss in value caused by negative influences outside the site; external depreciation is always incurable. External depreciation can be caused by political factors, such as a change in zoning; economic factors, such as the loss in value that may result from a recession; or environmental changes, as when property is located next to a shopping center, expressway or factory.

Depreciated Value of Improvements

Subtract the total dollar amount of property depreciation from the estimated cost new on the line above to find the depreciated value of the property improvements and enter this amount here. Note that what are considered "site improvements" (explained next) are not included in this calculation.

Site Imp. "as is"

Enter the present value of site improvements (in their current condition) that are not included in *ESTIMATED SITE VALUE* below or any other cost valuation category. These could include items such as drainage systems, grading and landscaping, driveways, fences or walls, sidewalks, curbs, gutters and so on. They could also include utility lines, sewer systems and other items, if those items are not considered in estimating site value.

As a practical matter, you should complete this entry *after* estimating site value, so that the basis for the site valuation will be known and any site improvements not included in that category can be included here.

ESTIMATED SITE VALUE

Estimate site value and indicate the method used to reach your estimate in the *BUILDING SKETCH* section at left or in an addendum. In appraisals of single-family residences, the sales comparison approach is most frequently used to estimate site value. Improvements included in the defined site may vary according to local appraisal custom. Be sure to avoid including any items valued in another part of the cost approach. For instance, if comparable sites in the area include all utilities as well as curbs and gutters, these items would be included in the site valuation here and not in the separate consideration of site improvements "as is" in the line above.

 ▶ **FNMA** If the estimate of site value is not typical for a comparable residential property in the subject neighborhood, comment on how the variance affects the marketability of the subject property.
 ▶ **VA** Only this value must be completed in every case proposed or existing, *excluding* condominiums.

INDICATED VALUE BY COST APPROACH

 ▶ **FmHA** Enter the indicated dollar value derived by the cost approach, as defined in Form 1007, "Square Foot Appraisal Form," line 34.
 ▶ **FNMA** In reviewing the appraisal report, the lender should make sure that the appraiser's analysis in the cost approach is consistent with comments and adjustments mentioned elsewhere in the report. For example, if the *NEIGHBORHOOD* or *SITE* description on page 1 reveals that the property backs up to a shopping center, the lender should expect to see an adjustment for external depreciation in the *COST APPROACH* section on page 2. Similarly, if the improvement analysis indicates that it is necessary to go through one bedroom to get to another bedroom, the lender should expect to see an adjustment for functional depreciation.

Does property conform to applicable HUD/VA property standards?

Figure 11 shows the minimum property standards that appear as Section 4905.1 of the HUD Handbook. You must determine whether the subject property meets these standards.

p... ...
containing one to four living ... ...
which they are located. The buildings may be detached,
semi-detached, duplex, or row houses. These requirements
also cover the immediate site environment for the dwellings, including streets, and other services and facilities for
the site.

1-2 *Proposed Additions and Alterations.* Any proposed additions to an existing property shall comply with the requirements of HUD Handbook 4900.1, MPS for one and two
family dwellings. This is only applicable to HUD programs.

1-3 *Compliance with Codes.* Enforcing, interpreting or determining compliance with local codes and regulations is the
responsibility of local authorities. When code compliance is
required by statute, responsibility to secure evidence of compliance rests with the respective agency.

Chapter 2—GENERAL ACCEPTABILITY CRITERIA

2-1 *General.* These requirements for existing housing together
with appropriate administrative rules and regulations pre-
scribe the basic qualifications necessary for eligibility of
existing properties.

2-2 *Real Estate Entity.* The property shall comprise a single plot
except that a primary plot with secondary plot for an appur-
tenant garage or for other use essential to the marketability
of the property may be acceptable provided the two plots are
in such proximity as to comprise a readily marketable real
estate entity.

2-3 *Party or Lot Line Wall.* A building constructed on or to a
property line shall be separated from the adjoining building, or from the adjoining lot, by a party or lot line wall.
Party or lot line walls shall extend the full height of the
building.

continued

SOURCE: *Handbook 4905.1* Federal Housing Commissioner. U.S. Department of
Housing and Urban Development, Washington, DC 20410.

Figure 11. HUD Minimum Property Standards (*continued*)

2-4 *Services and Facilities.*

a. *Trespass.* Each living unit shall be one that can be used and maintained individually without trespass upon adjoining properties. Any easements granted shall run with the land to protect future owners.

b. *Utilities.* Utilities shall be independent for each living unit except that common services, such as water, sewer, gas and electricity, may be provided for living units under a single mortgage or ownership. Separate utility service shut-offs for each unit shall be provided. For living units under separate ownership, common utility services may be provided from the main to the building line when protected by easement or covenant and maintenance agreement acceptable to HUD. Individual utilities serving a living unit shall not pass over, under or through another living unit, unless provision is made for repair and maintenance of utilities without trespass on adjoining properties or legal provision is made for permanent right of access for maintenance and repair of utilities.

c. *Other Facilities.* Other facilities shall be independent for each living unit, except that common services, such as laundry and storage space or heating, may be provided for up to four living units under a single mortgage.

2-5 *Required Provisions.*

a. *Each living unit* shall contain each of the following:
    (1) A continuing supply of safe and potable water.
    (2) Sanitary facilities and a safe method of sewage disposal.
    (3) Heating adequate for healthful and comfortable living conditions. The Field Office may determine that climatic conditions are such that mechanical heating is not required.
    (4) Domestic hot water.
    (5) Electricity for lighting and for equipment used in the living unit.

b. *When individual water supply* and sewage disposal systems apply, the following shall be required:
    (1) Water quality shall meet the requirements of the health authority having jurisdiction. If the local health authority having jurisdiction does not have specific requirements, the maximum contaminant levels established by the Environmental Protection Agency (EPA) shall apply.
    (2) Connection shall be made to a public or community water system whenever feasible.

continued

Figure 11. HUD Minimum Property Standards (*continued*)

(3) Each living unit shall be provided with a water-carried sewage disposal system adequate to dispose of all domestic wastes in a manner which will not create a nuisance, or in any way endanger the public health. Individual pit privies are permitted where such facilities are customary and are the only feasible means of waste disposal, provided they are installed in accordance with the recommendations of the local Department of Health or, in the absence of such recommendations, with the requirements of the U.S. Public Health Service publication, "Individual Sewage–Disposal Systems."

(4) Whenever feasible, connection shall be made to a public or community sewage disposal system.

2-6 *Nonresidential Use.*
　　a. *Design Limitations.*

(1) Any nonresidential use of the property shall be subordinate to its residential use and character. A property, any portion of which is designed or used for nonresidential purposes, is eligible only if the type or extent of the nonresidential use does not impair the residential character of the property.

(2) Areas designed or used for nonresidential purposes shall not exceed 25 percent of the total floor area. Storage areas or similar spaces which are integral parts of the nonresidential portion shall be included in the total nonresidential area.

2-7 *Access.*
　　a. *Streets.*

(1) Each property shall be provided with vehicular or pedestrian access from a public or private street. Private streets shall be protected by permanent easements.

(2) The required street and provisions for its continued maintenance shall include a safe and suitable vehicular access to and from the property at all times.

2-8 *Access to the Living Unit.* A means of access to each living unit shall be provided without passing through any other living unit.

2-9 *Access to the Rear Yard.*
　　a. Access to the rear yard shall be provided without passing through any other living unit.

continued

Figure 11. HUD Minimum Property Standards (*continued*)

b. For a row type dwelling, the access may be by means of alley, easement, passage through the dwelling, or other acceptable means.

2-10 *Defective Conditions.* Existing or partially completed construction which indicates defective construction, poor workmanship, evidence of continuing settlement, excessive dampness, leakage, decay, termites, or other conditions impairing the safety or sanitation of the dwelling shall render the property unacceptable until the defects or conditions have been remedied and the probability of further damage eliminated.

2-11 *Space Requirements.* Each living unit shall be provided with space necessary to assure suitable living, sleeping, cooking and dining accommodations and sanitary facilities.

2-12 *Mechanical Systems.* Mechanical systems shall assure safety of operation, be protected from destructive elements, have reasonable durability and economy, and have adequate capacity and quality.

2-13 *Ventilation.* Natural ventilation of structural spaces, such as attics and crawl spaces, will be provided to reduce the effect of conditions which are conducive to decay and deterioration of the structure.

2-14 *Roof Covering.* Roof covering shall prevent entrance of moisture and provide reasonable durability and economy of maintenance.

2-15 *Hazards.* The property shall be free of those hazards which may adversely affect the health and safety of the occupants or the structural soundness of the improvements, or which may impair the customary use and enjoyment of the property by occupants. The hazards can be subsidence, flood, erosion, defective lead base paint, or the like.

As a general rule, federal property standards have deferred in recent years to local building codes. These codes typically follow the Uniform Building Codes of the International Conference of Building Officials, headquartered in Los Angeles.

▶ **FmHA** Note the building code standard(s) used.
▶ **HUD/FHA** The appraiser must also consider the existence of hazards due to lead-based paint. For improvements built *before 1978*, if there is *no* evidence of cracking, chipping, peeling or loose paint, then the question may be answered by checking the *Yes* box. If any of these deficiencies exist, however, the *No* box should be checked and the following explanation entered: "Property built prior to 1978. Lead-based paint abatement required." You must also check the lead-based paint abatement requirement of the V.C. sheet.
▶ **FHLMC** As indicated on the form, this information is not required for a Freddie Mac appraisal.
▶ **FNMA** As indicated on the form, this information is not required for a Fannie Mae appraisal.

Construction Warranty

Various types of warranties will pay the cost of repair or replacement of defects to property improvements. The most widely used form of warranty is the Homeowner's Warranty (HOW) covering major appliances and mechanical systems, such as the furnace and air-conditioning unit. Newer structures are likely to have a Home Builder's Warranty (HBW) covering structural components. The warranty may be included in the buyer's purchase price, or it may be separately itemized and paid by buyer, seller or even the real estate agent, as negotiated.

If the subject property improvements are covered by any type of warranty, check the *Yes* box. If there is no warranty, check the *No* box. Note the influence on property value, if any, that results from the presence or absence of a warranty.

▶ **FmHA** Leave this section blank.
▶ **HUD/FHA** Check the *Yes* box only if there is a HUD-approved warranty such as HOW or HBW.

Name of Warranty Program

Enter the name of the warranty policy program.

Warranty Coverage Expires

Enter the date that is the last day covered by the warranty.

▶ Appraisal 1

BUILDING SKETCH (SHOW GROSS LIVING AREA ABOVE GRADE)
If for Freddie Mac or Fannie Mae, show only square foot calculations and cost approach comments in this space.

COST APPROACH

SEE SKETCH FOR MEASUREMENT ANALYSIS.
LIVING AREA: 2,119 SQUARE FEET

THE PROPERTY'S VALUE IS WELL SUPPORTED BY ITS
FUNCTIONAL UTILITY AND ITS LOCATION'S EXTERNAL
INFLUENCES. THE DEPRECIATION ESTIMATE REFLECTS
OBSERVED EFFECTIVE AGE, BASED ON AREA SALES.

THE APPRAISAL IS BASED ON A CASH OR EQUIVALENT
SALE AND NO PERSONAL PROPERTY IS INCLUDED IN THE
VALUATION. LAND VALUE IS BASED ON AREA LAND
SALES. THE LAND/VALUE RATIO OF THE SUBJECT
PROPERTY IS SUPPORTED BY THOSE FOR COMPARABLE
PROPERTIES.

ESTIMATED REPRODUCTION COST—NEW—OF IMPROVEMENTS:

Dwelling	2,119 Sq. Ft. @ $ 40.00	= $	84,760
ENTRY	60 Sq. Ft. @ $ 12.00	=	720
Extras		=	18,000
		=	
Special Energy Efficient Items INCLUDED		=	
Porches, Patios, etc. 458 SF @ $25		=	11,450
Garage/~~Carport~~ 525 Sq. Ft. @ $ 18.00		=	9,450
Total Estimated Cost New		= $	124,380

	Physical	Functional	External		
Less					
Depreciation	13M	N/A	N/A	= $	13,000
Depreciated Value of Improvements				= $	111,380
Site Imp. "as is" (driveway, landscaping, etc.)				= $	9,020
ESTIMATED SITE VALUE				= $	45,000
(If leasehold, show only leasehold value.)					165,400
INDICATED VALUE BY COST APPROACH				= $	

(Not Required by Freddie Mac and Fannie Mae)	Construction Warranty ☐ Yes ☒ No
Does property conform to applicable HUD/VA property standards? ☐ Yes ☐ No	Name of Warranty Program N/A
If No, explain: _____	Warranty Coverage Expires N/A

In Appraisal 1, the subject property, as sketched in an addendum (shown on page 23), has 2,119 square feet of living area. The appraiser has determined that the property's value is well supported by its functional utility and its location's external influences. The depreciation estimate reflects observed effective age, based on area sales. The appraisal is based on a cash or equivalent sale, and no personal property is included in the valuation. Land value is based on area land sales. The Land/Value ratio of the subject property is supported by those for comparable properties.

The dwelling has a living area of 2,119 square feet; at an estimated current construction cost in this area of $40 per square foot, the cost estimate is $84,760. In addition, there is a covered entry area of 60 square feet, valued at $12 per square foot for an estimated cost of $720. Extras include a swimming pool enclosed in a bronze A-frame cage, valued at $18,000. All energy-efficient items, such as wall and ceiling insulation, are included in the living area valuation. There is an enclosed porch of 458 square feet, valued at $25 per square foot for an estimated cost of $11,450. The attached garage of

525 square feet is valued at $18 per square foot for an estimated cost of $9,450. The total estimated cost new of the subject dwelling is thus $124,380.

Depreciation due to physical deterioration is based on the effective age of the subject in relation to other properties in the area. Because of its overall good condition, although the subject is 11 years old, it has an effective age of only about 5 years. The loss in value attributable to overall wear and tear is thus $13,000. There is no evidence of functional or external depreciation. The depreciated value of the improvements, then, is $111,380.

Site improvements, including the driveway and landscaping, are valued at $9,020. Site value, including all amenities commonly found in comparable sites (such as underground utilities, storm and sanitary sewers, and concrete curbs and gutters) is estimated by analysis of comparable properties at $45,000. The indicated value of the subject property by the cost approach is thus $165,400.

This appraisal is not for HUD or VA purposes. There is no applicable construction warranty.

▶ Exercise: Appraisal 2

COST APPROACH

BUILDING SKETCH (SHOW GROSS LIVING AREA ABOVE GRADE)
If for Freddie Mac or Fannie Mae, show only square foot calculations and cost approach comments in this space

ESTIMATED REPRODUCTION COST-NEW-OF IMPROVEMENTS:

Dwelling _____ Sq. Ft. @ $ _____ = $ _____
_____ Sq. Ft. @ $ _____ = _____
Extras _____ = _____
_____ = _____
Special Energy Efficient Items _____ = _____
Porches, Patios, etc. _____ = _____
Garage/Carport _____ Sq. Ft. @ $ _____ = _____
Total Estimated Cost New . . . . = $ _____

	Physical	Functional	External
Less			
Depreciation			

= $ _____
Depreciated Value of Improvements . . . . = $ _____
Site Imp. "as is" (driveway, landscaping, etc.) = $ _____
ESTIMATED SITE VALUE . . . . = $ _____
(If leasehold, show only leasehold value.)
INDICATED VALUE BY COST APPROACH . . . . = $ _____

(Not Required by Freddie Mac and Fannie Mae)
Does property conform to applicable HUD/VA property standards? ☐ Yes ☐ No
If No, explain: _____

Construction Warranty ☐ Yes ☐ No
Name of Warranty Program _____
Warranty Coverage Expires _____

Complete the blank URAR *COST APPROACH* section provided above for Appraisal 2, using the following information. When you have finished, you can check your work against the completed Appraisal 2 in the Answer Key.

The subject property is a rectangle, 60 feet wide and 33 feet deep. There is a center front entrance but no front porch. There is a rear sliding glass door to the left of the house, opening onto a deck that is 20 feet wide by 15 feet deep. There is a detached garage of 25 feet by 25 feet, directly behind and to the right of the house at the end of an asphalt driveway. The energy-efficient items on the property are the same as those enjoyed by other homes in the neighborhood —well-insulated walls, ceilings and floors. There are no special energy-efficient fixtures. A red-wood board fence encloses the rear yard.

Cost estimates are based on $95 per square foot for residential construction of this quality, $12 per square foot for decking and $25 per square foot for a detached garage.

The subject is 18 years old and in average overall condition. Depreciation due to physical deterioration is estimated at 25%. There is no evidence of functional or external obsolescence.

Site value, including all utilities, grading, and concrete curbs and gutters, is estimated by comparison with comparable properties as $90,000. The value "as is" of site improvements not considered in any other category (such as the driveway, landscaping and fencing) is estimated to be $16,000.

The appraisal is not being performed for HUD or FHA purposes. The property has no construction warranties.

Sales Comparison Analysis

The undersigned has recited three recent sales of properties most similar and proximate to subject and has considered these in the market analysis. The description includes a dollar adjustment, reflecting market reaction to those items of significant variation between the subject and comparable properties. If a significant item in the comparable property is superior to, or more favorable than, the subject property, a minus (−) adjustment is made, thus reducing the indicated value of subject; if a significant item in the comparable is inferior to, or less favorable than, the subject property, a plus (+) adjustment is made, thus increasing the indicated value of the subject.

ITEM	SUBJECT	COMPARABLE NO. 1		COMPARABLE NO. 2		COMPARABLE NO. 3	
Address							
Proximity to Subject							
Sales Price	$	$		$		$	
Price/Gross Liv. Area	$	$		$		$	
Data Source							
VALUE ADJUSTMENTS	DESCRIPTION	DESCRIPTION	+ (−) $ Adjustment	DESCRIPTION	+ (−) $ Adjustment	DESCRIPTION	+ (−) $ Adjustment
Sales or Financing Concessions							
Date of Sale/Time							
Location							
Site/View							
Design and Appeal							
Quality of Construction							
Age							
Condition							
Above Grade Room Count	Total Bdrms Baths	Total Bdrms Baths		Total Bdrms Baths		Total Bdrms Baths	
Gross Living Area	Sq. Ft.	Sq. Ft.		Sq. Ft.		Sq. Ft.	
Basement & Finished Rooms Below Grade							
Functional Utility							
Heating/Cooling							
Garage/Carport							
Porches, Patio, Pools, etc.							
Special Energy Efficient Items							
Fireplace(s)							
Other (e.g. kitchen equip., remodeling)							
Net Adj. (total)		+ − $		+ − $		+ − $	
Indicated Value of Subject		$		$		$	

Comments on Sales Comparison: _____

INDICATED VALUE BY SALES COMPARISON APPROACH .... $ _____

The sales comparison approach is the most widely used appraisal method for valuing residential properties. In this approach, value is estimated by comparing the subject property to recently sold, similar nearby, properties. The basic premise of the sales comparison approach is that the value of the subject is directly related to the sales prices of the comparables. The mathematical formula for the sales comparison approach is:

$$\text{Sales Price of Comparable Property} \pm \text{Adjustments} = \text{Indicated Value of Subject Property}$$

The *SALES COMPARISON ANALYSIS* section of the URAR form lists most of the significant property variables that may require price adjustments. To arrive at a value estimate using this approach, the appraiser must:

- Describe the subject property and comparables.
- Adjust the sales price of each comparable to account for property differences.
- Determine the indicated value that best reflects the market value of the subject property.

THE ADJUSTMENT PROCESS

In an ideal market for applying the sales comparison approach, a large number of recent sales would be available between buyers and sellers who are knowledgeable and familiar with the local market, the sold properties would be substantially similar to the subject property, and financing would be consistent with current terms and conditions.

In reality two properties are seldom, if ever, exactly alike. Therefore each comparable must be compared to the subject and the sales prices *adjusted* to account for any dissimilar features. Adjustments are made to the sales price of a comparable property by *adding* the value of features present in the subject but not in the comparable, and *subtracting* the value of features present in the comparable but not in the subject. The adjusted sales prices of the comparables represent the probable value range of the subject property. From this range a single market value estimate can be selected that most accurately reflects the unique nature of the subject property.

The objective of the adjustment process, then, is to estimate the price at which the comparable property would have sold if its significant characteristics were the same as those of the subject property.

The most difficult step in using the sales comparison approach is determining the dollar amount of each adjustment. The accuracy of an appraisal using this approach depends on the use of reliable adjustment values.

Ideally, if properties could be found that were exactly alike except for one variable, the adjustment value of that variable would be the difference in selling prices of the two properties.

Example: House A is very similar to house B, except that house A has central air-conditioning and house B does not. House A sold for $108,500; house B sold for $105,000. Because central air-conditioning is the only significant difference between the two properties, its market value is the difference between the selling price of $108,500 and the selling price of $105,000. Thus the value of central air-conditioning *in this market and as of the time of these sales* is $3,500.

This reasoning is called *matched pair,* or *paired data,* analysis. However, an adjustment supported by just one matched pair, as in the example, may be unreliable. In actual practice, the appraiser should analyze as many properties as needed to isolate each significant variable and to substantiate the accuracy of an adjustment value. Most neighborhoods have very similar properties, so usually this is not as difficult as it may first appear.

ADVANTAGES AND LIMITATIONS

The most obvious advantage of the sales comparison approach is its simplicity. It is not complex either as a concept or as a mechanical technique. Furthermore, its simplicity and directness appeal to both clients and the courts. When there are sufficient, recent and reliable market transactions, the sales comparison approach is probably the most logical and objective approach to value.

The chief limitation of the sales comparison approach is that it depends on a substantial volume of reliable information for its validity. When the number of market transactions is insufficient, the reliability of the approach is seriously reduced. Adjustments may be lengthy and complex in some cases, with relatively little available basis for evaluating differences. Finally, it is sometimes difficult to determine whether a transaction is a bona fide, arm's-length sale or whether the sales price was distorted by a hidden motive.

The undersigned has recited three recent sales of properties most similar and proximate to subject and has considered these in the market analysis. The description includes a dollar adjustment, reflecting market reaction to those items of significant variation between the subject and comparable properties. If a significant item in the comparable property is superior to, or more favorable than, the subject property, a minus (–) adjustment is made, thus reducing the indicated value of subject; if a significant item in the comparable is inferior to, or less favorable than, the subject property, a plus (+) adjustment is made, thus increasing the indicated value of the subject.

Although adjustments may be made for some differences between the subject property and the comparables, most of the following factors should be similar:

style of house	size of lot
age	size of dwelling
number of rooms	terms of sale
number of bedrooms	type of construction
number of bathrooms	general condition

If possible the comparable properties should be from the same neighborhood as the subject property.

Even though the URAR requires data on only three comparable sales, you should have investigated many more properties before determining the three most appropriate for the appraisal. The number of sales needed for an accurate estimate of market value cannot be easily specified, but the fewer the sales, the more carefully they need to be investigated. The amount of data considered by you to support conclusions may be much more extensive than the specific data shown in the appraisal report. For example, an analysis of the sales properties not used directly in the report may be helpful in establishing neighborhood values, price trends and time adjustments.

▶ **FNMA** The sales comparison approach to value, traditionally referred to as the market data approach, is the analysis of comparable sales, contract offerings and current listings of properties that are the most comparable to the subject property. However, Fannie Mae requires the appraiser to report only the comparable sales in the appraisal report. The comparable sales must be verified, analyzed and adjusted for differences between the comparable properties and the subject property.

Analyze each comparable sale used in the sales comparison approach for differences and similarities between it and the property being appraised. Make appropriate adjustments for location, terms and conditions of sale, date of sale and physical characteristics of the properties.

Comparable sales must be adjusted *to* the subject property— except for sales and financing concessions, which are adjusted to the market at the time of sale. The subject property is the standard against which the comparable sales are evaluated and adjusted. Thus if an item in the comparable property is superior to that in the subject property, a minus (–) adjustment is required to make that item equal to that in the subject property. Conversely, if an item in the comparable property is inferior to that in the subject property, a plus (+) adjustment is required to make the item equal to that in the subject property.

The proper selection of comparable properties minimizes both the need for, and the size of, any dollar adjustments. Occasionally there may be no similar or truly comparable sales for a particular property, because of the uniqueness of the property or other conditions. In such cases, you must use your knowledge and judgment to select comparable sales that represent the best indicators of value for the subject property and to make adjustments to reflect the actions of typical purchasers in the market. Dollar adjustments should reflect the market's reaction to the difference in the properties, not necessarily the cost of the difference. Swimming pools, electronic air filters, intercom systems, elaborately finished basements, carpets and other special features generally do not affect value to the extent of their cost.

▶ **HUD/FHA** Always select the comparables that have the fewest dissimilarities for the URAR report.

ITEM

The important factors that affect property value are listed here.

SUBJECT

Enter in this column the required information for the subject property. The easiest way to complete the sales comparison section is to enter all details of the subject property, then do the same for each comparable in turn.

COMPARABLE NO. 1

Enter the required information for the first comparable selected.

COMPARABLE NO. 2

Enter the required information for the second comparable selected.

COMPARABLE NO. 3

Enter the required information for the third comparable selected.

Address

Enter the street address or rural route number. Enough information must be provided to locate the property. Be sure the subject's address is the same as the address entered in the *SUBJECT* section on page 1.

▶ **HUD/FHA** Enter the address that can be used to locate each property. If necessary include the name of the community. For rural properties list the location by road name and nearest intersection and indicate on which side of the road the property is located.

Proximity to Subject

Enter the approximate distance and the direction of each comparable property from the subject; for example, ¼ MILE NE.

▶ **FNMA** Be specific when describing the comparable's proximity to the subject property; for example, TWO BLOCKS SOUTH. Whenever possible, use comparable sales from the same neighborhood as the subject, because those sales should reflect the same positive and negative locational characteristics.

Sales Price

Enter the reported sales price of each comparable property. If there is no current pending sales price for the subject, leave that space blank.

▶ **FNMA** The sales price of each comparable sale should be within the general range of the estimate of market value for the subject property. A $100,000 comparable sale for a $75,000 subject property would raise questions about the validity of the comparable.

▶ **HUD/FHA** Enter the total price paid by the buyer, including extras.

Price/Gross Liv. Area

Enter the price per square foot of gross living area for the subject and comparables. Divide the sales price of the dwelling by the number of square feet of gross living area it contains. For example, if the sales price is $150,000 and the gross living area is 2,000 square feet, then the *Price/Gross Liv. Area* is $75 per square foot.

Gross living area for the subject dwelling can be found in three different sections of the URAR form: the *ROOM LIST* on page 1, the *COST APPROACH* on page 2 and the *SALES COMPARISON ANALYSIS* discussed here.

Note: The price per square foot of living area computed here is *not* the same as the price per square foot used to estimate reproduction cost at the top of page 2 of the URAR form. In the sales comparison approach, the price per square foot is used simply as a way to compare the relative sales prices of the subject and comparables and is not intended to be an accurate reflection of the reproduction or replacement cost of their improvements.

▶ **HUD/FHA** Enter the price per square foot based on the number of square feet of living area *above grade*.

▶ **VA** Compute the price per square foot of gross living area *only* if it is considered a valid method of comparison.

Data Source

Enter the source of the market data used, such as personal inspection, lender, public records, multiple listing service or some similar response.

▶ **FNMA** Because an appraiser's estimate of market value is no better than the reliability of the comparable data used, you must exercise due diligence to ensure the reliability of comparable sales data. When comparable sales data are provided by a party having a financial interest in either the sale or financing of the subject property, you must reverify the data with a party who does not have a financial interest in the subject transaction.

▶ **HUD/FHA** Enter the name of the source or location where price and property information was obtained, such as tax stamps, MLS, and so on. Also show the type of financing, such as CONV., FHA or VA.

Value Adjustments

Up to this point you have recorded only descriptive or factual data about the subject and comparables. The remaining items in the property variables list may require plus or minus adjustments.

In most home appraisals, good comparables usually are available, thus requiring few adjustments. Remember, however, that all adjustments must be supported by documented market evidence. In most cases market-based price adjustments can be developed through paired data (or matched pair) analysis.

▶ **HUD/FHA** The value factors of *Location, Site/View, Design and Appeal, Quality of Construction, Age, Condition* and *Functional Utility* (Column 1) are all subjective factors that require subjective adjustments. Make sure that your adjustments are reasonable—that is, not excessive. If property is ever overvalued, a high probability exists that the reason can be traced to an excessive adjustment somewhere in this section.

DESCRIPTION

Enter all of the required information on the listed property or transaction characteristics for the subject property, then the comparables.

+ (−) $ Adjustment

Enter a dollar value for any listed feature that differs significantly between the subject and a comparable. The dollar value will be a plus adjustment to the sales price of the comparable if the feature makes the subject more valuable than the comparable. The dollar value will be a minus adjustment to the sales price of the comparable if the feature makes the subject less valuable than the comparable.

Sales or Financing Concessions

Describe any financing arrangements that may have affected the sales price of a comparable property, such as mortgage assumptions, buydowns, installment sales contracts and wraparound loans. Then enter the estimated value of the adjustment, if any.

▶ **FNMA** The dollar amount of sales or financing concessions paid by the seller must be reported for the comparables if the information is reasonably available. Generally, sales or financing data for comparable sales—such as the mortgage amount, loan type, interest rate, term and any fees or concessions the seller paid—are available. Be sure to obtain this information from an individual who was a party to the comparable transaction (the broker, buyer or seller) or from a data source you consider reliable. Fannie Mae recognizes that there may be some situations in which sales or financing information is not available because of legal restrictions or other disclosure-related problems. In such cases, you must explain why the information is not available; however, FNMA will not accept an explanation indicating that you did not make an effort to verify the information. In all other cases, you must provide the sales and financing concession information that was available (and verified) for the comparables. If the appraisal report form does not provide enough space to discuss this information, make adjustments for the concessions on the form and explain them in an addendum to the appraisal report.

Examples of sales or financing concessions include interest rate buydowns or other below-market-rate financing, loan discount points, loan origination fees, closing costs customarily paid by the buyer, payment of condominium or PUD association fees, refunds of (or credit for) the borrower's expenses, absorption of monthly payments, assignment of rent payments and the inclusion of nonrealty items in the transaction. The amount of the negative adjustment to be made to each comparable with sales or financing concessions is equal to any increase in the purchase price of the comparable that the appraiser determines to be attributable to the concessions.

The need to make negative adjustments and the amount of the adjustments to the comparables for sales and financing concessions are not based on how typical the concessions might be for a segment of the market area—large sales concessions can be relatively typical in a particular segment of the market and still result in sales prices that reflect more than the value of the real estate. Adjustments based on mechanical, dollar-for-dollar deductions that are equal to the cost of the concessions to the seller (as a strict cash equivalency approach would dictate) are not appropriate. FNMA recognizes that the effect of the sales concessions on sales prices can vary with the amount of the concessions and differences in various markets. The adjustments must reflect the difference between what the comparables actually sold for with the sales concessions and what they would have sold for without the concessions so that the dollar amount of the adjustments will approximate the market's reaction to the concessions.

Positive adjustments for sales or financing concessions are not acceptable. For example, if local tradition or law results in virtually all of the property sellers in the market area paying a 1% loan origination fee for the purchaser, and a property seller in that market did not pay any loan fees or concessions for the purchaser, the sale would be considered a cash equivalent sale in that market. Note comparable sales that sold for all cash or with cash equivalent financing and use them as comparables if they are the best indicators of value for the subject property. Such sales also can be useful in determining those costs normally paid by sellers as the result of tradition or law in the market area.

▶ **HUD/FHA** Enter any necessary adjustments for sales or financing concessions here. Adjust each comparable in accordance with the instructions in mortgage letter 86-15. Explain the adjustment in *Comments on Sales Comparison* and, if appropriate, use an addendum.

▶ **VA** You *must* consider and report the effect of any sales or financing incentives that were involved in the comparable sales transactions. Fee appraisers should consult local release 86-18 (DVB Circular 26-86-9, par. 4f), stating the VA's policy regarding seller incentives.

Date of Sale/Time

Enter the closing date of each comparable sale and, if needed, an adjustment for time.

In an active market, comparable properties that sold within the past four to six months should be readily available. Most underwriters require the appraiser to explain the use of any comparable sale that occurred more than six months before the date of appraisal. In a slow market, however, it may be necessary to use comparable sales from as long as a year ago. In that event, market conditions may have changed, thus creating the need for a time adjustment.

If other types of properties have increased in value over the same period, a general rise in prices may be indicated. If the market has shown little price fluctuation over that period, no adjustment may be necessary. A downward adjustment may be indicated if prices have tended to fall over the period since the sale of the comparable—a situation that has become increasingly common throughout the country. You must determine whether the comparable property which sold a year ago is part of the general trend (upward, stable or downward) and, if necessary, adjust the sales price of the comparable accordingly.

▶ **FNMA** Provide the date of the sales contract and the settlement or closing date for each comparable sale. Unless you believe the exact date is critical to understanding the adjustments, only the month and year of the sale need be reported. If you do not report both the contract date and settlement or closing date, identify the reported sale date as either the "contract date" or the "settlement or closing date." If you report only the contract date, state whether the contract resulted in a settlement or a closing.

Time adjustments must be representative of the market and should be supported by the comparable sales whenever possible. The adjustments must reflect the time that elapsed between the contract date (or the date of the "meeting of the minds") for the comparable sale and the effective date of the appraisal for the subject property.

In general, use comparable sales that have been settled or closed within the past 12 months. However, you may use older comparable sales as additional supporting data, if you believe that it is appropriate. You must comment on the reasons for using any comparable sales that are more than six months old.

In addition, you may use the subject property as a fourth comparable sale or as supporting data if the property previously was sold (and closed or settled). If you believe that it is appropriate, you also may use contract offerings and current listings as supporting data.

▶ **HUD/FHA** Enter the month and year of closing. A specific date is not necessary unless it is meaningful, e.g., occurring in a rapidly changing market.

Use older sales only if more recent ones are not available. If older sales are used as comparables, explain their use in the *Comments on Sales Comparison* part of this section of the URAR.

Location

Two comparisons are required in this entry, followed by the adjustment value (plus or minus) for any significant locational difference between the subject and comparable.

1. Rate the overall location of the subject within the neighborhood or market area. Enter GOOD, AVG, FAIR or POOR as appropriate. Some lenders also require reference to an actual map page and grid number.
2. Rate the location of each comparable against the subject. Enter SUPERIOR, EQUAL or INFERIOR as appropriate. Again, reference to an actual map page and grid number may be required.

▶ **FNMA** For properties in established subdivisions or for units in established condominium or PUD projects (those that have resale activity), you should use comparable sales from within the subject property's subdivision or project if any are available. Resale activity from within the subdivision or project should be the best indicator of value for properties in that subdivision or project. If you use sales of comparable properties located outside of the subject neighborhood, you must include an explanation with the analysis.

For properties in new subdivisions or for units in new (or recently converted) condominium or PUD projects, you must compare the subject property to other properties in its general market area as well as to properties within the subject subdivision or project. This comparison should help demonstrate market acceptance of new developments and the properties within them. Generally, you should select one comparable sale from the subject subdivision or project, one comparable sale from outside the subject subdivision or project and one comparable sale from inside *or* outside the subject subdivision or project provided you consider it to be a good indicator of value for the subject property. In selecting the comparables, keep in mind that sales or resales from within the subject subdivision or project are preferable to sales from outside the subdivision or project *as long as the developer or builder of the subject property is not involved in the transactions.*

▶ **HUD/FHA** Enter GOOD, AVG or FAIR for each comparable as compared to the subject property, using the same standard as that used for the subject.

Site/View

Give the size of each site in square feet; your figure for the subject should agree with the entry in the *SITE* section on page 1. Rate each site *and* view as GOOD, AVG, FAIR or POOR as appropriate. If possible, give a brief description of the view along with the rating; for example, WATER/GOOD or NBHD/AVG. (If necessary, use a single letter abbreviation for your rating; for example, WATER/G or NBHD/A.)

Adjustments for this entry can reflect differences in site, view or both. Site adjustments may reflect differences in size, shape, topography, landscaping, drainage, streets, sidewalks or other features. In most neighborhoods, view adjustments are uncommon; however, adjustments for houses with water or mountain views may be very substantial.

If both site and view values are adjusted, the adjustment amounts are usually added together and shown as one figure. For example, separate adjustments for site (+$4,500) and view (−$8,500) can be combined and recorded as −$4,000.

▶ **HUD/FHA** Enter the size of the lot and explain the view, if appropriate. Adjustments may come from the size of the lot as well as a view rated SUPERIOR or INFERIOR to that of the subject property. If the property's size is typical for the area, small differences in lot sizes usually do not call for an adjustment.

Design and Appeal

First identify the architectural design or style of the subject and comparables (ranch, Cape Cod, two-story and so on). Then rate the subject as GOOD, AVG, FAIR or POOR. (This entry should be consistent with the subject's rating in the *IMPROVEMENT ANALYSIS* section on page 1 of the form.) Next rate each comparable against the subject by entering SUPERIOR, EQUAL or INFERIOR. Finally, enter the value of any required adjustment.

This category refers to exterior design, interior qualities, special features and any other characteristics that would make a property appealing to the typical buyer and affect its livability, marketability and value. The style of a house probably should follow the rule of conformity; that is, the design should be compatible with that of others in the neighborhood.

> ▸ **HUD/FHA** Describe the style according to local custom and indicate the property's appeal by G, A, F or P.

Quality of Construction

Rate the construction quality of the subject and comparables as GOOD, AVG, FAIR or POOR and enter appropriate adjustments. The subject property's entry should be consistent with its rating in the *IMPROVEMENT ANALYSIS* section on page 1.

Remember that this entry covers *all* aspects of construction, from foundation to finish work. The quality of workmanship and quality and durability of materials used in the construction of the structure must be considered. If adjustments are to be made for differences in materials, these should be identified by the appraiser.

> ▸ **HUD/FHA** Enter GOOD, AVERAGE or FAIR and the construction type, such as aluminum siding, wood siding, brick and so on.

Age

Enter the actual age (or the actual year of construction) of the subject dwelling and comparables and, if necessary, make adjustments indicated by the market.

If good comparables are available, the ages of the subject and comparables will be very close, and no adjustment will be necessary.

Note: In some appraisals, *effective* age may be used as the basis for comparison. In that event write EFFECTIVE in the space to the right of the word *Age.*

> ▸ **HUD/FHA** If both actual and effective age are used, enter and note both, such as A-25, E-20. A difference between actual and effective age typically is caused by modernization or significant maintenance, or the lack of either. Any difference is the basis for a plus or minus adjustment.

Condition

Rate the overall condition of the subject and comparables as GOOD, AVG, FAIR or POOR. The subject's rating must be consistent with the rating in the *IMPROVEMENT ANALYSIS* section on page 1. An adjustment is indicated if the comparable is in better or worse condition than the subject.

Note: Be careful not to "double adjust" for age and condition, because both variables require judgments on elements of deterioration.

▶ **HUD/FHA** Enter GOOD, AVERAGE, FAIR or POOR when compared to the subject. Be consistent with the ratings used on page 1.

Above Grade Room Count/Gross Living Area

Enter the number of finished above-grade rooms, the number of bedrooms and baths, and the total above-grade, square-foot living area for the subject and comparables. The living area and room count for the subject must correspond to the information entered in the *ROOM LIST* section on page 1.

If an adjustment is necessary, it is usually to reflect differences in the number of baths or minor differences in square footage.

▶ **FNMA** Include only finished above-grade areas in calculation of gross living area. Report the basement and other partially below-grade areas separately and adjust for them accordingly. Room count and gross living area should be similar for the subject property and all comparables; for example, a four-bedroom comparable generally is not acceptable to support the value of a two-bedroom subject property. Address large differences between the subject property and the comparable sales, because they raise doubts about the validity of the comparables as good indicators of value.

▶ **HUD/FHA** Enter room count, being consistent with page 1 of the report. There are three common adjustments:

1. An adjustment for "expendable space," such as a bath, with a deficiency in the number of baths adjusted first;
2. A separate adjustment for a difference in square feet; and
3. An adjustment for room count.

These can be entered separately or combined, but all adjustment values should be extracted from the market.

Typically an appraiser will *not* make an adjustment for a difference in square footage as well as an adjustment for a difference in room count; for example, a very large home may have a small room count. Any property requiring an adjustment for both square footage *and* room count should be explained.

Basement & Finished Rooms Below Grade

If a house has a basement, enter FULL or PARTIAL, as appropriate. A percentage indicating basement space could be given instead; for example, **100%** or **50%**. If the house has no basement or finished rooms below grade, enter **NONE** or **0%**.

Indicate whether there are any finished rooms below grade (including the basement). If there are, identify the room types; for example, **REC RM**, **DEN**, **BDRM** and so on.

Make appropriate adjustments to reflect differences between comparables and subject property. As in all adjustments, value is dictated by the market and not by construction cost.

▶ **HUD/FHA** Enter the type of improvements in the basement, such as **BEDROOM**, **REC ROOM**, **LAUNDRY** and so on. Explain any special features. Show the number of square feet of *finished* below-grade area.

Functional Utility

Rate the subject and comparables as **GOOD**, **AVG**, **FAIR** or **POOR**. Adjust for differences. Be sure your entry for the subject property is consistent with the *Room Sizes/Layout* rating in the *IMPROVEMENT ANALYSIS* block of the *INTERIOR* section on page 1.

Functional utility refers to a dwelling's overall compatibility with its intended use and environment, as defined by market standards. This category includes design features (such as layout, room size, storage area, security and privacy) that are in line with current trends in the market area. A layout has functional *inutility* if it has poor traffic patterns. For example, people should not have to walk through bedrooms to get to other parts of the house. As another example, bathrooms should be accessed directly or through a hall and not through a second bedroom.

Marketability is the ultimate test of functional utility. When judging the functional utility of homes, the appraiser must interpret the reaction of typical buyers in the subject market area.

▶ **FNMA** Sometimes improvements can be overimprovement for the neighborhood but still be within the neighborhood price range. An example would be a property with an in-ground swimming pool, a large addition or an oversized garage, in a market that does not demand these kinds of improvements. Comment on such overimprovements and indicate their contributory value in the *SALES COMPARISON ANALYSIS* adjustment grid.

Because an overimproved property may not be acceptable to the typical purchaser, the lender's underwriter must review appraisals on this type of property carefully to ensure that the appraiser has reflected only the contributory value of the overimprovement in the analysis.

▶ **HUD/FHA** Enter **EQUAL**, **SUPERIOR** or **INFERIOR** as a total of the items rated in the *IMPROVEMENT ANALYSIS* block in the *INTERIOR* section, compared to the subject. Make your analysis consistent with the factors reported in that section. Make liberal use of the *Comments on Sales Comparison* section and explain special features.

Typically this is the category in which to deduct for functional obsolescence observed in the subject property and recorded on page 1 but not found in the comparables. The value of any necessary adjustments should be extracted from the market. For example, a negative adjustment for functional obsolescence would be made for a poor floor design that includes two bedrooms located so that entrance to one is possible only by passing through the other. In such a case, the bedroom without separate access would not be counted as a bedroom.

Heating/Cooling

Identify the types of heating and cooling systems present in the subject house and comparable houses. Adjustments should be based on such things as type of system, presence or absence of air-conditioning and the condition and effectiveness of the equipment. Adjustments should be derived from market data, not cost data.

▶ **HUD/FHA** If appropriate, enter an adjustment for heating and cooling systems; adjustment values should be based on local market expectations.

Garage/Carport

Indicate whether the subject and comparables have garages or carports and the number of cars they hold. If a property does not have a garage or carport, enter **NONE**.

Adjustments should be based on the typical value buyers place on garages or carports, not on cost data.

▶ **HUD/FHA** Enter any required adjustment for car storage. Adjustments should be calculated in accordance with market acceptance of carport versus garage, as well as the impact of size on market value.

Porches, Patio, Pools, etc.

Porches, patios, pools, decks, greenhouses, fences and any other structure not considered part of the primary house should be noted here. Adjustments for such features should reflect local market expectations and buyer requirements.

▶ **FNMA** Dollar adjustments should reflect the market's reaction to the differences between properties, not necessarily the cost of the difference in actual dollars. Items such as swimming pools, electronic air filters, intercom systems, elaborately finished basements, carpets and other special features generally do not affect value to the extent of their cost.

▶ **HUD/FHA** Enter any necessary adjustments for these features, based on local market expectations. For example, a property with a swimming pool in an area where a swimming pool is an expected feature might bring a dollar premium, compared with a comparable property without a pool. On the other hand, an improvement such as a swimming pool in a low-income area might bring a negative adjustment because of increased maintenance expenses.

Special Energy Efficient Items

Identify any energy-efficient items contained in the homes. Price adjustments for energy conservation features should reflect how much more the market will pay for the property because of their existence.

▶ **FNMA** FNMA recommends that lenders give special underwriting consideration to buyers of properties with energy-efficient improvements. In such cases, higher monthly housing expenses and debt payment ratios may be justified because of the potential savings in energy costs.

▶ **HUD/FHA** Enter an adjustment for any energy-efficient items, such as storm windows and doors, solar installations and so on, as appropriate.

Fireplace(s)

Record the type and number of fireplaces in the subject house and comparables. If a house does not have a fireplace, enter NONE. If an adjustment is necessary, base it on how much the typical buyer is willing to pay for a house with a fireplace—*not* on the cost of construction.

▶ **HUD/FHA** Enter any adjustment required by the presence or absence of a fireplace.

Other (e.g. kitchen equip., remodeling)

This is a catchall entry in which you can adjust for differences between the subject and comparables for items such as built-in kitchen appliances, fire and burglar alarm systems, modernization and remodeling or other features not categorized elsewhere in the *SALES COMPARISON ANALYSIS* section.

▶**HUD/FHA** Enter adjustments for any features not covered elsewhere.

Net Adj. (total)

Total the dollar amounts of the positive (+) and negative (–) adjustments for each comparable to find the net adjustment and enter that amount, checking the + or – box as appropriate. Very substantial adjustments suggest that the properties are not comparable.

▶ **FNMA** FNMA has established guidelines for the net and gross percentage adjustments that underwriters may rely on as a general indicator of whether a property should be used as a comparable sale. Generally the total dollar amount of the net adjustments for each comparable sale should not exceed 15% of the comparable's sales price. If the adjustments exceed 15%, you must comment on the reasons for not using a more similar comparable.

Further, the dollar amount of the *gross* adjustment for each comparable sale should not exceed 25% of the comparable's sales price. The amount of the gross adjustment is determined by adding all individual adjustments without regard to the plus or minus signs. If the adjustments exceed 25% you must comment on the reasons for not using a more similar comparable. You should explain individual adjustments that are excessively high, and they should be reviewed carefully by the lender's underwriter. In some circumstances, the use of comparables with higher-than-normal adjustments may be warranted, but you must satisfactorily justify your use of them.

You must research the market and select the most comparable sales available for the subject property. Then adjust those sales to reflect the market's reaction to the differences (except for sales and financing concessions) between the comparable sales and the subject property, without regard for the percentage or amount of the dollar adjustments. If your adjustments do not fall within FNMA's net and gross percentage adjustment guidelines but you believe the comparable sales used to be the best available, as well as the best indicators of value for the subject property, you simply have to provide an appropriate explanation.

If the extent of your adjustments to the comparable sales is great enough to indicate that the property may not conform to the general market area, the lender's underwriter must give special consideration to the case. An atypical property might require more conservative mortgage terms because it might not appeal to a typical purchaser in the market area.

▶ **HUD/FHA** Check either the (+) or (–) box to indicate whether the total net adjustment will increase or decrease the sales price. If any adjustment is excessive, the comparables should be reviewed to determine whether the best ones were selected. Any adjustment that appears excessive should be explained.

Indicated Value of Subject

The net adjustment is added to or subtracted from the sales price of the comparable property to obtain an adjusted sales price. This is the appraiser's best estimate of what the comparable property would have sold for had it possessed all the significant characteristics of the subject property.

▶ **HUD/FHA** Total all adjustments and add or subtract them to the sales price of each comparable.

Keep track of the magnitude of the adjustments by comparing each one to the sales price of the comparable property. In general the total adjustments should not exceed 10% of the sales price.

Comments on Sales Comparison:

Use this space to:

- Explain the reconciliation process that supports your conclusion of value;
- Expand on any significant adjustments developed; or
- Record additional comments concerning the sales comparison approach.

If more space is needed, supply additional remarks on an addendum attached to the form.

▸ **FNMA** Your comments should reflect your reconciliation of the adjusted (or indicated) values for the comparable sales and identify the comparable(s) you gave the most weight in arriving at the indicated value for the subject property.

▸ **VA** Provide an adequate, supportable explanation of any adjustments made to the comparables, either in the *Comments on Sales Comparison* block or in an addendum.

INDICATED VALUE BY SALES COMPARISON APPROACH

Enter the dollar amount of your estimate of market value by the sales comparison approach. The adjusted values of the comparable properties probably will not be identical. It is your task to choose the adjusted value that best reflects the characteristics of the subject property. There is no formula for reconciling the indicated values. The reconciliation process involves application of careful analysis and judgment for which no mathematical or mechanical formula can be substituted.

▸**FNMA** The lender's underwriter should make a thorough review of the *SALES COMPARISON ANALYSIS* adjustment grid. The sales comparison analysis provides many places in which an error can be made in the use of dollar adjustments. A spot check must always be made of the adjustment calculations and the use of plus (+) and minus (−) signs. Errors in arithmetic can have a significant effect on the value conclusion, making it necessary for the lender to contact the appraiser.

▶ Appraisal 1

The undersigned has recited three recent sales of properties most similar and proximate to subject and has considered these in the market analysis. The description includes a dollar adjustment, reflecting market reaction to those items of significant variation between the subject and comparable properties. If a significant item in the comparable property is superior to, or more favorable than, the subject property, a minus (–) adjustment is made, thus reducing the indicated value of subject; if a significant item in the comparable is inferior to, or less favorable than, the subject property, a plus (+) adjustment is made, thus increasing the indicated value of the subject.

ITEM	SUBJECT	COMPARABLE NO. 1		COMPARABLE NO. 2		COMPARABLE NO. 3	
Address	456 CHERRY HILL ROAD	403 BENT TREE LANE		475 CHERRY HILL ROAD		191 FOREST TRAIL	
Proximity to Subject		1/4 MILE NW		SAME STREET		1 MILE NE	
Sales Price	$ 165,000	$160,000		$ 149,500		$ 149,000	
Price/Gross Liv. Area	$ 77.87	$ 75.65		$ 78.89		$ 86.78	
Data Source	LENDER	PUBLIC RECORDS		PUBLIC RECORDS		PUBLIC RECORDS	
VALUE ADJUSTMENTS	DESCRIPTION	DESCRIPTION	+ (–) $ Adjustment	DESCRIPTION	+ (–) $ Adjustment	DESCRIPTION	+ (–) $ Adjustment
Sales or Financing Concessions		CONV MTG		CONV MTG		CONV MTG	
Date of Sale/Time	CURRENT	1 MONTH AGO		2 MONTHS AGO		5 MONTHS AGO	
Location	GOOD	EQUAL		EQUAL		INFERIOR	+5,000
Site/View	13,907/AVG	14,200/EQUAL		11,370/INF	+5,000	10,000/INF	+7,100
Design and Appeal	RANCH/GOOD	RANCH/EQUAL		RANCH/EQUAL		RANCH/EQUAL	
Quality of Construction	AVG/ASPH R	AVG/ASPH R		AVG/TILE/SUP	–2,000	AVG/RANCH R	
Age	11	11		10		5	–3,000
Condition	GOOD	GOOD		GOOD		GOOD	
Above Grade Room Count	Total 7 Bdrms 3 Baths 2	Total 7 Bdrms 3 Baths 2		Total 7 Bdrms 3 Baths 2		Total 7 Bdrms 3 Baths 2	
Gross Living Area	2,119 Sq. Ft.	2,115 Sq. Ft.		1,895 Sq. Ft.		1,717 Sq. Ft.	
Basement & Finished Rooms Below Grade	NONE	NONE		NONE		NONE	
Functional Utility	GOOD	GOOD		GOOD		GOOD	
Heating/Cooling	FA/CENT	FA/CENT		FA/CENT		FA/CENT	
Garage/Carport	GARAGE/2	GARAGE/2		GARAGE/2		GARAGE/2/SM	+1,000
Porches, Patio, Pools, etc.	ENCL/PORCH CAGED POOL	EQUAL SMALLER	+4,000	SMALLER EQUAL	+5,000	SMALLER EQUAL	+5,000
Special Energy Efficient Items	H/C SYSTEM FANS	EQUAL EQUAL		EQUAL EQUAL		EQUAL EQUAL	
Fireplace(s)	STONE/1	NONE	+1,500	NONE	+1,500	EQUAL	
Other (e.g. kitchen equip., remodeling)	BUILT-INS KITCHEN	EQUAL		EQUAL		EQUAL	
Net Adj. (total)		X + ☐ – $	5,500	X + ☐ – $	9,500	X + ☐ – $	15,100
Indicated Value of Subject			$ 165,500		$ 159,000		$ 164,100

Comments on Sales Comparison: ALL THREE SALES ARE LOCATED WITHIN THE SAME GENERAL AREA.   SALE 1 WAS GIVEN THE MOST WEIGHT IN THE FINAL ANALYSIS BECAUSE IT REQUIRED THE FEWEST ADJUSTMENTS AND IS MOST SIMILAR OVERALL.

INDICATED VALUE BY SALES COMPARISON APPROACH .... $ 165,000

SALES COMPARISON ANALYSIS

▶ Appraisal 1 (*continued*)

In Appraisal 1, the subject property is located at 456 Cherry Hill Road. The house is a three-bedroom, two-bath ranch with a total of seven rooms above grade, excluding the foyer, baths, attic and laundry area. The lender has verified a current pending sales price of $165,000.

Three properties have been selected as comparables. According to public records, all are current sales with conventional mortgage financing:

- *Sale 1* is located at 403 Bent Tree Lane—1/4 mile NW of the subject. It sold one month ago for $160,000.

- *Sale 2* is located at 475 Cherry Hill Road, just up the street from the subject. It sold two months ago for $149,500.
- *Sale 3* is located at 191 Forest Trail—approximately one mile NE of the subject. It sold five months ago for $149,000.

Based on matched pair analysis, the appraiser has assigned the adjustment values shown in the table to account for significant differences between the subject property and the three comparables.

	Subject	Comp. 1	Comp. 2	Comp. 3
Location	GOOD	GOOD	GOOD	INF/$5,000
Site Size	13,908	14,200	11,370/$5,000	10,000/$7,100
Roofing Material	ASPHALT	ASPHALT	SUP/TILE/$2,000	ASPHALT
Age	11	11	10	5/$3,000
Gross Living Area	2,119	2,115	1,895/$4,500	1,717/$8,100
Garage	YES/2-CAR	YES/2-CAR	YES/2-CAR	SMALLER/2/$1,000
Enclosed Porch	YES	YES	SMALLER/$5,000	SMALLER/$5,000
Caged Pool	YES	SMALLER/$4,000	SIMILAR	SIMILAR
Fireplace	YES/1	NO/$1,500	NO/$1,500	YES

► Exercise: Appraisal 2

The undersigned has recited three recent sales of properties most similar and proximate to subject and has considered these in the market analysis. The description includes a dollar adjustment, reflecting market reaction to those items of significant variation between the subject and comparable properties. If a significant item in the comparable property is superior to, or more favorable than, the subject property, a minus (−) adjustment is made, thus reducing the indicated value of subject; if a significant item in the comparable is inferior to, or less favorable than, the subject property, a plus (+) adjustment is made, thus increasing the indicated value of the subject.

ITEM	SUBJECT	COMPARABLE NO. 1		COMPARABLE NO. 2		COMPARABLE NO. 3	
Address							
Proximity to Subject							
Sales Price	$		$		$		$
Price/Gross Liv. Area	$ ⊡	$ ⊡		$ ⊡		$ ⊡	
Data Source							
VALUE ADJUSTMENTS	DESCRIPTION	DESCRIPTION	+ (−) $ Adjustment	DESCRIPTION	+ (−) $ Adjustment	DESCRIPTION	+ (−) $ Adjustment
Sales or Financing Concessions							
Date of Sale/Time							
Location							
Site/View							
Design and Appeal							
Quality of Construction							
Age							
Condition							
Above Grade Room Count	Total ¦ Bdrms ¦ Baths	Total ¦ Bdrms ¦ Baths		Total ¦ Bdrms ¦ Baths		Total ¦ Bdrms ¦ Baths	
Gross Living Area	Sq. Ft.	Sq. Ft.		Sq. Ft.		Sq. Ft.	
Basement & Finished Rooms Below Grade							
Functional Utility							
Heating/Cooling							
Garage/Carport							
Porches, Patio, Pools, etc.							
Special Energy Efficient Items							
Fireplace(s)							
Other (e.g. kitchen equip., remodeling)							
Net Adj. (total)		+ ☐ − ☐ $		+ ☐ − ☐ $		+ ☐ − ☐ $	
Indicated Value of Subject		$		$		$	

Comments on Sales Comparison: _____

INDICATED VALUE BY SALES COMPARISON APPROACH .... $ _____

Complete the blank URAR *SALES COMPARISON ANALYSIS* section provided above for Appraisal 2, using the following information. When you have finished, you can check your work against the completed Appraisal 2 in the Answer Key.

The description of the subject property was verified by the appraiser through personal inspection. It is a single-family, ranch-style residence, containing eight rooms, four bedrooms and two baths; gross living area is 1,980 square feet. The property is located at 1053 Locust Lane, a typical residential street for this neighborhood, which is considered good for the area. The house is 18 years old, with an effective age of 18 years; remaining economic life is estimated to be 38 to 42 years.

The subject lot is a rectangle, 75′ × 150′; site

▶ Exercise: Appraisal 2 *(continued)*

and view are average for this market area. The improvements conform in design and appeal to the market area. Construction is average, as is condition of exterior and interior. There is a partial finished basement. The functional utility of the home is average. The heating and cooling systems are gas-fired, forced-air with central air-conditioning. There is a two-car detached garage.

There are no special energy-efficient items. The home has a wood deck in back and a masonry fireplace in the family room. The financing is a conventional mortgage, typical of the area.

Adjustment values based on local market data are: garage, $15,000; fireplace, $3,000; wood deck, $3,500; finished basement, $6,000; updated kitchen, $5,000 (comp 4); lot size, $20,000 (comp 4); living area, $20,000 (comp 4).

Comparable sales data, which have been verified by brokers involved in the transactions, are shown below.

	Comp 1	Comp 2	Comp 3	Comp 4
Address	310 Minagua St.	1091 Locust Lane	453 Chelsea Ct.	565 Lord Ave.
Proximity to Subject	½ mi. NW	Same Block	¾ mi. NE	2 mi. S
Sales Price	$255,500	$240,000	$259,000	$309,000
Financing	Conv. Mortg.	Conv. Mortg.	Conv. Mortg.	Conv. Mortg.
Date of Sale	3 mos. ago	4 mos. ago	3 mos. ago	7 mos. ago
Location	Average	Avg.	Avg.	Avg.
Site/View	Average	Avg.	Avg.	Avg.
Size of Lot	11,000 sq. ft.	10,875 sq. ft.	10,500 sq. ft.	15,000 sq. ft.
Design & Appeal	Ranch/Avg.	Ranch/Avg.	Ranch/Avg.	Ranch/Avg.
Construction	Average	Avg.	Avg.	Avg.
Age	18 Yrs.	18 Yrs.	19 Yrs.	17 Yrs.
Condition	Average	Average	Average	Average
No. of Rms./ Bedrms./Baths	8/4/2	8/4/2	8/4/2	8/4/2
Sq. Ft. of Living Space	2,000	1,950	1,975	2,500
Other Space (Basement)	Crawl Space	Crawl Sp.	Crawl Sp.	Fin. Bsmt.
Functional Utility	Average	Avg.	Avg.	Avg.
Heating/Cooling	FA/Central	FA/Cent.	FA/Cent.	FA/Cent.
Garage	2-car Det.	None	2-car Det.	2-car Det.
Other Exterior Improvements	None	Wood Deck	Wood Deck	None
Special Energy Efficient Items	None	None	None	None
Fireplace(s)	Masonry/1	None	Masonry/1	Masonry/1
Other Interior Improvements	None	None	None	Mod. Kit.

Income Approach

INDICATED VALUE BY INCOME APPROACH (If Applicable) Estimated Market Rent $ _____ /Mo. x Gross Rent Multiplier _____ = $ _____

The income approach can be the most technically complex method of appraisal when applied to large commercial properties. A far simpler method can be applied to single-family residences, however, based on the assumption that value is related to the market rent the property can be expected to earn.

Market rent is the rental income that a property would most probably command on the open market as indicated by current rentals paid for comparable space. To find market rent, an appraiser must know what rent tenants have paid, and are currently paying, on comparable properties. By comparing present and past performances of properties similar to the subject, the appraiser should be able to determine the subject property's rent potential. By analyzing sales prices of comparable properties, the factor, or *gross rent multiplier*, represents the relationship between market rent and market value, can be determined. When the appropriate gross rent multiplier is applied to the rental income the subject property is expected to produce, the result is an estimate of market value.

The steps in this method of applying the income approach are summarized below and explained in this section. The appraiser must:

- Estimate the subject property's monthly market rent.
- Calculate gross rent multipliers from recently sold comparable properties that were rented at the time of sale.
- Based on rent multiplier analysis, derive the appropriate GRM for the subject property.
- Estimate market value by multiplying the amount of the monthly market rent by the subject property's GRM.

GROSS RENT MULTIPLIER

Gross rent multipliers (GRMs) are numbers that express the relationship between the sales price of a residential property and its gross monthly unfurnished rental. This ratio can be expressed by the formula:

$$\frac{\text{Sales Price}}{\text{Gross Rent}} = \text{GRM}$$

To establish a reasonably accurate GRM, the appraiser should have recent sales and rental data from at least 10 properties similar to the subject that have sold in the same market area and were rented at the time of sale. The resulting GRM can then be applied to the projected rental of the subject property to estimate its market value. The formula for that step is:

$$\text{Gross Rent} \quad \times \quad \text{GRM} \quad = \quad \text{Market Value}$$

Because even very similar properties rarely have the same rent or sales price, GRM analysis is likely to produce a range of multipliers. The appraiser must decide which multiplier is most appropriate for the subject property, in the appraiser's best judgment based on the property that is most comparable to the subject. No mathematical or mechanical formula can be substituted for careful analysis and judgment. Following is an example of the range of data that might be collected by an appraiser trying to determine an appropriate GRM for a single-family residence.

Sale No.	Sales Price	Monthly Rental	GRM (rounded)
1	$109,600	$800	137
2	109,500	800	137
3	112,200	825	136
4	110,000	815	135
5	111,700	840	133
6	110,300	815	135
7	108,200	790	137
8	113,000	850	133
9	110,900	820	135
10	112,500	840	134
11	111,100	835	133
Subject	?	815	?

In the example above, the appraiser has determined that the market rent for the subject property is $815. The range of GRMs derived from recent sales of comparable properties is from 133 to 137. When applied to the subject's market rent estimate, the GRMs place value between

$108,395 ($815 × 133) and $111,655 ($815 × 137). These comparisons bracket the estimate of value within reasonable limits. Because property sales 4, 6 and 9 are most comparable to the subject property, the appraiser concludes that the subject property's GRM should be 135. The GRM is applied to the subject's projected monthly rental: $815 × 135 = $110,000 (rounded), the estimated value of the subject property by the income approach.

The income approach can be a valid indicator of market value if the subject property is located in a rental-oriented neighborhood. In areas that are almost exclusively owner-occupied, however, rental data may be too scarce to permit the use of this approach.

If the right kinds of data are available to develop valid market rent and GRM estimates, the income approach for single-family residences should be used, if only to serve as a check against the sales comparison and cost approaches.

INDICATED VALUE BY INCOME APPROACH (If Applicable) Estimated Market Rent $_____/Mo. × Gross Rent Multiplier _____ = $_____

Enter the subject property's monthly market rent estimate derived from the marketplace. Then enter the GRM applicable to the subject property. Finally, multiply the monthly market rent estimate by the GRM and enter the value estimate indicated by the income approach.

▶ **FNMA** The income approach to value is based on the assumption that market value is related to the market rent or income that a property can be expected to earn. Its use generally is appropriate in neighborhoods of single-family properties when there is a substantial rental market, and it is an important approach in the valuation of a two- to four-family property. However, it generally is not appropriate in areas that consist mostly of owner-occupied properties because adequate rental data generally do not exist for those areas. FNMA will not accept an appraisal if the appraiser relies solely on the income approach as an indicator of market value.

To arrive at the indicated value by the income approach, multiply the estimated market rent for the subject property by a gross rent multiplier.

- *Estimated market rent* is based on an analysis of comparable rentals in the neighborhood. After appropriate adjustments are made to the comparables, their adjusted (or indicated) values are reconciled to develop an estimated monthly market rent for the subject property.
- The *gross rent multiplier* is determined by dividing the sales prices of comparable properties that were rented at the time of sale by their monthly market rent, which is then recon-

ciled to create a single gross rent multiplier (or a range of multipliers) for the subject property.

When the property being appraised is a single-family property that will be used as an investment property, you must prepare a *Single-Family Comparable Rent Schedule* (Form 1007) in addition to the appropriate appraisal report form. This form is not required for a two-to four-family property because the *Appraisal Report—Small Residential Income Property* (Form 1025) provides substantially the same information. When you are relying on the income approach, you should attach the supporting comparable rental and sales data, and the calculations used to determine the gross rent multiplier, as an addendum to the appraisal report form.

> ▶ **HUD/FHA** This section must be completed for three-and four-unit properties only. When used, you must show the gross rent from each of the comparables near the bottom of page 2, under *Final Reconciliation*, such as **COMP. #1 GROSS RENT = $1,000.00; COMP. #2 GROSS RENT = $1,200;** and so on.
>
> If you do not use the income approach, draw a line through the words *INDICATED VALUE BY INCOME APPROACH (If Applicable)* and enter the estimated market rent. The rest of the line items should be marked *N/A*.
>
> ▶ **VA** Complete this section only if applicable and a valid indicator of value (for example, if the subject property is a multiunit building).

▶ Appraisal 1

INDICATED VALUE BY INCOME APPROACH (If Applicable) Estimated Market Rent $ __N/A__ /Mo. x Gross Rent Multiplier __N/A__ = $ _____

In Appraisal 1, the income approach was not considered applicable for single-family homes in this area.

▶ Exercise: Appraisal 2

INDICATED VALUE BY INCOME APPROACH (If Applicable) Estimated Market Rent $ _____ /Mo. x Gross Rent Multiplier _____ = $ _____

Complete the blank URAR *INCOME AP-PROACH* section for Appraisal 2, using the following information. When you have finished, you can check your work against the completed Appraisal 2 in the Answer Key.

The subject property is a single-family house located in a neighborhood that is predominantly owner-occupied, yet a small number of homes are rented out. Although the house being ap-praised has always been owner-occupied, current market information indicates that a potential rental income of $1,750 monthly is in line with recent comparable rentals in the area. A thorough rent multiplier analysis produced a GRM range of 140 to 153. The appraiser concluded that the median of the range, 148, was the appropriate GRM for the subject property.

Reconciliation

This appraisal is made ☐ "as is" ☐ subject to the repairs, alterations, inspections or conditions listed below ☐ completion per plans and specifications.
Comments and Conditions of Appraisal:

Final Reconciliation: _____

This appraisal is based upon the above requirements, the certification, contingent and limiting conditions, and Market Value definition that are stated in

☐ FmHA, HUD &/or VA instructions.

☐ Freddie Mac Form 439 (Rev. 7/86)/Fannie Mae Form 1004B (Rev. 7/86) filed with client _____ 19 ___ ☐ attached.

I (WE) ESTIMATE THE MARKET VALUE, AS DEFINED, OF THE SUBJECT PROPERTY AS OF _____ 19 ___ **to be $** _____

I (We) certify: that to the best of my (our) knowledge and belief the facts and data used herein are true and correct; that I (we) personally inspected the subject property, both inside and out, and have made an exterior inspection of all comparable sales cited in this report; and that I (we) have no undisclosed interest, present or prospective therein.

Appraiser(s) SIGNATURE _____	Review Appraiser SIGNATURE _____	☐ Did ☐ Did Not
NAME _____	(if applicable) NAME _____	Inspect Property

In the *RECONCILIATION*, the final section of the URAR form, the appraiser brings all elements of the appraisal together to present and comment on the final conclusion of the market value of the subject property.

The separate value estimates reached by the different appraisal approaches rarely will be identical. Through the process of reconciliation the appraiser compares and analyzes the estimates derived from the approaches used (sales comparison, cost and/or income). By considering the appropriateness of each approach for the property appraised, the value estimate that most accurately represents the market value of the subject can be determined.

The process of reconciliation is *not* a simple averaging of figures. One approach may have more validity for certain properties at certain times. Another approach may have little utility for the type of property being appraised. For instance, because most single-family residences are not purchased for their income-producing capability, the value reached by applying the income approach in the appraisal of a single-family residence is rarely a significant determinant of market value.

Overall, the approach likely to receive the most weight in appraising a single-family residence is the *sales comparison approach*. The sales comparison approach tells the appraiser what buyers in the market-place have been willing to pay for properties similar to the subject property. Of course, accurate data must be collected concerning market forces in the area and neighborhood, and there must be a sufficient number of recent comparable property sales.

Even when using the sales comparison approach to appraise a single-family residence, however, the appraiser must remember that past performance is never a guarantee of future performance and must always be alert to changing market conditions. Layoffs by a major employer, for instance, could signal decreased demand for housing as well as an increased supply of homes on the market. Either result could have a devastating effect on sales prices.

In recent years, more than one area of the country has seen a boom turn to a bust with frightening speed. Rising expectations can blind homebuyers and investors to the harsh realities of the marketplace. An appraiser always must be aware of the potential for the real estate market to turn down as well as up. In the process of reconciliation the appraiser will:

- Note and explain any work to be performed as a condition of the appraised valuation.
- Reconcile the value estimates resulting from the appraisal approaches used to reach a final estimate of market value and explain the conclusion.
- Provide the definition of market value used.
- State the terms under which the appraisal is performed and the limitations on its use.
- Certify by signature that the appropriate property inspections have been made by the appraiser personally and that the appraisal is based on the appraiser's knowledge and belief that the facts and data used in the appraisal are true and correct.

This appraisal is made. . . .

Indicate whether the final value estimate is based on the present condition of the property "as is" or, if not, how the condition of the property is expected to change. Building or remodeling work may be under way, as may repairs necessitated by termite damage or other property inspection reports. If the appraisal is based on any work that is not yet completed, the value estimate must be made *subject to* the work described.

▶ **FmHA** Check the appropriate box.

Comments and Conditions of Appraisal:

▶ **FmHA** Provide additional comments regarding any work to be completed or conditions to be met.

Final Reconciliation:

State the reasons why the final estimate of value chosen is the best estimate of market value.

▶ **FNMA** The reconciliation process that leads to the estimate of market value is an ongoing process throughout the appraiser's analysis. In the final reconciliation, you must reconcile the reasonableness and reliability of each approach to value and the reasonableness and validity of the indicated values and the available data, and then you must select and report the approach(es) that were given the most weight. The final reconciliation must never be an averaging technique. If you have provided a comprehensive and logical analysis of the neighborhood and property, the lender's underwriter should be able to reach a sound conclusion on the adequacy of the property as security for the mortgage.

▶ **FmHA** Briefly explain the basis for the final reconciliation, including the type and availability of data.

▶ **HUD/FHA** This section should contain the appraiser's reasoning for arriving at the final value.

This appraisal is based. . . .

Every appraisal will be qualified to some extent. To estimate property value accurately, you must define the type of value sought and the conditions under which the appraisal is made. As an appraiser, you also want to place limits on representations you are making with regard to the appraisal or its use. Various agencies require use of a particular form stating the terms under which the appraisal is conducted.

▶ **FmHA** Check the appropriate box, indicating the terms under which the appraisal is performed.

▶ **FNMA** Fannie Mae will not purchase a mortgage loan unless the underlying property appraisal is based on the most recent version of Form 1004B, as revised in July 1986 (current as of publication of this book), shown on page 122. Indicate that the form has been used by checking the second box in this section. If Form 1004B is attached to the URAR form, check the box labeled *attached.* Otherwise use the space provided to enter the date on which the form was presented to the client.

FNMA's definition of *market value* takes into account the effect on value of special or creative financing or sales concessions, such as seller contributions, interest rate buydowns and so on. Market value is reduced by whatever adjustments are necessary to adequately reflect such concessions. No adjustment is made for ". . . those costs which are normally paid by sellers as a result of tradition or law in a market area; these costs are readily identifiable since the seller pays these costs in virtually all sales transactions. . . ." The term "sellers" refers to all sellers in the market area, whether builders, developers or individuals in the resale market. A practice of one seller, or even a group of sellers, that is not followed by other sellers would qualify as "special." For example, if a seller is paying part of the purchaser's closing costs (or an interest rate buydown or in some other way is helping to provide below-market financing for the buyer), but virtually no other sellers in the market are doing the same, an adjustment must be made by the appraiser. This is true even if another *group* of sellers, such as builders, is also offering concessionary financing.

The sales price of a comparable property that has special or creative financing or sales concessions can be adjusted by comparing it to properties that had third-party institutional lenders (conventional financing), as long as the lender is not involved in the appraisal's subject property or transaction. "The appraiser should use his or her judgment in establishing the dollar amount for any adjustment to assure that it approximates the market's reaction to the financing or concession at the time of the sale."

The appraiser's *certification* states that:

1. The appraiser has no present or contemplated future interest in the property. Neither the appraiser's employment nor the appraiser's compensation is based on the appraised value of the property.
2. The appraiser has no bias with respect to either the subject property or the participants in the subject transaction. The appraisal report will *not* be based—completely or partly—on the race, color or national origin of *either* the prospective owners or occupants of the subject property *or* the present owners or occupants of properties in the vicinity of the subject property.
3. The appraiser has personally inspected the subject property inside and out and has made an outside inspection of comparable properties. To the best of the appraiser's knowledge and belief, all statements and information in the report are true and correct. The appraiser has not knowingly withheld any significant information.
4. All contingent and limiting conditions are stated in the report, whether they were imposed by the terms of the assignment or are an outcome of the appraiser's analyses, opinions and conclusions in the report.
5. The appraisal has been performed in conformity with and subject to the Code of Professional Ethics and Standards of Professional Conduct of the appraisal organizations with which the appraiser is affiliated.
6. Unless signing as Review Appraiser, the appraiser has personally prepared the report's conclusions and opinions. Only the appraiser is allowed to change any item in the report; the appraiser will not be responsible for unauthorized changes.

The *limiting conditions* of the appraisal are:

1. The appraiser assumes no responsibility for matters that are legal in nature. The appraiser offers no opinion on the condi-

tion of the subject property's title. The appraisal assumes that title is good and marketable and that the property is under responsible ownership.

2. The appraiser has made no property survey. Any property sketch in the report shows approximate dimensions only and is included only to assist in visualizing the property.

3. The appraiser will not appear in court on any matter relating to the appraisal, unless specific arrangements to do so have already been made.

4. Any distribution of value between land and buildings has been made on the basis of the present property use only, and is not to be used for any other purpose.

5. The appraiser assumes that there are no latent (hidden) defects of the property, including subsoil and structures, that would affect property value. The appraiser takes no responsibility for such conditions that might exist, or for engineering that might be required to reveal any such conditions.

6. The appraiser has used information, estimates and opinions believed to be true and correct, received from sources considered reliable; however, the appraiser accepts no responsibility for the accuracy of such items.

7. The appraiser will reveal the contents of the appraisal report only as provided by the bylaws and regulations of the professional appraisal organizations with which the appraiser is affiliated.

8. Use of all or any part of the report is strictly limited to the client, borrower (if paying the appraisal fee), lender and other parties specified, unless the appraiser consents to other use in writing. The report can be made public only with the written consent and approval of the appraiser.

9. If the report is subject to satisfactory completion, repairs or alterations to any property improvements, the report and value conclusions are contingent upon the required work being performed in a workmanlike manner.

▶ **HUD/FHA** Fee appraisers are required to base their value estimate on the Veterans Administration's regulatory definition of *reasonable value* (38 CFR 36.4301), which the VA considers synonymous with *market value.* Reasonable value is "that figure which represents the amount a reputable and qualified appraiser, unaffected by personal interest, bias, or prejudice, would recommend to a prospective purchaser as a property price or cost in the light of prevailing conditions." This definition is considered consistent with that used by Fannie Mae, Freddie Mac, the American Institute of Real Estate Appraisers and the Society of Real Estate Appraisers. "It is the VA fee appraiser's responsibility to develop a market value for the subject property which is consistent with the current standard definition of market value and the VA regulatory definition of reasonable value."

I (WE) ESTIMATE THE MARKET VALUE....

Enter the date of the appraisal. If the purpose of the appraisal is to determine current market value, this is typically the date of the property inspection. Next enter the amount of the market value estimate determined by the reconciliation process.

> ▶ **FmHA** Enter date of appraiser's property inspection and the market value of the subject property based on analysis of the market data and cost approach, in accordance with FmHA Instruction 1922-C.

I (We) certify....

This is a summary of the most important elements of the certification and statement of limiting conditions: to the appraiser's best knowledge and belief the facts and data used in the report are true and correct; the appraiser has personally inspected the subject property inside and out; the exterior of all comparables has been inspected; the appraiser has no undisclosed present or prospective future interest in the subject property.

Appraiser(s)

This space is for the signature of the appraiser who performed the appraisal, carrying out the necessary property inspection, collecting and examining the necessary data and reconciling the derived value estimates to reach a final conclusion of value for the subject property.

> ▶ **FmHA** Appraiser signs.
> ▶ **HUD/FHA** The appraiser signs his or her name and prints the name below the signature with the assigned CHUMS identification number. The report is dated as of the day the property is inspected.

Review Appraiser

This space is for the signature of the review Appraiser, if there was one. The review appraiser also indicates whether he or she personally inspected the subject property by checking the appropriate box. The boxes are for the use of the review appraiser *only*—not the appraiser who performed the appraisal.

> ▶ **FmHA** Review appraiser signs as appropriate.
> ▶ **HUD/FHA** If the report is approved, the review appraiser signs, enters the CHUMS identification number and date of review and then completes the Data Entry Sheet.

▶ Appraisal 1

This appraisal is made [X] "as is" [ ] subject to the repairs, alterations, inspections or conditions listed below   [ ] completion per plans and specifications.

Comments and Conditions of Appraisal: THE INCOME APPROACH IS NOT CONSIDERED APPLICABLE FOR PROPERTIES IN THIS AREA.   THERE ARE NO SPECIAL FINANCING CONSIDERATIONS.

Final Reconciliation: THE FINAL VALUE ESTIMATE IS BASED ON THE SALES COMPARISON APPROACH, AS THAT IS A REASONABLE AND SUPPORTABLE METHOD FOR THIS TYPE OF PROPERTY.

This appraisal is based upon the above requirements, the certification, contingent and limiting conditions, and Market Value definition that are stated in

[ ] FmHA, HUD &/or VA instructions.

[ ] Freddie Mac Form 439 (Rev. 7/86)/Fannie Mae Form 1004B (Rev. 7/86) filed with client _____ 19 ___ [ ] attached.

I (WE) ESTIMATE THE MARKET VALUE, AS DEFINED, OF THE SUBJECT PROPERTY AS OF SEPTEMBER 8 **19** 90 **to be $** 165,000

I (We) certify: that to the best of my (our) knowledge and belief the facts and data used herein are true and correct; that I (we) personally inspected the subject property, both inside and out, and have made an exterior inspection of all comparable sales cited in this report; and that I (we) have no undisclosed interest, present or prospective therein.

Appraiser(s) SIGNATURE *James Havlic*   NAME JAMES HAVLIC

Review Appraiser SIGNATURE *Todd Simpson* (if applicable)   NAME TODD SIMPSON   [ ] Did [X] Did Not Inspect Property

In Appraisal 1, the subject property is appraised "as is." There are no repairs or other ongoing construction work to which the appraisal is subject. The appraiser has used the *Comments and Conditions of Appraisal* section to begin the explanation of how the reconciliation process was carried out. The income approach was not considered applicable for properties in this area. There are no special financing considerations affecting market value.

The final value estimate is based on the sales comparison approach, because it is a reasonable and supportable method for this type of property. Fannie Mae Form 1004B is attached to the appraisal. The market value estimate is $165,000.

The appraiser has signed the certification statement, as has the review appraiser, who did not personally inspect the subject property.

▶ **Exercise: Appraisal 2**

This appraisal is made ☐ "as is" ☐ subject to the repairs, alterations, inspections or conditions listed below ☐ completion per plans and specifications.
Comments and Conditions of Appraisal: _____

Final Reconciliation: _____

This appraisal is based upon the above requirements, the certification, contingent and limiting conditions, and Market Value definition that are stated in
☐ FmHA, HUD &/or VA instructions.
☐ Freddie Mac Form 439 (Rev. 7/86)/Fannie Mae Form 1004B (Rev. 7/86) filed with client _____ 19 ___ ☐ attached.
I (WE) ESTIMATE THE MARKET VALUE, AS DEFINED, OF THE SUBJECT PROPERTY AS OF _____ 19_ ___ **to be $** _____

I (We) certify: that to the best of my (our) knowledge and belief the facts and data used herein are true and correct; that I (we) personally inspected the subject property, both inside and out, and have made an exterior inspection of all comparable sales cited in this report; and that I (we) have no undisclosed interest, present or prospective therein.

Appraiser(s) SIGNATURE _____ Review Appraiser SIGNATURE _____ ☐ Did ☐ Did Not
NAME _____ (if applicable) NAME _____ Inspect Property

RECONCILIATION

Complete the blank URAR *RECONCILIATION* section for Appraisal 2, using the following information. When you have finished, you can check your work against the completed Appraisal 2 in the Answer Key.

There is no ongoing or uncompleted construction work, repairs or alterations to the subject property improvements. The property is appraised "as is."

The income approach is not considered a valid indicator of value for this appraisal, because few similar properties in the area are rented out. No new properties are being built in the area. The most reasonable and supportable conclusion of market value is reached by analyzing the sales prices of comparable properties.

The appraisal is subject to the market value definition, certification and limiting conditions of FNMA Form 1004B (Rev. 7/86), attached. As of the date of property inspection, market value is estimated at $265,000.

The appraiser and review appraiser both certify the contents of the appraisal. The review appraiser did not inspect the subject property.

PART FOUR

Putting It All Together

Appraisal 3

Now that you have finished the discussion of the URAR form and practiced making entries in each section of the form, you should be ready to attempt an entire sample appraisal.

Using the information supplied here for Appraisal 3, complete the blank URAR form on pages 180–183. Fill in as many items on the form as you can, then compare your entries against those in the completed Appraisal 3 in the Answer Key.

SUBJECT

The subject property is a single-family detached residence located at 582 Augustina Lane, Brandywine, Anystate 99999. The owners of record are Cindi and George Rattan. The census tract number is 27.04. The lender's file number is 80808C8. The property's legal description is:

Lot 58, Sunnyside Tennis Club Estates, as shown on page 36 of book 25, records of King County.

This appraisal is being made at the request of the owners' lender, First State Bank, as part of a refinancing transaction. The map reference number is 95-2. The real estate taxes for the tax year 1991 are $1,028.90. The homeowners' association dues on this property are $120 yearly.

NEIGHBORHOOD DATA

The 25-year-old subdivision is 100% developed with single-family residences ranging in value from $95,000 to $195,000. Most are valued at about $140,000 and virtually all are owner-occupied with little or no vacancies. Although most houses are 15 years old, they range in age from 2 to 25 years. There has been an adequate demand for housing in the subject neighborhood, with a steady uptrend in values during the past few years. Although recent economic conditions have slowed overall demand in the metropolitan area, most houses in this desirable subdivision are sold within 120 days of being put on the market.

The subject neighborhood is favorably affected by its proximity to the interstate highway and its convenience to area employment centers. Public bus transportation, which is provided to the neighborhood, is somewhat limited and not as good as in competing areas. Except for this, all other subject neighborhood amenities are normal for the market area.

SITE DATA

The subject lot has a frontage of 80 feet and a depth of 132 feet and is not located on a corner. It is rectangular in shape, level and has a well-drained sandy subsoil. The lot size is typical of those found in the market area. Landscaping is good and typical of this area. The view from the subject house is of street, parkway and surrounding houses—typical of most houses in the neighborhood.

The site has public electricity, water and sanitary and storm sewers. The street is asphalt with concrete sidewalks, curbs and gutters—all publicly maintained. There are no streetlights or alleys in this neighborhood. The driveway is concrete. The property is not located in a FEMA flood hazard zone.

The subject property is zoned R-1/Single-Family Residential and represents the highest and best use of the site. The zoning ordinance, which is strongly enforced, has many provisions controlling lot size and building dimensions. All special assessments for water, sewer, sidewalk, curb, gutter and street surfacing have been paid in full by the developers of the subdivison. There are no apparent adverse influences, easements or encroachments.

DESCRIPTION OF IMPROVEMENTS

All of the following have been verified by the appraiser through personal inspection.

The subject property has good market appeal and compatibility within the neighborhood. The dwelling is a 14-year-old ranch-style house with foyer, living room, dining room, kitchen, family room, four bedrooms and two full baths. Gross area, based on outside dimensions, is 2,030 square feet. The effective age of the structure is estimated at 10 years, remaining economic life at 50 years and remaining physical life at 60 years.

Exterior: Poured concrete foundation with no apparent settlement or infestation problems; wood frame with brick veneer walls; asphalt shingle roof with aluminum gutters and downspouts, wood-frame, double-hung windows with aluminum screens.

Insulation: Batts over ceilings and in walls, R-values unknown; insulation appears typical for the area.

Interior: All features typical of competing houses, including quality of construction, condition of improvements, room sizes and layout, adequacy of closets and other storage space, overall energy efficiency, plumbing and fixtures, electrical system and kitchen amenities.

Floors: Wall-to-wall carpeting in the living room, hallways and bedrooms; finished oak in the dining room and foyer; vinyl tile in the kitchen and family room; all floor coverings in average condition.

Walls/Ceilings: Drywall, taped and painted; good condition.

Kitchen: Built-in range and oven, dishwasher, garbage disposal and hood-type exhaust fan; refrigerator and microwave not included in valuation process.

Baths: Ceramic tile floor; ceramic tile wainscot around tub and shower area; good condition.

Trim/Finish: Wood trim throughout the house; average condition.

Interior doors: Wood, hollow core; average condition.

Exterior doors: Steel; good condition.

Fireplace: Masonry in family room; average condition.

Attic: None.

Heating/Cooling: Central forced-air heating and cooling fueled by electricity; the system is in average shape with adequate output.

Garage: Two-car, 25' × 25', detached; electric overhead door; meets neighborhood standards; average condition.

Additional Features: Attractive masonry fireplace in family room; ceiling fans in every room.

COST DATA

The square footage of the subject house can be computed from the diagram below.

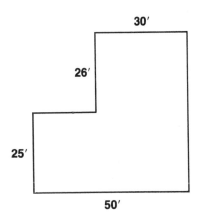

House	$39 per square foot
Garage	$16 per square foot

Landscaping/driveway $7,500

Site value, estimated by
analysis of comparable properties $31,000

DEPRECIATION

Overall, the house and garage are in good condition, with normal wear and tear. Depreciation due to physical deterioration is estimated at 12%. There is no evidence of functional or external obsolescence.

This appraisal is not for HUD or VA purposes. The property has no construction warranties.

INCOME DATA

Current market analysis indicates that the subject property would rent for $800 per month with a GRM of 138.

SALES COMPARISON DATA

The value of the subject property, as indicated by the sales comparison approach, was estimated after careful comparison with three recently sold similar properties. All sales data were verified by the brokers involved in the transactions. Several other sales were considered but not included in this report because of a too-wide spread in cost, type of construction, location or time of sale.

Sale 1 is located at 205 Briarwood Drive—½ mile NW of the subject. It sold for $112,500. The property is 14 years old, has a gross living area of 2,025 square feet and, like the subject, is located in a good area of the neighborhood.

Sale 2 is located at 570 Shanter Court, three blocks south of the subject. It sold for $114,200. The property is 14 years old, has a gross living area of 2,010 square feet and is in a good location.

Sale 3 is located at 308 Crafton Street, five blocks SE of the subject. It sold for $108,000. It is 14 years old, has a gross living area of 2,050 square feet and is in a good location.

Additional data are shown in the accompanying chart.

	Subject	Comp 1	Comp 2	Comp 3	Adjustment
Date of Sale		1 mo. ago	3 mos. ago	4 mos. ago	
Financing		Conv. Mtg.	Conv. Mtg.	Conv. Mtg.	
Site/View	Average	Same	Same	Same	
Size of Lot	12,000 SF	Same	Same	10,000 SF	$4,000
Design & Appeal	Ranch/Avg.	Same	Same	Same	
Cosntruction	Average	Same	Same	Same	
No. of Rms/ Bedrms/Baths	8/4/2	Same	Same	Same	
Basement	None	None	None	None	
Functional Utility	Good	Same	Same	Same	
Heating/Cooling	FA/Cent.	Same	Same	Same	
Garage	2-Car/Det.	Same	Same	Same	
Other Exterior Improvements	None	None	Wood Deck	None	$1,200
Special Energy- Efficient Items	Fans	Same	Same	Same	
Fireplace(s)	Masonry/1	Same	Same	None	$2,000
Other Interior Improvements	None	None	None	None	
General Condition	Average	Same	Same	Same	

CONCLUSION

The property has been appraised by the three traditional approaches, and the results indicated are:

Cost approach	$116,970
Income approach	$110,400
Sales comparison approach	$112,500 to $114,000

The cost approach is felt to reflect the upper limit of value; it has been given consideration because the cost data were sufficiently accurate and the depreciation factors reflect the actions in the market.

The income approach shows a lower value. Much of the data used to indicate rent and rent multipliers were drawn from areas outside the subject neighborhood and possibly are not indicative of the market in this area. This approach could reflect the lower value of a like property if bought for investment purposes. The appraiser has given little weight to this approach.

The sales comparison approach is based on sales of similar properties in the immediate area. Sufficient sales data were available; because sales were made within a relatively short period, data were not influenced by a time adjustment. This approach is the most factual and accurate because it measures actions of buyers in the market.

Because the value range is fairly close and comparable 1 required no adjustment, it can be assumed that the subject property has a market value of $112,500.

▶ Appraisal 3

☐☐　　　　　　　　　　　　　　　　　　　　　　　　　　　　　　☐☐

Property Description & Analysis　**UNIFORM RESIDENTIAL APPRAISAL REPORT**　**File No.**

SUBJECT			
Property Address		Census Tract	LENDER DISCRETIONARY USE
City	County	State　　Zip Code	Sale Price　$
Legal Description			Date
Owner/Occupant		Map Reference	Mortgage Amount　$
Sale Price $　　Date of Sale		PROPERTY RIGHTS APPRAISED	Mortgage Type
Loan charges/concessions to be paid by seller $		☐ Fee Simple	Discount Points and Other Concessions
R.E. Taxes $　　Tax Year　　HOA $/Mo.		☐ Leasehold	Paid by Seller　$
Lender/Client		☐ Condominium (HUD/VA)	
		☐ De Minimis PUD	Source

NEIGHBORHOOD

LOCATION	☐ Urban	☐ Suburban	☐ Rural	NEIGHBORHOOD ANALYSIS	Good	Avg.	Fair	Poor
BUILT UP	☐ Over 75%	☐ 25-75%	☐ Under 25%	Employment Stability	☐	☐	☐	☐
GROWTH RATE	☐ Rapid	☐ Stable	☐ Slow	Convenience to Employment	☐	☐	☐	☐
PROPERTY VALUES	☐ Increasing	☐ Stable	☐ Declining	Convenience to Shopping	☐	☐	☐	☐
DEMAND/SUPPLY	☐ Shortage	☐ In Balance	☐ Over Supply	Convenience to Schools	☐	☐	☐	☐
MARKETING TIME	☐ Under 3 Mos.	☐ 3-6 Mos.	☐ Over 6 Mos.	Adequacy of Public Transportation	☐	☐	☐	☐

PRESENT LAND USE　%	LAND USE CHANGE	PREDOMINANT	SINGLE FAMILY HOUSING	Recreation Facilities	☐	☐	☐	☐
Single Family ____	Not Likely ☐	OCCUPANCY	PRICE　　AGE	Adequacy of Utilities	☐	☐	☐	☐
			$ (000)　　(yrs)					
2-4 Family ____	Likely ☐	Owner ☐		Property Compatibility	☐	☐	☐	☐
Multi-family ____	In process ☐	Tenant ☐		Protection from Detrimental Cond.	☐	☐	☐	☐
Commercial ____	To: _____	Vacant (0-5%) ☐	Low	Police & Fire Protection	☐	☐	☐	☐
Industrial ____		Vacant (over 5%) ☐	High	General Appearance of Properties	☐	☐	☐	☐
Vacant ____			Predominant	Appeal to Market	☐	☐	☐	☐
			—					

Note: Race or the racial composition of the neighborhood are not considered reliable appraisal factors.

COMMENTS: _____

_____

_____

_____

SITE

Dimensions	Topography
Site Area	Size
Corner Lot	Shape
Zoning Classification　　Zoning Compliance	Drainage
HIGHEST & BEST USE: Present Use　　Other Use	

UTILITIES	Public	Other	SITE IMPROVEMENTS	Type	Public	Private		
Electricity	☐		Street		☐	☐	View	
Gas	☐		Curb/Gutter		☐	☐	Landscaping	
Water	☐		Sidewalk		☐	☐	Driveway	
Sanitary Sewer	☐		Street Lights		☐	☐	Apparent Easements	
Storm Sewer	☐		Alley		☐	☐	FEMA Flood Hazard　Yes* ____　No ____	
							FEMA* Map/Zone	

COMMENTS (Apparent adverse easements, encroachments, special assessments, slide areas, etc.): _____

▶ Appraisal 3 (continued)

IMPROVEMENTS

GENERAL DESCRIPTION	EXTERIOR DESCRIPTION	FOUNDATION	BASEMENT	INSULATION
Units	Foundation	Slab	Area Sq. Ft.	Roof
Stories	Exterior Walls	Crawl Space	% Finished	Ceiling
Type (Det./Att.)	Roof Surface	Basement	Ceiling	Walls
Design (Style)	Gutters & Dwnspts.	Sump Pump	Walls	Floor
Existing	Window Type	Dampness	Floor	None
Proposed	Storm Sash	Settlement	Outside Entry	Adequacy
Under Construction	Screens	Infestation		Energy Efficient Items:
Age (Yrs.)	Manufactured House			
Effective Age (Yrs.)				

ROOM LIST

ROOMS	Foyer	Living	Dining	Kitchen	Den	Family Rm.	Rec. Rm.	Bedrooms	# Baths	Laundry	Other	Area Sq. Ft.
Basement												
Level 1												
Level 2												

Finished area **above** grade contains: _____ Rooms; _____ Bedroom(s); _____ Bath(s); _____ Square Feet of Gross Living Area

INTERIOR

SURFACES	Materials/Condition	HEATING	KITCHEN EQUIP.	ATTIC	IMPROVEMENT ANALYSIS	Good	Avg.	Fair	Poor
Floors		Type	Refrigerator	None	Quality of Construction				
Walls		Fuel	Range/Oven	Stairs	Condition of Improvements				
Trim/Finish		Condition	Disposal	Drop Stair	Room Sizes/Layout				
Bath Floor		Adequacy	Dishwasher	Scuttle	Closets and Storage				
Bath Wainscot		COOLING	Fan/Hood	Floor	Energy Efficiency				
Doors		Central	Compactor	Heated	Plumbing-Adequacy & Condition				
		Other	Washer/Dryer	Finished	Electrical-Adequacy & Condition				
		Condition	Microwave		Kitchen Cabinets-Adequacy & Cond.				
Fireplace(s) #		Adequacy	Intercom		Compatibility to Neighborhood				

AUTOS

CAR STORAGE:			Attached	Adequate	House Entry	Appeal & Marketability				
No. Cars	Carport		Detached	Inadequate	Outside Entry	Estimated Remaining Economic Life			Yrs.	
Condition	None		Built-In	Electric Door	Basement Entry	Estimated Remaining Physical Life			Yrs.	

Garage (first row CAR STORAGE)

Additional features: _____

COMMENTS

Depreciation (Physical, functional and external inadequacies, repairs needed, modernization, etc.): _____

General market conditions and prevalence and impact in subject/market area regarding loan discounts, interest buydowns and concessions: _____

▶ **Appraisal 3** *(continued)*

Valuation Section   **UNIFORM RESIDENTIAL APPRAISAL REPORT**   **File No.**

Purpose of Appraisal is to estimate Market Value as defined in the Certification & Statement of Limiting Conditions.

COST APPROACH

BUILDING SKETCH (SHOW GROSS LIVING AREA ABOVE GRADE)
If for Freddie Mac or Fannie Mae, show only square foot calculations and cost approach comments in this space.

ESTIMATED REPRODUCTION COST-NEW-OF IMPROVEMENTS:

Dwelling _____ Sq. Ft. @ $ _____ = $ _____
_____ Sq. Ft. @ $ _____ = _____
Extras _____ = _____
_____ = _____
Special Energy Efficient Items _____ = _____
Porches, Patios, etc. _____ = _____
Garage/Carport _____ Sq. Ft. @ $ _____ = _____
Total Estimated Cost New .... = $ _____

| | Physical | Functional | External |
Less
Depreciation _____ = $ _____
Depreciated Value of Improvements .... = $ _____
Site Imp. "as is" (driveway, landscaping, etc.) = $ _____
ESTIMATED SITE VALUE .... = $ _____
(If leasehold, show only leasehold value.)
INDICATED VALUE BY COST APPROACH ...... = $ _____

(Not Required by Freddie Mac and Fannie Mae)
Does property conform to applicable HUD/VA property standards? ☐ Yes ☐ No
If No, explain: _____

Construction Warranty ☐ Yes ☐ No
Name of Warranty Program _____
Warranty Coverage Expires _____

▶ **Appraisal 3** *(continued)*

The undersigned has recited three recent sales of properties most similar and proximate to subject and has considered these in the market analysis. The description includes a dollar adjustment, reflecting market reaction to those items of significant variation between the subject and comparable properties. If a significant item in the comparable property is superior to, or more favorable than, the subject property, a minus (−) adjustment is made, thus reducing the indicated value of subject; if a significant item in the comparable is inferior to, or less favorable than, the subject property, a plus (+) adjustment is made, thus increasing the indicated value of the subject.

ITEM	SUBJECT	COMPARABLE NO. 1		COMPARABLE NO. 2		COMPARABLE NO. 3	
Address							
Proximity to Subject							
Sales Price	$	$		$		$	
Price/Gross Liv. Area	$	$		$		$	
Data Source							
VALUE ADJUSTMENTS	DESCRIPTION	DESCRIPTION	+ (−) $ Adjustment	DESCRIPTION	+ (−) $ Adjustment	DESCRIPTION	+ (−) $ Adjustment
Sales or Financing Concessions							
Date of Sale/Time							
Location							
Site/View							
Design and Appeal							
Quality of Construction							
Age							
Condition							
Above Grade Room Count	Total Bdrms Baths	Total Bdrms Baths		Total Bdrms Baths		Total Bdrms Baths	
Gross Living Area	Sq. Ft.	Sq. Ft.		Sq. Ft.		Sq. Ft.	
Basement & Finished Rooms Below Grade							
Functional Utility							
Heating/Cooling							
Garage/Carport							
Porches, Patio, Pools, etc.							
Special Energy Efficient Items							
Fireplace(s)							
Other (e.g. kitchen equip., remodeling)							
Net Adj. (total)		+ − $		+ − $		+ − $	
Indicated Value of Subject		$		$		$	

Comments on Sales Comparison: _____

INDICATED VALUE BY SALES COMPARISON APPROACH .... $_____
INDICATED VALUE BY INCOME APPROACH (If Applicable) Estimated Market Rent $_____ /Mo. x Gross Rent Multiplier _____ = $_____
This appraisal is made ☐ "as is" ☐ subject to the repairs, alterations, inspections or conditions listed below ☐ completion per plans and specifications.
Comments and Conditions of Appraisal: _____

Final Reconciliation: _____

This appraisal is based upon the above requirements, the certification, contingent and limiting conditions, and Market Value definition that are stated in
☐ FmHA, HUD &/or VA instructions.
☐ Freddie Mac Form 439 (Rev. 7/86)/Fannie Mae Form 1004B (Rev. 7/86) filed with client _____ 19___ ☐ attached.
I (WE) ESTIMATE THE MARKET VALUE, AS DEFINED, OF THE SUBJECT PROPERTY AS OF _____ 19___ to be $_____
I (We) certify: that to the best of my (our) knowledge and belief the facts and data used herein are true and correct; that I (we) personally inspected the subject property, both inside and out, and have made an exterior inspection of all comparable sales cited in this report; and that I (we) have no undisclosed interest, present or prospective therein.

Appraiser(s) SIGNATURE _____ NAME _____ Review Appraiser SIGNATURE _____ (if applicable) NAME _____ ☐ Did ☐ Did Not Inspect Property

ANSWER KEY
Appraisal 3

Property Description & Analysis **UNIFORM RESIDENTIAL APPRAISAL REPORT** File No.

SUBJECT

Property Address 582 AUGUSTINA LANE — Census Tract 27.04
City BRANDYWINE   County KING   State ANY-STATE   Zip Code 99999
Legal Description LOT 58 SUNNYSIDE TENNIS CLUB ESTATES
Owner/Occupant CINDI AND GEORGE RATTAN   Map Reference 95-2
Sale Price $ REFINANCE   Date of Sale N/A
Loan charges/concessions to be paid by seller $ N/A
R.E. Taxes $ 1,028.90   Tax Year 1990   HOA $/Mo. 10.00
Lender/Client FIRST STATE BANK

LENDER DISCRETIONARY USE
Sale Price $
Date
Mortgage Amount $
Mortgage Type
Discount Points and Other Concessions
Paid by Seller $
Source

PROPERTY RIGHTS APPRAISED
[X] Fee Simple
[ ] Leasehold
[ ] Condominium (HUD/VA)
[ ] De Minimis PUD

NEIGHBORHOOD

LOCATION				NEIGHBORHOOD ANALYSIS	Good	Avg.	Fair	Poor
LOCATION	[ ] Urban	[X] Suburban	[ ] Rural	Employment Stability		X		
BUILT UP	[X] Over 75%	[ ] 25-75%	[ ] Under 25%	Convenience to Employment		X		
GROWTH RATE	[ ] Rapid	[X] Stable	[ ] Slow	Convenience to Shopping		X		
PROPERTY VALUES	[X] Increasing	[ ] Stable	[ ] Declining	Convenience to Schools		X		
DEMAND/SUPPLY	[ ] Shortage	[X] In Balance	[ ] Over Supply	Adequacy of Public Transportation			X	
MARKETING TIME	[ ] Under 3 Mos.	[X] 3-6 Mos.	[ ] Over 6 Mos.	Recreation Facilities		X		

PRESENT LAND USE %: Single Family 100; 2-4 Family; Multi-family; Commercial; Industrial; Vacant
LAND USE CHANGE: Not Likely [X]; Likely; In process; To:
PREDOMINANT OCCUPANCY: Owner [X]; Tenant; Vacant (0-5%) [X]; Vacant (over 5%)
SINGLE FAMILY HOUSING PRICE $(000) AGE (yrs): 95 Low 2; 195 High 25; Predominant 140 — 15

Adequacy of Utilities — X
Property Compatibility — X
Protection from Detrimental Cond. — X
Police & Fire Protection — X
General Appearance of Properties — X
Appeal to Market — X

Note: Race or the racial composition of the neighborhood are not considered reliable appraisal factors.
COMMENTS: THE NEIGHBORHOOD IS COMPOSED OF MEDIUM TO HIGHER PRICED RESIDENCES, MOSTLY SINGLE-FAMILY HOMES. THE SUBJECT'S MARKET APPEAL IS FAVORABLY AFFECTED BY THE NEIGHBORHOOD'S PROXIMITY TO THE INTERSTATE AND ITS CONVENIENCE TO AREA EMPLOYMENT CENTERS.

SITE

Dimensions 80 X 132   Corner Lot NO
Site Area 10,560 SF
Zoning Classification R-1 SINGLE-FAMILY RES   Zoning Compliance YES
HIGHEST & BEST USE: Present Use YES   Other Use N/A

Topography LEVEL
Size 10,560 SF/TYPICAL
Shape RECTANGULAR
Drainage TYPICAL/GOOD
View TYPICAL/STREETS & HOUSES
Landscaping TYPICAL /GOOD
Driveway CONCRETE
Apparent Easements NONE
FEMA Flood Hazard Yes* No [X]
FEMA* Map/Zone

UTILITIES	Public	Other	SITE IMPROVEMENTS	Type	Public	Private
Electricity	X		Street	ASPHALT	X	
Gas			Curb/Gutter	CONCRETE	X	
Water	X		Sidewalk	CONCRETE	X	
Sanitary Sewer	X		Street Lights	NONE		
Storm Sewer	X		Alley	NONE		

COMMENTS (Apparent adverse easements, encroachments, special assessments, slide areas, etc.): NO APPARENT ADVERSE INFLUENCES, EASEMENTS OR ENCROACHMENTS WERE OBSERVED.

IMPROVEMENTS

GENERAL DESCRIPTION: Units 1; Stories 1; Type (Det./Att.) DET; Design (Style) RANCH; Existing YES; Proposed N/A; Under Construction N/A; Age (Yrs.) 14; Effective Age (Yrs.) 10
EXTERIOR DESCRIPTION: Foundation CONCRETE; Exterior Walls FRM/BRICK/VEN; Roof Surface ASPH SHGLS; Gutters & Dwnspts. ALUMINUM; Window Type WD/DBL-HUNG; Storm Sash N/A; Screens ALUMINUM; Manufactured House N/A
FOUNDATION: Slab YES; Crawl Space N/A; Basement N/A; Sump Pump N/A; Dampness N/A; Settlement NO; Infestation NO
BASEMENT N/A: Area Sq. Ft.; % Finished; Ceiling; Walls; Floor; Outside Entry
INSULATION: Roof; Ceiling BATTS [X]; Walls BATTS [X]; Floor; None; Adequacy A [X]; Energy Efficient Items: FIREPLACE, FANS R-VALUE UNKNOWN

ROOM LIST

ROOMS	Foyer	Living	Dining	Kitchen	Den	Family Rm.	Rec. Rm.	Bedrooms	# Baths	Laundry	Other	Area Sq. Ft.
Basement												
Level 1	1	1	1	1		1		4	2			2,030
Level 2												

Finished area above grade contains: 8 Rooms; 4 Bedroom(s); 2 Bath(s); 2,030 Square Feet of Gross Living Area

INTERIOR

SURFACES Materials/Condition: Floors CPT/WD/VINYL/AVG; Walls DRYWALL/GOOD; Trim/Finish WD/AVG; Bath Floor CT/GOOD; Bath Wainscot CT/GOOD; Doors EXT/STEEL/GD, INT/HC/AVG
Fireplace(s) 1 /MASONRY/FR AVG
HEATING: Type FA/CENT; Fuel ELECT; Condition AVG; Adequacy ADEQ
COOLING: Central YES; Other; Condition AVG; Adequacy ADEQ
KITCHEN EQUIP.: Refrigerator P; Range/Oven X; Disposal X; Dishwasher X; Fan/Hood X; Compactor; Washer/Dryer; Microwave P; Intercom
ATTIC: None X; Stairs; Drop Stair; Scuttle; Floor; Heated; Finished

IMPROVEMENT ANALYSIS (Good/Avg/Fair/Poor): Quality of Construction X; Condition of Improvements X; Room Sizes/Layout X; Closets and Storage X; Energy Efficiency X; Plumbing-Adequacy & Condition X; Electrical-Adequacy & Condition X; Kitchen Cabinets-Adequacy & Cond. X; Compatibility to Neighborhood X; Appeal & Marketability X

CAR STORAGE: Garage [X]; No. Cars 2; Carport; Condition AVG; None
Attached [ ]; Detached [X]; Built-In
Adequate [X]; Inadequate
House Entry; Outside Entry [X]; Electric Door [X]; Basement Entry

Estimated Remaining Economic Life 50 Yrs.
Estimated Remaining Physical Life 60 Yrs.

Additional features: ATTRACTIVE MASONRY FIREPLACE IN FAMILY ROOM; CEILING FANS IN EVERY ROOM.

COMMENTS

Depreciation (Physical, functional and external inadequacies, repairs needed, modernization, etc.): OVERALL, THE HOUSE AND GARAGE ARE IN GOOD CONDITION, WITH NORMAL WEAR AND TEAR. NO SIGNIFICANT ITEMS WERE OBSERVED THAT REQUIRE IMMEDIATE REPAIR. THERE IS NO EVIDENCE OF FUNCTIONAL OR EXTERNAL OBSOLESCENCE.

General market conditions and prevalence and impact in subject/market area regarding loan discounts, interest buydowns and concessions: THE SUBJECT IS LOCATED IN A FAIRLY ACTIVE MARKET WITH A STEADY UPTREND IN VALUES. NO SPECIAL FINANCING, LOAN DISCOUNTS, INTEREST BUYDOWNS OR CONCESSIONS WERE FOUND FOR THE SUBJECT OR COMPARABLE SALES IN THIS MARKET.

Freddie Mac Form 70 10/86 (10 ch)   U.S. Forms Inc. 2 Central Square, Grafton, MA 01519-0446, 1-800-225-9583   Fannie Mae Form 1004 10/86

ANSWER KEY
Appraisal 3
(*continued*)

UNIFORM RESIDENTIAL APPRAISAL REPORT   File No.

Valuation Section

Purpose of Appraisal is to estimate Market Value as defined in the Certification & Statement of Limiting Conditions.

COST APPROACH

BUILDING SKETCH (SHOW GROSS LIVING AREA ABOVE GRADE)
If for Freddie Mac or Fannie Mae, show only square foot calculations and cost approach comments in this space.

```
            30'
      26'
  25'
            50'
```

50' X 25' = 1,250 SF
30' X 26' = 780
TOTAL GLA = 2,030 SF

ESTIMATED REPRODUCTION COST - NEW - OF IMPROVEMENTS:

Dwelling	2,030 Sq. Ft. @ $ 39	= $	79,170
	Sq. Ft. @ $	=	
Extras		=	
		=	
Special Energy Efficient Items	INCLUDED	=	
Porches, Patios, etc.		=	
Garage/Carport 625 Sq. Ft. @ $ 16		=	10,000
Total Estimated Cost New		= $	89,170

	Physical	Functional	External	
Less	12%			
Depreciation	10,700	N/A	N/A	= $ 10,700

Depreciated Value of Improvements	= $	78,470
Site Imp. "as is" (driveway, landscaping, etc.)	= $	7,500
ESTIMATED SITE VALUE	= $	31,000
(If leasehold, show only leasehold value.)		
INDICATED VALUE BY COST APPROACH	= $	116,970

Construction Warranty		Yes	X No
Name of Warranty Program	N/A		
Warranty Coverage Expires	N/A		

(Not Required by Freddie Mac and Fannie Mae)
Does property conform to applicable HUD/VA property standards? ☐ Yes ☐ No
If No, explain:

SALES COMPARISON ANALYSIS

The undersigned has recited three recent sales of properties most similar and proximate to subject and has considered these in the market analysis. The description includes a dollar adjustment, reflecting market reaction to those items of significant variation between the subject and comparable properties. If a significant item in the comparable property is superior to, or more favorable than, the subject property, a minus (−) adjustment is made, thus reducing the indicated value of subject; if a significant item in the comparable is inferior to, or less favorable than, the subject property, a plus (+) adjustment is made, thus increasing the indicated value of the subject.

ITEM	SUBJECT	COMPARABLE NO. 1		COMPARABLE NO. 2		COMPARABLE NO. 3	
Address	582 AUGUSTINA LANE	205 BRIARWOOD DRIVE		570 SHANTER COURT		308 CRAFTON STREET	
Proximity to Subject		1/2 MILE NW		3 BLOCKS SOUTH		5 BLOCKS SE	
Sales Price	$ N/A	$ 112,500		$ 114,200		$ 108,000	
Price/Gross Liv. Area	$ N/A	$ 55.56		$ 55.62		$ 52.68	
Data Source	INSPECTION	BROKER		BROKER		BROKER	
VALUE ADJUSTMENTS	DESCRIPTION	DESCRIPTION	+ (−) $ Adjustment	DESCRIPTION	+ (−) $ Adjustment	DESCRIPTION	+ (−) $ Adjustment
Sales or Financing Concessions		CONV MORTG		CONV MORTG		CONV MORTG	
Date of Sale/Time		1 MONTH AGO		3 MONTHS AGO		4 MONTHS AGO	
Location	GOOD	EQUAL		EQUAL		EQUAL	
Site/View	12,000/AVG	12,000/EQUAL		12,000/EQUAL		10,000/INF	+4,000
Design and Appeal	RANCH/AVG	RANCH/EQUAL		RANCH/EQUAL		RANCH/EQUAL	
Quality of Construction	AVERAGE	EQUAL		EQUAL		EQUAL	
Age ACTUAL	14	14		14		14	
Condition	AVERAGE	EQUAL		EQUAL		EQUAL	
Above Grade	Total Bdrms Baths	Total Bdrms Baths		Total Bdrms Baths		Total Bdrms Baths	
Room Count	8 4 2	8 4 2		8 4 2		8 4 2	
Gross Living Area	2,030 Sq. Ft.	2,025 Sq. Ft.		2,010 Sq. Ft.		2,050 Sq. Ft.	
Basement & Finished Rooms Below Grade	NONE	NONE		NONE		NONE	
Functional Utility	GOOD	EQUAL		EQUAL		EQUAL	
Heating/Cooling	FA/CENT	FA/CENT		FA/CENT		FA/CENT	
Garage/Carport	2-CAR DET	SAME		SAME		SAME	
Porches, Patio, Pools, etc.	NONE	NONE		WD DECK	−1,200	NONE	
Special Energy Efficient Items	FANS	SAME		SAME		SAME	
Fireplace(s)	MASONRY/1	SAME		SAME		NONE	+2,000
Other (e.g. kitchen equip., remodeling)	NONE	NONE		NONE		NONE	
Net Adj. (total)		☐ + ☐ − $		☐ + ☒ − $ 1,200		☒ + ☐ − $ 6,000	
Indicated Value of Subject		$ 112,500		$ 113,000		$ 114,000	

Comments on Sales Comparison: MANY COMPS WERE CONSIDERED IN MAKING THIS APPRAISAL. HOWEVER, SALE 1 WAS GIVEN THE MOST WEIGHT BECAUSE IT WAS MOST SIMILAR TO THE SUBJECT AND REQUIRED NO ADJUSTMENTS. SALES 2 & 3 PROVIDE GOOD SUPPORT.

INDICATED VALUE BY SALES COMPARISON APPROACH .... $ 112,500

INDICATED VALUE BY INCOME APPROACH (If Applicable) Estimated Market Rent $ 800 /Mo. x Gross Rent Multiplier 138 = $ 110,400

This appraisal is made ☒ "as is" ☐ subject to the repairs, alterations, inspections or conditions listed below ☐ completion per plans and specifications.

Comments and Conditions of Appraisal: THE INCOME APPROACH WAS GIVEN THE LEAST WEIGHT SINCE RENT AND MULTIPLIER DATA WERE DRAWN FROM OUTSIDE AREAS AND MAY NOT REFLECT THE SUBJECT MARKET.

Final Reconciliation: THE SALES COMPARISON APPROACH IS CONSIDERED TO BE THE BEST INDICATOR OF THE SUBJECT PROPERTY'S MARKET VALUE. THE COST AND INCOME APPROACHES PROVIDE ADEQUATE SUPPORT

RECONCILIATION

This appraisal is based upon the above requirements, the certification, contingent and limiting conditions, and Market Value definition that are stated in
☐ FmHA, HUD &/or VA instructions.
☐ Freddie Mac Form 439 (Rev. 7/86)/Fannie Mae Form 1004B (Rev. 7/86) filed with client _____ 19____ ☐ attached.
I (WE) ESTIMATE THE MARKET VALUE, AS DEFINED, OF THE SUBJECT PROPERTY AS OF APPRAISAL DATE 19____ to be $ 112,500
I (WE) certify: that to the best of my (our) knowledge and belief the facts and data used herein are true and correct; that I (we) personally inspected the subject property, both inside and out, and have made an exterior inspection of all comparable sales cited in this report; and that I (we) have no undisclosed interest, present or prospective therein.

Appraiser(s) SIGNATURE	SIGNATURE	Review Appraiser SIGNATURE	SIGNATURE	☐ Did ☒ Did Not
NAME	TYPED NAME	(if applicable) NAME	TYPED NAME	Inspect Property

Freddie Mac Form 70 10/86   10CH USF#10110C   Fannie Mae Form 1004 10/86

Index

Excerpts From the Uniform Standards of Professional Appraisal Practice Applicable to Federally Related Transactions

(Based upon the Uniform Standards of Professional Appraisal Practice as promulgated by the Appraisal Standard Board of The Appraisal Foundation)

Section I – Introduction
Preamble

It is essential that a professional appraiser arrive at and communicate his or her analyses, opinions, and advice in a manner that will be meaningful to the client and will not be misleading in the marketplace. These Uniform Standard of Professional Appraisal Practice reflect the current standard of the appraisal profession.

The importance of the role of the appraiser places ethical obligations on those who serve in this capacity. These standards include explanatory comments and begin with an Ethics Provision setting forth the requirements for integrity, objectivity, independent judgement, and ethical conduct. In addition, these standards include a Competency Provision which places an immediate responsibility on the appraiser prior to acceptance of an assignment. The standards contain binding requirements, as well as specific guidelines. Definitions applicable to these standard are also included.

These standards deal with the procedures to be followed in performing an appraisal or review and the manner in which an appraisal or review is communicated. Standards 1 and 2 relate to the development and communication of a real property appraisal. Standard 3 establishes guidelines for reviewing an appraisal and reporting on that review.

These standards are for appraisers and the users of appraisal services. To maintain the highest level of professional practice, appraisers must observe these standards. The users of appraisal services should demand work performed in conformance with these standards.

Comment: Explanatory comments are an integral part of the Uniform Standard and should be viewed as extensions of the provisions, definitions, and standard rules. Comments provide interpretation from the Appraisal Standards Board concerning the background or application of certain provisions, definitions, or standards rules. There are no comments for provisions, definitions, and standards rules that are axiomatic or have not yet required further explanation; however, additional comments will be developed and others supplemented or revised as the need arises.

Ethics Provision

Because of the fiduciary responsibilities inherent in professional appraisal practice, the appraiser must observe the highest standards of professional ethics. This Ethics Provision is divided into four sections: conduct, management, confidentiality, and record keeping.

Comment: This provision emphasizes the personal obligations and responsibilities of the individual appraiser. However, it should also be emphasized that groups and organizations engaged in appraisal practice share the same ethical obligations.

Conduct. An appraiser must perform ethically and competently in accordance with these standards and not engage in conduct that is unlawful, unethical, or improper. An appraiser who could reasonably be perceived as a disinterested third party in rendering an unbiased appraisal, review, or consulting service must perform assignments with impartiality, objectivity, and independence and without accommodation of personal interests.

Comment: An appraiser is required to avoid any incident that could be considered misleading or fraudulent. In particular, it is unethical for an appraiser to use or communicate a misleading or fraudulent report or to knowingly permit an employee or other person to communicate a misleading or fraudulent report.

The development of an appraisal, review, or consulting service based upon a hypothetical condition is unethical unless:

(1) The use of the hypothesis is clearly disclosed;

(2) The assumption of the hypothetical condition is clearly required for legal purposes, for purposes of reasonable analysis, or for purposes of comparison and would not be misleading; and

(3) The report clearly describes the rationale for this assumption, the nature of the hypothetical condition, and its effect on the result of the appraisal, review, or consulting service.

An individual appraiser employed by a group or organization conducts itself in a manner that does not conform to these standards should take steps that are appropriate under the circumstances to ensure compliance with the standards.

Management. The acceptance of compensation that is contingent upon the reporting of a predetermined value or a direction in value that favors the cause of the attainment of a stipulated result, or the occurrence of a subsequent event is unethical.

The payment of undisclosed fees, commissions, or things of value in connection with the procurement of appraisal, review, or consulting assignments is unethical

Comment: Disclosure of fees, commissions, or things of value connected to the procurement of an assignment should appear in the certification of a written record and in any transmittal letter in which conclusions are stated. In groups or organizations engaged in appraisal practice, intracompany payments to employees for business development are not considered to be unethical. Competency, rather than financial incentives, should be the primary basis for awarding an assignment.

Advertising for or soliciting appraisal assignments in a manner which is false, misleading or exaggerated is unethical.

Comment: In groups or organizations engaged on appraisal practice, decisions concerning finder or referral fees, contingent compensation, and advertising may not be the responsibility of an individual appraiser, but for a particular assignment it is the responsibility of the individual appraiser to ascertain that there has been no breach of ethics, that the appraisal is prepared in accordance with these standards, and that the report can be properly certified as required by Standards Rules 2-3 or 3-2.

The restriction on contingent compensation in the first paragraph of this section does not apply to consulting assignments where the appraiser is not acting in a disinterested manner and would not reasonably be perceived as performing a service that requires impartiality. This permitted contingent compensation must be properly disclosed in the report.

Comment: The preparer of the written report of an assignment where the appraiser is not acting in a disinterested manner must certify that the compensation is contingent and must explain the basis for the contingency in the report, certification, executive summary and in any transmittal letter in which conclusions are stated.

Confidentiality. An appraiser must protect the confidential nature of the appraiser-client relationship.

Comment: A appraiser must not disclose confidential factual data obtained from a client or the result of an assignment prepared for a client to anyone other than: (1) The client and persons specifically authorized by the client; (2) such third parties as may be authorized by due process of law; and (3) a duly authorized professional peer review committee. As a corollary, it is unethical for a member of a duly authorized professional peer review committee to disclose confidential information or factual data presented to the committee.

Record Keeping. An appraiser must prepare written records of appraisal, review and consulting assignments-including oral testimony and reports-and retain such records for a period of at least five (5) years after preparation or at least two (2) years after final disposition of any judicial proceeding in which testimony was given, whichever period expires last.

Comment. Written records of assignments include true copies of written reports, written summaries of oral testimony and reports (or a transcript of testimony) all data and statements required by these standards, and other information as may be required to support the findings and conclusions of the appraiser. The term written records also includes information stored on electronic, magnetic, or other media. Such records must be made available by the appraiser when required by due process of law or by duly authorized professional peer review committee.

Competency Provision

Prior to accepting an assignment or entering into an agreement to perform any assignment, an appraiser must properly identify the problem to be addressed and have the knowledge and experience to complete the assignment competently; or alternatively:

1. Disclose the lack of knowledge and/or experience to the client before accepting the assignment; and

2. Take all steps necessary or appropri-

ate to complete the assignment competently; and

3. Describe the lack of knowledge and/or experience and the steps taken to complete the assignment competently in the report.

Comment: The background and experience of appraisers varies widely and a lack of knowledge or experience can lead to inaccurate or inappropriate appraisal practice. The competency provision requires the appraiser to perform a specific appraisal service competently. If an appraiser is offered an opportunity to perform an appraisal service but lacks the necessary knowledge or experience to complete it competently, the appraiser must disclose his or her lack of knowledge or experience to the client before accepting the assignment and then take the necessary or appropriate steps to complete the appraisal service competently. This may be accomplished in various ways including, but not limited to, personal study by the appraiser; association with an appraiser believed to have the necessary knowledge or experience; or retention of others who possess the required knowledge or experience.

Although this provision requires an appraiser to identify the problem and disclose any deficiency in competence prior to accepting an assignment, facts or conditions uncovered during the course of an assignment could cause an appraiser to discover that he or she lacks the required knowledge or experience to complete the assignment competently. At the point of such discovery, the appraiser is obligated to notify the client and comply with items 2 and 3 of the provision.

The concept of competency also extends to appraisers who are requested or required to travel to geographic area wherein they have no recent appraisal experience. An appraiser preparing an appraisal in an unfamiliar location must spend sufficient time to understand the nuances of the local market and the supply and demand factors relating to the specific property type and the location involved. Such understanding will not be imparted solely from a consideration of specific data such as demographics, costs, sales and rentals. The necessary understanding of the local market conditions provides the bridge between a sale and a comparable sale or a rental and a comparable rental. If an appraiser is not in a position to spend the necessary amount of time in a market area to obtain this understanding, affiliation with a qualified

local appraiser may be the appropriate response to ensure the development of a competent appraisal.

Jurisdictional Exception

If any part of these standards is contrary to the law or public policy of any jurisdiction, only that part shall be void and of no force or effect in that jurisdiction.

Supplemental Standards

These Uniform Standards provide the common basis for all appraisal practice. Supplemental standard applicable to appraisals prepared to specific purposes or property types may be issued by public agencies and certain client groups, e.g., regulatory agencies, eminent domain authorities, asset managers, and financial institutions. Appraiser and clients ascertain whether any supplemental standards in addition to these Uniform Standard apply to the assignment being considered.

Definitions

For the purpose of these standards, the following definitions apply:

Appraisal: (noun) The act or process of estimating value; an estimate of value. (adjective) of or pertaining to appraising and related functions, e.g. appraisal practice, appraisal services.

Appraisal practice: The work or services performed by Appraisers, defined by three terms in these standards: appraisal, review, and consulting.

Comment: These three terms are intentionally generic, and are not mutually exclusive. For example, an estimate of value may be required as a part of a review or consulting service. The use of other nomenclature by an appraiser (e.g. analyses, counseling, evaluation, study, submission, valuation) does not exempt an appraiser from adherence to these standards.

Cash Flow Analysis: A study of the anticipated movement of cash into or out of an investment.

Client: Any party for whom an appraiser performs a service.

Consulting: The act or process of providing information, analyses of real estate data, and recommendations or conclusions on diversified problems in real estate, other than estimating value.

Feasibility Analysis: A study of the cost benefit relationship of an economic endeavor.

Investment Analysis: A study that reflects the relationship between acquisition price and anticipated future benefits of a real estate investment.

Market Analysis: A study of real estate market conditions for a specific type of property.

Market Value: Market value is the major focus of most real property appraisal assignments. Both economic and legal definitions of market value have been developed and refined.

A current economic definition agreed upon by federal financial institutions in the United States of America is:

The most probable price which a property should bring in a competitive and open market under all conditions requisite to a fair sale, the buyer and the seller each acting prudently and knowledgeably, and assuming the price is not affected by undue stimulus. Implicit in this definition is the consummation of a sale as of a specified date and the passing of title from buyer to seller under conditions whereby:

1. Buyer and seller are typically motivated;

2. Both parties are well informed or well advised, and acting in what they consider their best interests;

3. A reasonable time is allowed for exposure in the open market;

4. Payment is made in the terms of cash in United States dollars or in terms of financial arrangements comparable thereto; and

5. The price represents the normal consideration for the property sold unaffected by special or creative financing or sales concessions granted by anyone associated with the sale.

Substitution of another currency for *United States dollars* in the fourth condition is appropriate in countries or in reports addressed to clients from other countries.

Persons performing appraisal services that may be subject to litigation are cautioned to seek the exact legal definition of market value in the jurisdiction in which the services are being performed.

Mass Appraisal: The process of valuing a universe of properties as of a given date utilizing standard methodology, employing common data, and allowing for statistical testing.

Mass Appraisal Model: A mathematical expression of how supply and demand factors interact in a market.

Personal Property: Identifiable portable and tangible objects which are considered by the public as being "personal," e.g.

furnishings, artwork, antiques, gems and jewelry, collectibles, machinery and equipment; all property that is not classified as real estate.

Real Estate: An identifiable parcel or tract of land, including improvements, if any.

Real Property: The interests, benefits, and rights inherent in the ownership of real estate.

Comment: In some jurisdictions, the terms "real estate" and "real property" have the same legal meaning. The separate definitions recognize the traditional distinction between the two in appraisal theory.

Report: Any communication, written or oral, of an appraisal, review or analysis; the document that is transmitted to the client upon completion of an assignment.

Comment: Most reports are written and most clients mandate written reports. Oral report guidelines (See Standards Rule 2-4) and restrictions (See Ethics Provision: Record Keeping) are included to cover court testimony and other oral communications of an appraisal, review, or consulting service.

Review: The act or process of critically studying a report prepared by another.

Section II–Real Property Appraisals

Standard 1

In developing a real property appraisal, an appraiser must be aware of, understand, and correctly employ those recognized methods and techniques that are necessary to produce a credible appraisal.

Comment: Standard 1 is directed toward the substantive aspects of developing a competent appraisal. The requirements set forth in Standard Rule 1-1, the appraisal guidelines set forth in Standards Rules 1-2, 1-3, 1-4, and the requirements set forth in Standards Rule 1-5 mirror the appraisal process in the order of topics addressed and can be used by appraisers and the users of appraisal services as a convenient checklist.

Standards Rule 1-1. In developing a real property appraisal, an appraiser must:

(a) Be aware of, understand, and correctly employ those recognized methods and techniques that are necessary to produce a credible appraisal;

Comment: Departure from this binding requirement is not permitted. This rule recognizes that the principle of change continues to affect the manner in which appraisers perform appraisal services.

Changes and developments in the real estate field have a substantial impact on the appraisal profession. Important changes in the cost and manner of constructing and marketing commercial, industrial, and residential real estate and changes in legal framework in which real estate property rights and interests are created, conveyed, and mortgaged have resulted in corresponding changes in appraisal theory and practice. Social change has also had an effect on appraisal theory and practice. To keep abreast of these changes and developments, the appraisal profession is constantly reviewing and revising appraisal methods and techniques and devising new methods and techniques to meet new circumstances. For this reason it is not sufficient for appraisers to simply maintain the skills and the knowledge they possess when they become appraisers. Each appraiser must continuously improve his or her skills to remain proficient in real property appraisal.

(b) Not commit a substantial error of omission or commission that significantly affects an appraisal;

Comment: Departure from this binding requirement is not permitted. In performing appraisal services an appraiser must be certain that the gathering of factual information is conducted in a manner that is sufficiently diligent to ensure that the data would have a material or significant effect on the resulting opinions or conclusions are considered. Further an appraiser must use sufficient care in analyzing such data to avoid errors that would significantly affect his or her opinions or conclusions.

(c) Not render appraisal services in a careless or negligent manner, such as a series of errors that, considered individually, may not significantly affect the results of an appraisal, but which, when considered in the aggregate, would be misleading.

Comment: Departure from this binding requirement is not permitted. Perfection is impossible to attain and competence does not require perfection. However, an appraiser must not render appraisal services in a careless of negligent manner. This rule requires an appraiser to use due diligence and due care. The fact that the carelessness and the negligence of an appraiser has not caused an error that significantly affects his or her opinions or conclusions and thereby seriously harms a client or a third party does not excuse such carelessness or negligence.

Standards Rule 1-2. In developing a real property appraisal, an appraiser must observe the following specific appraisal guidelines:

(a) Adequately define the real estate, identify the real property interest, consider the purpose and intended use of the appraisal, consider the extent of the data collection process, identify any special limiting conditions, and identify the effective date of the appraisal;

(b) Define the value being considered; if the value to be estimated is market value, the appraiser must clearly indicate whether the estimate is the most probable price:

(i) In terms of cash; or

(ii) In terms of financial arrangements equivalent to cash; or

(iii) In such other terms as may be precisely defined; if an estimate of value is based on submarket financing or financing with unusual conditions or incentives, the terms of such financing must be clearly set forth, their contributions to or negative influence on value must be described and estimated, and the market data supporting the valuation must be described and explained;

Comment: For certain types of appraisal assignments in which a legal definition of market value has been established and takes precedence, the Jurisdictional Exception may apply to this guideline.

If the concept of reasonable exposure in the open market is involved, the appraiser should be specific as to the estimate of marketing time linked to the value estimate.

(c) Consider easements, restrictions, encumbrances, leases, reservations, covenants, contracts, declarations, special assessments, ordinances, or other items of a similar nature;

(d) Consider whether an appraised fractional interest, physical segment, or partial holding contributes pro rata to the value of the whole;

Comment: This guideline does not require an appraiser to value the whole when the subject of the appraisal is a fractional interest, a physical segment, or a partial holding. However, if the value of the whole is not considered, the appraisal must clearly reflect that the value of the property being appraised cannot be used to estimate the value of the whole by mathematical extension.

(e) Identify and consider the effect on value of any personal property, trade fixtures or intangible items that are not real property but are considered in the appraisal.

Comment: This guideline requires the appraiser to recognize the inclusion of items that are not real property in an overall value estimate. Additional expertise in personal property or business appraisal may be required to allocate the overall value to its various components. Separate valuation of such items is required when they are significant to overall value.

Standards Rule 1-3. In developing a real property appraisal, an appraiser must observe the following specific appraisal guidelines:

(a) Consider the effect on use and value of the following factors: existing land use regulations, reasonably probable modifications of such land use regulations, economic demand, the physical adaptability of the real estate, neighborhood trends, and the highest and best use of the real estate;

Comment: This guideline sets forth a list of factors that affect use and value. In considering neighborhood trends, an appraiser must avoid stereotyped or biased assumptions relating to race, age, color, religion, gender, or national origin or an assumption that racial, ethnic, or religious homogeneity is necessary to maximize value in a neighborhood. Further, an appraiser must avoid making an unsupported assumption or premise about neighborhood decline, effective age, and remaining life. In considering highest and best use, an appraiser should develop the concept to the extent that is required for a proper solution of the appraisal problem being considered.

(b) Recognize that land is appraised as though vacant and available for development to its highest and best use and that the appraisal of improvements is based on their actual contribution to the site.

Comment: This guideline may be modified to reflect that, in various legal and practical situations, a site may have a contributory value that differs from the value as if vacant.

Standards Rule 1-4. In developing a real property appraisal, an appraiser must observe the following specific guidelines, when applicable:

(a) Value the site by an appropriate appraisal method or technique;

(b) Collect, verify, analyze, and reconcile: (i) Such comparable cost data as are available to estimate the cost new of the improvements (if any); (ii) Such comparable data as are available to estimate the difference between cost new and the present worth of the improvements (accrued depreciation); (iii) Such comparable sales data, adequately identified and described, as are available to indicate a value conclusion;

(iv) Such comparable rental data as are available to estimate the market rental of the property being appraised;

(v) Such comparable operating expense data as are available to estimate the operating expenses of the property being appraised;

(vi) Such comparable data as are available to estimate rates of capitalization and/or rates of discount.

Comment: This rule covers the three approaches to value. See Standards Rule 2-2 (j) for corresponding reporting requirements.

(c) Base projections of future rent and expenses on reasonably clear and appropriate evidence;

Comment: Although the value of the whole may be equal to the sum of the separate estates or parts, it also may be greater than or less than the sum of the separate estates or parts. Therefore, the value of the whole must be tested by reference to appropriate market data and supported by an appropriate analysis of such data.

A similar procedure must be followed when the value of the whole has been established and the appraiser seeks to estimate the value of a part. The value of any such part must be tested by reference to appropriate market data and supported by appropriate analysis of such data.

(f) Consider and analyze the effect on value, if any, of anticipated public or private improvements, located on or off the site, to the extent that market actions reflect such anticipated improvements as of the effective appraisal date;

Comment: In condemnation evaluation assignments in certain jurisdictions, the Jurisdictional Exception may apply to this guideline.

(g) Identify and consider the appropriate procedures and market information required to perform the appraisal, including all physical, functional, and external market factors as they may effect the appraisal;

Comment: The appraisal may require a complete market analysis.

(h) Appraise proposed improvements only after examining and having available for future examination:

(i) plans, specifications, or other documentation sufficient to identify the scope and character of the proposed improvements;

(ii) evidence indicating the probable time of completion of the proposed improvements; and

(iii) Reasonably clear and appropriate

evidence supporting development costs, anticipated earnings, occupancy projections, and the anticipated competition at the time of completion.

Comment: The evidence required to be examined and maintained under this guideline may include such items as contractor's estimates relating to cost and the time required to complete construction. Market and feasibility studies; operating cost data; and the history of recently completed similar developments. The appraisal may require a complete feasibility analysis.

(i) All pertinent data in items (a) through (h) above shall be used in the development of an appraisal.

Comment: See Standards Rule 2-2 (k) for corresponding reporting requirements.

Standards Rule 1-5. In developing a real property appraisal, an appraiser must:

(a) Consider and analyze any current Agreement of Sale, option, or listing of the property being appraised, if such information is available to the appraiser in the normal course of business;

(b) Consider and analyze any prior sales of the property being appraised that occurred in the following time periods:

(i) One year for one-to-four-family residential property; and

(ii) Three years for all other property types;

Comment: The intent of this requirement is to encourage the research and analysis of prior sales of the subject; the time frames cited are minimums.

(c) Consider and reconcile the quality and quantity of data available and analyzed within the approaches used and the applicability or suitability of the approaches used.

Comment: Departure from this binding requirement is not permitted. See Standards Rule 2-2 (k) Comment for corresponding reporting requirements.

Standard 2

In reporting the results of a real property appraisal an appraiser must communicate each analysis, opinion, and conclusion in a manner that is not misleading.

Comment: Standard 2 governs the form and content of the report that communicates the results of an appraisal to clients and third parties.

Standards Rule 2-1. Each written or oral real property appraisal report must:

(a) Clearly and accurately set forth the appraisal in a manner that will not be misleading;

Comment: Departure from this binding requirement is not permitted. Since most reports are used and relied upon by third parties, communications considered adequate by the appraiser's client may not be sufficient. An appraiser must take extreme care to make certain that his or her reports will not be misleading in the marketplace or to the public.

(b) Contain sufficient information to enable the person(s) who receive or rely on the report to understand it properly;

Comment: Departure from this binding requirement is not permitted. A failure to observe this rule could cause a client or other users of this report to make a serious error even though each analysis, opinion, and conclusion in the report is clearly and accurately stated. To avoid this problem and the dangers it presents to clients and other users of reports, this rule requires an appraiser to include in each report sufficient information to enable the reader to understand it properly. All reports, both written and oral, must clearly and accurately present the analyses, opinions, and conclusions of the appraiser in sufficient depth and detail to address adequately the significance of the particular appraisal problem.

(c) Clearly and accurately disclose any extraordinary assumption or limiting condition that directly affects the appraisal and indicate its impact on value.

Comment: Departure from this binding requirement is not permitted. Examples of extraordinary assumptions or conditions might include items such as the execution of a pending lease agreement, atypical financing, or completion of onsite or offsite improvements. In a written report the disclosure would be requires in conjunction with statements of each opinion conclusion that is affected.

Standards Rule 2-2. Each written real property appraisal report must:

(a) identify and describe the real estate being appraised;

(b) identify the real property interest being appraised;

Comment on (a) and (b): These two requirements are essential elements in any report. Identifying the real estate can be accomplished by any combination of a legal description, address, map reference, copy of a survey or map, property sketch and/or photographs. A property sketch and photographs also provide some description of the real estate in addition to written comments about the physical attributes of

the real estate. Identifying the real property rights being appraised requires a direct statement substantiated as needed by copies or summaries of legal descriptions or other documents setting forth any encumbrances.

(c) State the purpose of the appraisal;

(d) Define the value to be estimated;

(e) Set forth the active date of the appraisal and the date of the report;

Comment on (c), (d), and (e): These three requirements call for clear disclosure to the reader of a report the "what, why, and when" surrounding the appraisal. The purpose of the appraisal is used generically to include both the task involved and rationale for the appraisal. Defining the value to be estimated requires both an appropriately referenced definition and any comments needed to clearly indicate to the reader how the definition is being applied [See Standards Rule 1-2 (b)]. The effective date for the appraisal establishes the context for the value estimate, while the date of the report indicates whether the perspective of the appraiser on the market conditions was prospective, current, or retrospective. Reiteration of the date of the report and the effective date of the appraisal at various stages of the report in tandem is important for the clear understanding of the reader whenever market conditions on the date of the report are different from the market conditions on the effective date of the appraisal.

(f) Describe the extent of the processes of collecting, confirming, and reporting data;

Comment: It is suggested that assumptions and limiting conditions be grouped together in an identified section of the report.

(h) Set forth the information considered, the appraisal procedures followed, and the reasoning that supports the analyses, opinions, and conclusions;

Comment: This requirement calls for the appraiser to summarize the data considered and the procedures that were followed. Each item must be addressed in the depth and detail required by its significance to the appraisal. The appraiser must be certain that sufficient information is provided so that the client, the users of the report, and the public will understand it and will not be misled or confused. The substantive content of the report, not its size, determines its compliance with this guideline.

(i) Set forth the appraiser's opinion of the highest and best use of the real estate, when such an opinion is necessary and appropriate;

Comment: This requirement calls for written report to contain a statement of the appraiser's opinion as to the highest and best use of the real estate, unless an opinion as to highest and best use is unnecessary, e.g., insurance valuation or value in use appraisals. If an opinion as to highest and best use is required; the reasoning in support of the opinion must also be included.

(j) Explain and support the exclusion of any of the usual valuation approaches;

(k) set forth any additional information that may be appropriate to show compliance with, or clearly identify and explain permitted departures from, the requirements of Standard 1;

Comment: This requirement calls for a written appraisal report or other written communication concerning the results of an appraisal to contain sufficient information to indicate that the appraiser complied with requirements of Standard 1, including the requirements governing any permitted departure from the appraisal guidelines. The amount of detail required will vary with the significance of the information to the appraisal.

Information considered and analyzed in compliance with Standards Rule 1-5 is significant information that deserves comment in any report. If such information is unattainable, comment on the efforts undertaken by the appraiser to obtain the information required.

(l) include a signed certification in accordance with Standards Rule 2-3.

Comment: Departure from binding requirements (a) through (l) above is not permitted.

Standards Rule 2-3. Each written real property appraisal report must contain a certification that is similar in content to the following form:

I certify that, to the best of my knowledge and belief:

- The statements of fact contained in this report are true and correct.

- The reported analyses, opinions, and conclusions are limited only by the supporting assumptions and limiting conditions, and are my personal, unbiased professional analyses, opinions, and conclusions.

- I have no (or the specified) present or prospective interest in the property that is the subject of this report, and I have no (or the specified) personal interest or bias with respect to the parties involved.

- My compensation is not contingent upon the reporting of a predetermined value or direction in that value that favors the cause of the client, the amount of the value estimate, the attainment of a stipulated result, or the occurrence of a subsequent event.

- My analyses, opinions, and conclusions were developed, and this report has been prepared, in conformity with the Uniform Standards of Professional Appraisal Practice.

- I have (or have not) made a personal inspection of the property that is the subject of this report. (If more than one person signs the report, this certification must clearly specify which individuals did and which individuals did not make a personal inspection of the appraised property.)

- No one provided significant professional assistance to the person signing this report. (If there are exceptions, the name of each individual providing significant professional assistance must be stated.)

Comment: Departure from this binding requirement is not permitted.

Standards Rule 2-4. To the extent that it is both possible and appropriate, each oral real property appraisal report (including expert testimony) must address the substantive matters set forth in Standards Rule 2-2.

Comment: In addition to complying with the requirements of Standards Rule 2-1, an appraiser making an oral report must use his or her best efforts to address each of the substantive matters in Standards Rule 2-2.

Testimony of an appraiser concerning his or her analyses, opinions, or conclusions is an oral report in which the appraiser must comply with the requirements of this Standards Rule.

See *Record Keeping* under the ETHICS PROVISION for corresponding requirements.

Standards Rule 2-5. An appraiser who signs a real property appraisal report prepared by another, even under the label of "review appraiser," must accept full responsibility for the contents of the report.

Comment: Departure from this binding requirement is not permitted. This requirement is directed to the employer or supervisor signing the report of an employee or subcontractor. The employer or the supervisor is as responsible as the individual preparing the appraisal for the content and the conclusions of the appraisal and the report. Using a conditional label next to the signature of the employer or supervisor or signing a form report on the line over the words "review appraiser" does not exempt that individual from adherence to these standards.

This requirement does not address the responsibilities of the review appraiser, the subject of Standard 3.

Section III–Review Appraisals

Standard 3

In reviewing an appraisal and reporting the results of that review, an appraiser must form an opinion as to the adequacy and appropriateness of the report being reviewed and must clearly disclose the nature of the review process taken.

Comment: The function of reviewing an appraisal requires the preparation of a separate report or a file memorandum by the appraiser performing the review setting forth results of the review process. Review appraisers go beyond checking for a level of completeness and consistency in the report under review by providing comment on the content and conclusions of the report. They may or may not have first-hand knowledge of the subject property or of data in the report. The COMPETENCY PROVISION applies to the appraiser performing the review as well as the appraiser who prepared the report under review.

Reviewing is a distinctly different function from that addressed Standards Rule 2-5. To avoid confusion in the marketplace between these two functions, review appraisers should not sign the report under responsibility of a cosigner.

Review appraisers must take appropriate steps to indicate to third parties the precise extent of the review process. A separate report or letter is one method. Another appropriate method is a form or checklist prepared and signed by the appraiser conducting the review and attached to the report under review. It is also possible that stamped impression on the appraisal report under review, signed or initialed by the reviewing appraiser, may be an appropriate method for separating the review function from the actual signing of the report. To be effective, however, the stamp must briefly indicate the extent of the review process and refer to a file memorandum that clearly outlines the review process conducted.

The review appraiser must exercise extreme care in clearly distinguishing between the review process and the appraisal or consulting process. Original work by the review appraiser may be governed by STANDARD 1 rather than this standard. A misleading or fraudulent review and/or report violates the ETHICS PROVISION.

Standards Rule 3-1. In interviewing an appraisal, an appraiser must:

(a) Identify the report under review, the real estate and real property interest being appraised, the effective date of the opinion in the report under review, and the date of the review;

(b) Identify the extent of the review process to be conducted;

(c) Form an opinion as to the completeness of the report under review in light of the requirements in these standards;

Comment: The review should be conducted in the context of market conditions as of the effective date of the opinion in the report being reviewed.

(d) Form an opinion as to the apparent adequacy and relevance of the data and the propriety of any adjustments to the data:

(e) Form an opinion as to the appropriateness of the appraisal methods and techniques used and develop the reasons for any disagreement;

(f) Form an opinion as to whether the analyses, opinions, and conclusions in the report under review are appropriate and reasonable, and develop the reasons for any disagreement.

Comment: Departure from binding requirements (a) through (f) above is not permitted. An opinion of a different estimate of value from that in the report under review may be expressed, provided the review appraiser:

1. Satisfies the requirements of STANDARD 1;

2. Identifies and sets forth any additional data relied upon and the reasoning and basis for the different estimate of value; and

3. Clearly identifies and discloses all assumptions and limitations connected with the different estimate of value to avoid confusion in the marketplace.

Standards Rule 3-2. In reporting the results of an appraisal review, an appraiser must: (a) Disclose the nature, extent, and detail of the review process undertaken;

(b) Disclose the information that must be considered in Standards Rule 3-1(a) and ((b);

(c) Set forth the opinions, reasons, and conclusions required in Standards Rule 3-1 (c), (d), (e) and (f);

(d) Include all known pertinent information;

(e) Include a signed certification similar in content to the following:

I certify that, to the best of my knowledge and belief:

-The facts and data reported by the review appraiser and used in the review process are true and correct.

-The analyses, opinions, and conclusions in this review report are limited only by the assumptions and limiting conditions stated in this review report, and are my personal, unbiased professional analyses, opinions and conclusions.

-I have no (or the specified) present or prospective interest in the property that is the subject of this report and I have no (or the specified) personal interest or bias with respect to the parties involved.

-My compensation is not contingent on an action or event resulting from the analyses, opinions, or conclusions in, or the use of this review report.

-My analyses, opinions, and conclusions were developed and this review report was prepared in conformity with the Uniform Standards of Professional Appraisal Practice.

-I did not (did) personally inspect the subject property of the report under review.

-No one provided significant professional assistance to the person signing this review report. (If there are exceptions, the name of each individual providing significant professional assistance must be stated.)

Comment: Departure from binding requirements (a) through (e) above is not permitted.